Faith, Morality, and
Civil Society

APPLICATIONS OF POLITICAL THEORY

Series Editors: Harvey Mansfield, Harvard University, and Daniel J. Mahoney, Assumption College

This series encourages analysis of the applications of political theory to various domains of thought and action. Such analysis will include works on political thought and literature, statesmanship, American political thought, and contemporary political theory. The editors also anticipate and welcome examinations of the place of religion in public life and commentary on classic works of political philosophy.

Faith, Morality, and Civil Society

Edited by Dale McConkey and
Peter Augustine Lawler

LEXINGTON BOOKS
Lanham • Boulder • New York • Toronto • Oxford

LEXINGTON BOOKS

Published in the United States of America
by Lexington Books
A Member of the Rowman & Littlefield Publishing Group, Inc.
4501 Forbes Boulevard, Suite 200, Lanham, Maryland 20706

PO Box 317
Oxford
OX2 9RU, UK

British Library Cataloguing in Publication Information Available

Library of Congress Cataloging-in-Publication Data

Faith, morality, and civil society / edited by Dale McConkey and Peter Augustine Lawler.
    p. cm. – (Applications of political theory)
    Includes bibliographical references and index.
    ISBN 0-7391-0482-9 (alk. paper) – ISBN 0-7391-0483-7 (pbk.: alk. paper)
    1. Religion and sociology—United States. 2. Religion and politics—United States.
3. United States—Religion—1960– 4. Religious ethics. I. McConkey, Dale, 1965–
II. Lawler, Peter Augustine. III. Series.

BL2525 .F35   2002
291.1'7—dc21   2002028302

Printed in the United States of America

♾™ The paper used in this publication meets the minimum requirements of American
National Standard for Information Sciences—Permanence of Paper for Printed Library
Materials, ANSI/NISO Z39.48–1992.

Contents

Acknowledgments

This book, together with a sister book already published by Lexington, originated from a conference held at Berry College on politics, religion, and community on March 9, 1999. Sponsored by the Departments of Government and Sociology at Berry College, Oglethorpe University, and the State University of West Georgia, the conference was the third in a series of annual conferences held jointly by Berry College and Oglethorpe University. We thank President Scott Colley of Berry College, West Georgia, and the Intercollegiate Studies Institute for their generous financial support.

Most of the authors first presented a draft version of their chapters at the conference. A few scholars who did not attend the conference were invited to submit chapters to bring their expertise to bear on the questions raised by the conference.

Deserving of our deepest thanks is Diane Land. Ms. Land's extraordinary competence in copyediting, her wonderful (but devilish) sense of humor, and her gentle but firm stewardship were the engines that saw this project through to completion. Also, heartfelt thanks to Michael Bailey, who shared the editing duties when the primary editor was called away by other obligations.

Alan Wolfe's chapter, "The Potential for Pluralism: Religious Responses to the Triumph of Theory and Method in American Academic Culture," first appeared in *Religion, Scholarship, & Higher Education: Perspectives, Models, and Future Prospects*, edited by Andrea Sterk (Notre Dame, Ind.: University of Notre Dame Press, 2002), 22-39. We thank the University of Notre Dame Press for granting us permission to reprint the article.

Introduction

Michael Bailey

In the immediate wake of the September 11 attacks, Americans were repeatedly told, and many Americans believed, that now "Everything is changed." A new and terrifying world of apocalyptic uncertainty seemed to loom on the horizon, threatening the freedom and security that Americans accept as their birthright. Yet to virtually everyone's surprise, the inevitable and imminent second attack has not come (as of this writing). And, in retrospect, our initial paralyzing worries seem inflated and perhaps even a little cowardly. By most objective measures, the actions that President Bush and the government took following the attack were surprisingly effective. Airports are safer, security agencies across the nation are in better communication with one another, and the military has had remarkable success (thus far). Even the 2002 Winter Olympics in Salt Lake City, which was ripe for terrorist activity, suffered more from disgruntled skaters and embarrassed French judges than from terrorism. In short, surprisingly little in American life has changed. True, negotiating the lines at the airport takes a bit more time, and the American military is engaged in a number of hot spots around the globe, but, for the most part, life goes on much as it did before tragedy struck. America is proving herself once again to be the land of perpetual virginity. From time to time America loses her innocence—be it from Vietnam, Watergate, Iran-gate, or September 11—only to regain it again.

Paradoxically, America's complacency, which is borne from the government's tremendous short-term successes following the September 11 tragedy, may now jeopardize the government's long-term goal of making the world fit for self-governance. Terrorism is still very much alive and well. As President Bush has repeatedly warned the nation, no one should fool himself or herself into believing that this goal will be quickly or easily achieved. It will almost certainly require war. It will also require virtue. Will Americans have the stomach to accept long-term sacrifice or commitment when the searing pain and sorrow of September 11 fades? Fighting the scope of evil to which Bush is committed requires, as he never ceases to remind us, resolve. It requires public spiritedness, the willingness of citizens to sacrifice to a greater good. It requires, in other words, the kinds of virtues and character traits generally associated with classical republicanism, not modern liberalism. It reminds us that liberal regimes cannot afford to be liberal all the way down. There is very little that liberal governments can do to generate virtue in the citizenry. That is the competency of families, religious institutions, neighborhoods, and schools. Therefore how these secondary agencies accomplish this hard task—and how government may assist them—is of interest to us in proportion to the extent we wish to preserve a free regime. This question reflects one important theme of this book.

The audacious task of making the world a safer and more receptive place for democracy requires more than self-sacrificing citizens. North Korea has self-sacrificing citizens in ample supply. It also requires citizens who understand what genuinely warrants sacrifice. This, in turn, requires citizens who understand what is good for human beings and how (and whether) politics may achieve these goods. Once more we discover that political philosophy, contrary to the end-of-history devotees, is not yet a dispensable human activity. It is, in fact, central to making liberal democracy decent and attractive. In that spirit, this book advances a rich and diverse collection of essays organized loosely on the connection between democratic political order in the United States, the diversity of beliefs that compete for recognition and power in the public sphere, and the faith and philosophical traditions that give rise to those beliefs.

Implicit in all the essays, and central to several, is the belief that the fundamental challenge of politics today is to redeem *pluralism*. Pluralism is that uniquely modern feature of liberal democracies which provides legal protection and status on an astonishingly diverse array of beliefs, life-styles, and institutions. Pluralism raises a host of questions for the friend of democratic government. Does pluralism require special virtues in the citizenry to sustain it? Does it require a morally neutral constitution? What institutional arrangements best sustain it peaceably? Can pluralism be principled and non-relativistic? How inclusive or deep can differences in society be without threatening all order? Does religion undermine the tolerance necessary for a pluralistic society? Does pluralism corrupt religion? Does pluralism in the private arena require uniformity in the public arena? Does the easy-going niceness associated with pluralism debase all beliefs? These and like questions are raised throughout the chapters of this volume.

The perspectives offered in this volume are offered at a high level of scholarship and learning. Several are genuinely innovative and surprising. Together they do not advance a single thesis, but they create an unusually thoughtful and nuanced overview of social life today. The problems of negotiating pluralism in the public square that have come to light in the aftermath of 9/11 make these essays, which were written before that sad day, even more relevant.

Alan Wolfe addresses some of the questions previously mentioned and sets the stage for the others by championing pluralism not only within society but also within the academic disciplines, especially the social sciences and the humanities. The academic disciplines, after all, are the place where aspiring and talented young men and women launch their careers and develop their notions of citizenship. Since the humanities and social sciences take as their subject the human person, it is only proper, Wolfe reasons, that students should encounter a bewildering array of perspectives, beliefs, and approaches in these fields. Humans are, after all, bewilderingly strange and complex creatures. It should alarm us then that sub-disciplinary wars between advocates of competing methodologies place enormous pressure on departments throughout the academy to speak with one methodological voice. In the field of political science, for instance, department after department has fallen under the sway of rational choice theory. Department members who dare approach the field through a different lens are marginalized and considered old-fashioned. Wolfe here explicitly appropriates Isaiah Berlin's insight that pluralism is a precondition for freedom, even academic freedom. Pluralism is also needed to clarify and strengthen one's own beliefs. As scholars no longer subject their work to the peer review of persons outside their sub-disciplines, the search for truth is greatly diminished.

In response to this situation, Wolfe calls for the return of pluralism *within* departments and not just between them. To demonstrate that pluralism is possible, Wolfe locates pluralism as the norm at many religious colleges, where it is often established of necessity. Religious people negotiate between secular and sacred understandings of their everyday experiences, and therefore thoughtful religious persons often develop a disposition for irony and an understanding that a multiplicity of perspectives is a normal feature of life. And it is this disposition that Wolfe cares about most. Pluralism for Wolfe is not simply the existence of diversity within a society. Every nation at civil war experiences that. Pluralism instead means that citizens would rather live with difference than engage in culture wars. For the academy it means that professionalism within departments can be coupled with a commitment to ultimate questions.

Like Wolfe, Kevin Pybas focuses on the compatibility of religion and pluralism. Moreso than Wolfe, Pybas believes that religion can embrace social pluralism without irony and even joyfully. Case in point, pluralism is a matter of *religious* principle for the neo-Calvinist tradition. Pybas argues that traditional liberal theory reduces natural social relations to a number of social contracts and grossly fails to provide justice to the diverse groups that compose society. In particular, its public education system, described by Pybas as a unitary system, claims to be neutral but in reality privileges liberal civic beliefs and values over alternative values. Worse yet, it claims to speak from reason alone, failing to recognize its own articles of faith. Drawing on the vibrant writings of neo-Calvinist theorists, especially their patron saint Abraham Kuyper (Father Abraham in some Reformed circles), Pybas artfully elaborates on the theory of sphere sovereignty, a Biblical account of the pluralistic structure of society. Sphere sovereignty holds that implicit in creation itself are social spheres, each with their own animating principle. The task of the government is to insure that the unchanging regulating principles within each of the social spheres is honored. It is decidedly *not* the task of government to *generate* those principles. Pybas draws out the implications of this theory by arguing for a more pluralistic and just education system.

If sphere sovereignty emphasizes the horizontal differentiation of society, the Catholic theory of subsidiarity recommends a vertical pattern of social life in which the individual is nestled in a community of lower and higher associations. The purpose of the higher associations, such as the state, is to assist lower associations, such as neighborhoods and schools, to perform their functions when assistance is needed, but otherwise to stay out of the way. Subsidiarity advances the integrity of the individual by blocking the interference of the state in matters of individual responsibility and competency. This formulation is common fare to those familiar with the literature. Joshua Hochschild's innovative piece moves beyond the standard formulation in two ways. First he emphasizes the obvious overlapping aspects between sphere sovereignty and subsidiarity. Occasionally in the past, disagreement between these two potential political allies has been so disrespectful as to be amusing were it not so sad. Hochschild's argument is again novel in his emphasis on the responsibilities that individuals have in resisting encroachment of the higher spheres, such as corporations. He uses the agrarian ideal as exemplary of proud self-assertiveness and responsibility. By insisting upon self-reliance, the agrarian ideal not only resists state interference, it also strengthens family ties, encourages the development of talents (such as building one's house), and strengthens community. To a degree I would have believed impossible before reading his piece, Hochschild is even convincing in depicting the Amish community as a plausible alternative to Lockean liberalism and our corporate industrialism.

The Amish have resisted modernity, but resistance is hard work. Followers of Kojève and Fukuyama even claim that it is futile. My own contribution to the volume laments the creeping tendency of our public ideals, especially equality, to undermine legitimate authority in the private spheres. At work is something like the *Invasion of the Body Snatchers* in reverse, a logic in which nearly every corporate body (family, church, university, and even government) is reconfigured as a collection of self-satisficing individuals. To stem the invasion I argue we adopt several of the normative recommendations of Alexis de Tocqueville. Tocqueville, who called for a "new political science," understood that the primary intellectual battle in the modern age would be over *which* variant of democracy will prevail. With this thought in mind, I argue that much about how we govern ourselves has yet to be settled once and for all, and so politics is still a meaningful and proud human activity.

Politics has yet to be settled and is therefore changing all the time. Beverly Gaddy details an important change in the rhetorical landscape of presidential elections, specifically the unusual degree of public receptivity in the 2000 election to faith-based remarks from candidates. Gaddy nicely articulates the common explanations for this phenomenon and offers a novel and interesting explanation herself, namely that changes in religion make "God talk" more palatable. Persons today are more likely than ever to describe themselves as spiritual rather than religious. Compared to old-time religion, spirituality is less wedded to denominations, more tolerant, more pluralistic, and less driven by specific issues in the political arena. As spirituality becomes more private and individualistic—more reflective of deeply personal inclinations—it also becomes more fluid, more relativistic, less wedded to ecclesiastical institutions, and therefore less threatening in the public arena. Lieberman, Bush, and Gore each peppered many of their remarks with talk about the importance of their own faith, but these remarks did not encourage a culture wars approach to the campaign.

Presidential candidates may be less than eager to engage in a rhetorical culture war, but cultural differences still matter enormously to how citizens vote. We may be a pluralistic notion, but when it comes to voting, the two-party electoral system encourages groups to coalesce around Democratic or Republican leadership. Cultural differences help explain the logic of how various groups choose their political allegiances. Dale McConkey's research puts forward robust data revealing that cultural emphases not only matter, they matter most of all in shaping how voters vote. His research refines and modifies David Brooks' famous contention that the nation is geographically and culturally divided between Red America (Republicans) and Blue America (Democrats). In demonstrating the dominance of culture over money, McConkey's contribution virtually puts to rest the tired notion that voters vote just with their pocketbooks. This finding does not contradict Gaddy's thesis that religion is more tolerant than ever, for McConkey readily admits that the nation gave a "collective yawn" to the fact that Lieberman is Jewish. What it does establish, however, is that one cannot altogether dismiss the idea that there is a stand-off between competing cultures. Several expressions of "Bubba" culture (my term) such as evangelical religion, pickup ownership, hunting licenses, subscriptions to *Reader's Digest* and *Field & Stream* are highly significantly correlated to the Bush vote. In contrast, several variables closely related to "Bobo" culture (coined by David Brooks) such as secular outlooks, subscriptions to *Gourmet*, and wine drinking all are positively and significantly related to voting for Gore.

In his presidential campaign Bush understood that the soft underbelly of conservatism is the wide-spread perception that it is a hard-hearted ideology. Compassion, after all, has historically been a uniquely liberal virtue. Liberals care about the poor and disadvantaged, the historically oppressed. Conservatives, it is thought, care about achievement, property, and protecting the rules that constitute civilization even when those rules generate hardship. As P. J. O'Rourke proudly asserts, God is a Republican (and a stern one at that) and Santa Claus is a Democrat. In the last few decades, however, under the intellectual leadership of the late John Rawls and his followers, the place of compassion in liberalism has become more ambiguous. Charity, for instance, is anathema to Rawls. Compassion is legitimate only in so far as it is indiscriminate and material in orientation. Compassion, in contrast to justice, too often flows from religious sensibilities, turns too greatly on conceptions of better and worse ways of living, and depends too heavily for its efficacy on the charity of the privileged to make it a worthy political ideal.

Bush sought to exploit these shifting political winds (not to suggest he first read *Theory of Justice*) by making Charitable Choice the heart of his compassionate conservative agenda. Bush's policy would greatly amplify the existing Charitable Choice provisions of the 1996 welfare reform law. John Bartkowski and Helen Regis here examine the prospects of faith-based anti-poverty efforts by examining the actions of two prominent Mississippi churches, one a Southern Baptist church, the other an African American Church of God in Christ. Their findings are that faith-based charities, while perhaps helpful in some respects, will be no panacea in the war on poverty. Results, they concluded, will vary in quality enormously from congregation to congregation. The two churches they studied exhibited worlds of difference in their approaches to charity, how they spent their resources, their beliefs about welfare recipients, and the competing moral logics of compassion and judgment they employed. Divisions among churches and between denominations, racial prejudice, and other problems therefore make local, faith-based empowerment an uncertain policy initiative. The African American Church of God in Christ had much more success in their programs for recipients who were church members than for non-church members, suggesting that results even within a single church effort will be uneven. The authors noted that even many church members on the front lines believe that churches cannot replace government involvement.

Just as the government is reaching into the religious realm in novel ways, religious interest groups are finding creative ways of using traditionally secular emphases to advance their political ends in the judiciary. In decades past, religious groups attempted to secure their liberty through the Free Exercise Clause of the First Amendment. This is less frequently the case. Steven P. Brown deftly traces and explains the meteoric rise in recent decades of Free Speech cases brought to the Court by the New Christian Right. The emphasis on speech rather than the Free Exercise Clause complicates our picture of pluralism. While many evangelical-friendly scholars such as Stephen Carter lament a neutralist Court that fails to accommodate the interests of the faithful, the New Christian Right today exploits that neutrality for the goal of equal treatment. Liberal neutralists in turn are crying foul, ironically claiming that religious language is somehow distinctive. Brown notes a further irony that by advancing an expansive interpretation of free speech to achieve their goals, the New Christian Right takes a constitutional page from the defenders of flag burning and peep shows. Pluralism again proves its wildly unpredictable and complex nature.

If one's goal is to turn conventional wisdom on its head, one can do little better than Beverly Gaddy's second contribution. Most social scientists, including those sympathetic to religious causes, accept as a truism that religion is closely correlated to intolerance. Gaddy's groundbreaking chapter argues that this conclusion is largely an artifact of outmoded methodology and a product of how tolerance and religion are measured. Using improved methodological tools and more precise measurements, Gaddy argues that religion and intolerance are unrelated. Religion contributes very little to either the attitudes of tolerance or intolerance. The most controversial aspect to Gaddy's approach will surely be her distinction between the "extrinsically" and "intrinsically" religious believers. Gaddy tackles the issue directly and mounts a fine defense, drawing on academic literature while appealing to the everyday experience we have of judging the sincerity of others.

With the exception of Gaddy, Bartkowski and Regis, a great deal of this volume has focused on the divide between religious and secular forces in liberal society today. Therefore this volume would not be complete without the contribution of David Oki Ahearn. Ahearn focuses on deep distinctions *within* Christian political thought. Ahearn argues that the proper relationship between church and the political realm in the United States has largely been a contest between narrative theology and public theology. Narrative theology's most prominent voice is Duke seminary professor, Stanley Hauerwas. Hauerwas famously describes the church as a resident alien in a foreign land. Critical of what he describes as the church's co-optation into political life (Constantinianism), Hauerwas calls for the church to maintain her purity by keeping the church community distinct from the broader society. Certainly the gulf between church and liberal democracy is too great to establish a public or universal moral discourse. Establishing such a discourse, however, is precisely the purpose of public theology, which sees its political position as that of a critical citizen who seeks to improve the nation. Ahearn is admirably even-handed in discussing both of these positions, but finally he takes the side of the public theologian. He gently criticizes Hauerwas for his appropriation of the term Constantinianism in describing the church in the American experience as being unhelpful and misleading. More importantly, Ahearn recognizes that while the church will always be in tension with society, justice and love need not be in tension with public reason.

Justice and love need not be in tension with reason but they are properly in tension with one another in the well-ordered liberal regime. Or, so says Brad Stone. Former President Carter once said that America deserves a government as good and honest as her citizens. Brad Stone would caution President Carter that one should be careful for what one wishes. Stone's very bold and elegantly argued thesis is that the problem with American social life today is not a bankrupt government or a corrupt business world; these spheres perform tolerably well. The problem with American social life today is rooted in the corruption of our private morality. In particular, too many Americans are miserable spouses and terrible mothers and fathers. When one measures the relative luxury by which even the poor live today in America with the poor in other nations or even in America's past, it becomes clear that centrality of poverty pales in comparison to the sad state of the American family as a source of our social ills.

Stone argues, like many other authors in the volume, that persons are situated in a host of nestled communities: family, church, work, community, nation, world. Each level removed from the individual makes it increasingly difficult to love persons in any meaningful way. The liberalism of John Locke and Adam Smith—the liberalism Stone endorses—puts forward its conception of public justice as a moral remedy for smoothing over relationships between strangers, where, in other words, love is impossible. That being said, the nonjudgmental cosmopolitanism associated with liberal justice was never meant to govern relationships between intimates. Intimate relationships must be guided by a different ethic altogether—by a sense of obligation to kin and friends that is exclusive, discriminating, and responsive to praise and censure. Shame is central to this ethic, and so it can never pass the high standards of political correctness of today's liberal justice. Love itself is unjust. To devote one's time, focus, tender affection, and labor on one person is inevitably to ignore other persons. When mothers and fathers change the diaper of their little ones, give them music lessons, help them with their homework, and help defray the cost of college, they are unjustly favoring their children over children who do not have these advantages. It is not accidental, then, that in *The Republic* Plato playfully pokes fun at the zeal of some for achieving justice by depicting children as being raised in the just state by the state itself. What else but collective child rearing can insure equal treatment? Accordingly, Locke and Smith had wisdom enough never to hope that their conception of public morality would replace private morality. Unfortunately, the more cosmopolitan liberalism of Kant and his followers have had precisely this effect. The transformation, Stone argues, has been an unmitigated disaster for society.

Alan Woolfolk notes another transformation in modernity of equal import, namely the move away from virtue and its attendant emphases to an emphasis on values. Woolfolk reminds us that traditionally all ethical life was forged through the discipline of self-denial. The great transformation came when a decidedly aesthetic approach to life gained acceptance among the most sophisticated persons of society. "Reprehensible" lost favor as a term of judgment; "in poor taste" gained ground. Because aesthetic appeals are difficult to establish in common, morality became emotivist, non-judgmental, and therapeutic. Emphasis on self-esteem has become all but universal, shaping even private Christian education. The upshot is a citizenry described by Alan Wolfe in *One Nation, After All.* At the heart of the highly personalized morality common to ordinary citizens today is a live-and-let-live ethic. Wolfe's position is that, on balance, this morality is defensible because it makes pluralism and peace possible. What Wolfe celebrates, Woolfolk laments, for the cost of easy-going niceness is too great. Woolfolk believes what is lost is the possibility of cultivating true human greatness.

Together the essays of this volume sharpen our understanding of political and social life in the American experience. In many respects the essays are critical of political life in the United States, but remarkably absent from most of the chapters is any hint of either despair or utopianism. Loving criticism seems to be the dominant attitude. Love of nation is, of course, a mildly embarrassing emotion for the most sophisticated persons in our nation today, people like professors and college administrators. It is perfectly acceptable to praise America, even in the Academy, as long as one makes absolutely clear that what one is praising is not America as she presently is but America as she can be. Praising the idea and ideals of America, in fact, our most sophisticated scholars will tell us, requires that we temper our love of America as she presently is.

The events of 9/11 have brought the question of patriotism front and center to our political debates. Should thoughtful Americans love their nation? One reason to love America is the same reason why we love our children: it is ours. This is the thinking of America's most influential political philosopher, Richard Rorty. It also happens to be the thinking of G. K. Chesterton. Chesterton argued that if we love our nation, we can make it great. If we wait until it is great before we love it, it will go to pieces, quickly. Therefore to choose whether to love America based on a balance sheet of her merits and faults is a risky proposition. And yet to accept America independently of any judgment of her promise and problems cuts sharply against the American experience itself. Defensible American patriotism, therefore, suggests two components: devotion to the political community simply because it is ours *as well as* a prophetic standard by which we may nudge society toward our highest common aspirations. We should be encouraged, then, that the essays in these volumes suggest that life in the United States offers genuine human goods worth defending. We should further be encouraged that together these essays teach us how we may improve America.

February 2003

Chapter 1

The Potential for Pluralism: Religious Responses to the Triumph of Theory and Method in American Academic Culture[1]

Alan Wolfe

Theory and Method in the American Academy

The recent death of Isaiah Berlin, together with the publication of a biography of him and a collection of his representative essays, suggests that, despite his failure to publish a systematic treatise, Berlin was among the most original philosophical voices of this century.[2] An appreciation of his work leads inevitably to a concern with pluralism, raising the question of whether human beings are better off attempting to maximize one particular good to the best of their ability or trying to live with diverse, sometimes mutually exclusive, goods, even if the cost of doing so is the inability to maximize any of them.

Berlin was a defender of pluralism not only in politics but also in understanding. He argued that, just as we seek diverse goods, we should also appreciate diverse ways of knowing the world. Indeed one of the least appreciated aspects of Berlin's writings are his passionate statements about what could be called, in contemporary parlance, academic culture. Berlin himself was trained in the hothouse environment of analytic philosophy at Oxford but eventually decided that its rigorous pursuit of relatively narrow questions did not fit his way of thinking about the world. He is often credited with developing the field now called "the history of ideas" as an alternative. At the time he did so, there was no real place for such an academic discipline at Oxford, leaving Berlin, although he was honored with extraordinarily prestigious positions from a relatively early age, somewhat marginal to the academic disciplines of his time. As his biographer makes clear, Berlin's fame rested largely on activities outside the academy: wartime work in Washington, BBC broadcasts, and an insatiable appetite for hobnobbing with influential figures.[3]

Perhaps because of his experiences outside of academia, Berlin became an effective critic of what might be called the imperial pretensions of academic theory. His study of Marxism, combined with his experiences as a child in St. Petersburg, had already led him to be critical of totalizing theories which ambitiously seek to explain the entire world through one causal law of history. But, in typical fashion, Berlin did not merely identify such efforts at totalization as synonymous with Marxism but instead tried to delineate a particular style of thought attractive to people with many different objectives but united in their commitment to the relentless pursuit of one idea. Condorcet and Comte, not Karl Marx, are in many ways Berlin's real target. Of Comte, Berlin writes that his understanding of the social sciences aimed at "one complete and all-embracing pyramid of scientific knowledge; one method; one truth; one scale of rational, 'scientific' values." "This naïve craving for unity and symmetry at the expense of experience," Berlin concluded, "is with us still."[4]

For Berlin all such attempts to reduce our understanding of human beings to one system threatened to deprive people of their freedom. Individuals must, in Berlin's view, have the freedom to make choices, for without that freedom they cannot be considered responsible. Yet totalistic theories of society, certain as they are that they have uncovered the secrets of how societies "really" work, base themselves on the denial of human choice. If people really understood what the social scientist does they would avoid ignorant and ill-informed choices—at least according to the social scientists. "The more we know," as Berlin summarizes their viewpoint, "the greater the relief from the burden of choice."[5] Worried about the arrogance and unfreedom of imperialistic social science, Berlin discovered in humanistic thinkers a tragic sense of life that warned against making individuals perfect—all too perfect. This did not lead him to conclude that social scientific knowledge was illegitimate or wrong. "It is plainly a good thing," he wrote, "that we should be reminded by social scientists that the scope of human choice is a good deal more limited than we suppose."[6] The obvious way to preserve the value of social science theorizing while also recognizing its limits was to be pluralistic. Because human beings are complicated creatures who desire contradictory goods, the study of human beings must itself be a complicated affair, devoted to many, sometimes incompatible, ways of knowing. No one approach to the understanding of human beings ought ever to be permitted to drive all others out of existence.

Yet a case could be made that, in the contemporary academy, something like this has indeed taken place. I am not referring here to scientific disciplines. The study of non-human phenomena (or creatures) does not raise issues of pluralism in the same way as the study of human beings, since the former not only fail to desire contradictory goods, they also, in some cases, fail to desire any goods at all. Scientific disciplines do have bitter controversies over method. Even when data is "hard," moreover, interpretation can be "soft." In science, like in every other field of knowledge, academic freedom and a willingness to consider divergent points of view are requirements for the pursuit of truth. But science is not, and need not be, pluralistic once truths are established, for the task of the scientist is to build upon fact in order to reach the next level of analysis. The social sciences, by contrast, have both an explanatory and a normative character, and to the degree that the latter plays a role—which it must if the subjects under study are norm-making and norm-altering creatures—pluralism of method and approach becomes essential. Unfortunately, developments in the social sciences in recent years can only be described as a setback for pluralist ways of understanding.

The example of the lack of pluralism in the contemporary academy comes from the field of political science, more interesting because the theory in question—rational choice theory—is one that, seemingly in contradiction to Berlin's fears, prides itself on its commitment to human freedom. Arising out of micro-economics, rational choice theory has its roots in versions of libertarianism distrustful of government and dedicated to advancing freedom of choice as a normative goal. Yet when adopted by political science departments as a model for how scholarship ought to be conducted, the success of rational choice theory does seem to confirm Berlin's fears. For one thing, this theory is reductionist, constantly seeking to show why behavior which might seem to contradict its premises—altruism, for example—can nonetheless be explained in terms of rational choice.[7] In its unwillingness to recognize other forms of behavior than the one it prefers, rational choice theory demonstrates quite well the illiberalism of certain forms of liberalism, as if the wide variety of human behavior throughout the world has to be channeled into one thing and one thing only.

At the same time, rational choice theory has little respect for pluralism in the organization of academic life. Departments committed to rational choice theory generally can never have enough rational choice theorists. Political science being what it is, there will in any department be some individuals who are not committed to rational choice: political theorists for example. But it is possible to redefine political theory as "formal theory," thereby bringing a rational choice perspective to that aspect of the discipline. Or if tenure has insured that the political theorists in a department otherwise committed to rational choice are feminists or Straussians, they can essentially be left alone while the serious business of political science takes place elsewhere. But whatever the strategy, pluralistic departments of political science are unlikely to result once strong commitments to rational choice have been established. Since this theory and only this theory is presumed to be the basis for a proper understanding of human political behavior, hiring people with a different orientation—say, a historical or institutional understanding of politics—seems a silly waste of valuable resources.

I confess to being flabbergasted by the popularity of rational choice theory. As a participant in the radical attack on "behavioral" political science in the 1960s, I was certain that the sheer irrelevance of the research then undertaken was matched only by its inability to establish findings beyond the obvious.[8] I neglected what could be called "sociology of knowledge" reasons for the perpetuation of scientific models as the proper way to study politics. Large numbers of students were attending graduate schools, hoping to become professors in the rapidly expanding universe of higher education. Social science research was increasingly being funded by federal agencies. Graduate education came to wag the tail of undergraduate education. The only research model which seemed to be compatible with the evolving structure of academic organization in the United States was a form of knowledge production emphasizing the publication of journal articles rather than books, based on research carried out by teams, and emphasizing quantity of publication over quality.

My own attraction to the social sciences came about as a result of an undergraduate course I took at Temple University which introduced students to works of social criticism by scholars such as David Riesman, C. Wright Mills, and William F. Whyte. (I am teaching very much the same course now.) As someone "politicized" by the civil rights movement and Vietnam, furthermore, I was attracted to the political sociology then being practiced by scholars like Seymour Martin Lipset and Daniel Bell. Although I imagined myself in those days far too radical to be comfortable with their centrist political viewpoints, I viewed them as first-rate scholars and writers, dealing with important subjects in well-researched and well-written books. They also taught at America's leading universities, leading me to conclude that work along the lines they did was the key to academic success.

Only much later did I learn how marginal many of these scholars were to their universities and their disciplines. Riesman, a lawyer without a social science doctorate, was all but ignored by Harvard's majordomo, Talcott Parsons. Daniel Bell and Nathan Glazer had worked in journalism, making them always somewhat tainted among professional academics. Lipset wrote books when it was far more prestigious within the academic world to publish articles in refereed journals. Reinhard Bendix, like other European émigrés and refugees who had studied in the shadow of Max Weber and Karl Mannheim, could never be replaced. To my somewhat naïve eye, American social science departments were pluralistic because Columbia had both Paul Lazarsfeld and Robert K. Merton to do the science and C. Wright Mills to do the social criticism, while Harvard had both social relations and social studies. But such pluralism was more of a façade than a reality, since rarely did one faction hold the other in any respect.

Academic pluralism, if that is what it was, also proved to be tenuous. Once upon a time the fields with which I identify—sociology and political science—were also bifurcated geographically. There was something called "Midwestern social science." Led primarily by Michigan and Wisconsin, political scientists at Big Ten universities concentrated on studies of the American electorate, developing comprehensive data bases and taking the lead in article publication. Ivy League and West Coast universities, by contrast, were more "book" oriented and more likely to contain at least a few scholars who leaned in the direction of becoming public intellectuals.[9] Over the past twenty years, however, the coastal universities have been thoroughly "midwesternized." Harvard's sociology department never replaced Riesman, Bell, and Glazer after their retirements. With the exception of Orlando

Patterson, who has been in the department for nearly thirty years, and Theda Skocpol, who was tenured only after a lawsuit and who has in any case moved into political science, Harvard's sociology department built itself up by recruiting full professors from Wisconsin, North Carolina, Northwestern, and Ohio State. Much the same took place at Columbia (where Herbert Gans and Allan Silver no longer fit the department's profile) and Cornell (the home of Robin Williams). With a few exceptions—the University of Virginia, New York University, Berkeley—there is generally only one way to be considered professionally serious in the social sciences, and that is the one rooted in a model borrowed from the natural sciences.

I have no doubt that a great deal of good has emerged from the efforts I have described to make the social sciences more rigorous. Much of our understanding of social life has been enriched by systematic efforts to gather data that are then treated rigorously so that ideas about reality can be tested against measured dollops of that reality. Even the sociology of religion, a subject matter that comes closest to exploring the most subjective and meaning-laden aspects of human experience, can benefit from an emphasis on rational choice, as witnessed in the work of Rodney Stark.[10] Social science without the quantitative imagination would be hardly worth having. But neither would social science without the sensibility of a David Riesman or Daniel Bell. Because social science studies human beings, creatures who, as Isaiah Berlin insists, pursue many competing goods, they can only be studied by methods which also reflect many different, and sometimes contrasting, understandings of their actions. If pluralism in method and approach ought to be the guiding way to organize academic life in the social sciences and the humanities, that test has been failed.

Religious Institutions as One Exception

As a student entering college in the somehow appropriate year of 1960, I knew that there were religious institutions of higher education, although it never occurred to me to think about attending one. Catholic universities, in the circles in which I traveled, were best known for their basketball teams, while their academic qualities, as far as I could see, lay more in conveying dogma than in understanding the world. (Villanova, St. Joseph's, and LaSalle were the leading ones around where I grew up). I barely knew that Protestant institutions existed, and when I discovered one for the first time, called David Libscomb College in Nashville, and learned of the strict rules governing campus life, I could not believe that the place was in the twentieth century. As for Jewish universities, they were not even on my family's radar screen, since the whole point of being Jewish was to succeed in secular America. Call this prejudice, if you want, for no doubt I knew too little about what was actually happening in those places for which I had so little respect. But I also do not think my reaction can be completely attributed to ignorance. There was something insular about many of those institutions at that time. They did make claims to already know what they needed to know, making instruction seem more like the conveyance of dogma than the search for understanding. It was more important for them to keep the loyalty of their alumni than to attract the best faculty. If one were looking for a model of how to educate people broadly so that they could, upon graduation, go out into the world not only learned but with strong critical sensibilities, one would hardly think first of faith-based institutions.

There are ironies in the transformation of religious colleges and universities over the past thirty years fully as surprising as those by which the 1960s generation of student radicals became the apologists for the 1990s university. At the time I was active in protesting the nature of political science, I would have been aghast had anyone told me that someday I would be relatively sympathetic toward religious institutions of higher learning. But now, as I try to survey the American academic landscape, the conspicuous exception to the antipluralist pattern I have been describing are America's faith-based colleges and universities. Here one can find an academic culture less completely transformed by the single-minded drive toward theory in the humanities and data in the social sciences witnessed elsewhere in American academic life. While there will always be exceptions, philosophy departments at many institutions of higher learning which take their religious mission seriously continue to be interested in Continental philosophy and thus are relatively untouched by the emphasis in the rest of the discipline on analytic methods or the clarification of scientific concepts. A concern with religious themes in poetry, the novel, works of art, and music makes it difficult for departments in the humanities to treat those forms of "cultural production" as if their actual content was irrelevant to the questions we have about them. And political science departments in many faith-based colleges pay more attention to political theory and to the actual institutions of politics in the real world than political science departments in the secular culture, often, in the process, resisting some of the trends toward empirical methods and formal theorizing.

This is not to say that faith-based institutions can be characterized as pluralist. Many of them insist on the priority of the faith which guides them, inevitably assigning second-class status to approaches or beliefs associated with other faiths—or with no faith at all. Careful to preserve the tradition, religious institutions are less impressed by work that offers itself as the "cutting-edge" of new ways of theorizing the world. Often unable to compete with the salaries paid to academic superstars in the humanities, religious institutions try to do the best with what they have. If they retain more of a commitment to the liberal arts and to general education than the more prestigious private universities, this may be because they are more successful in recruiting excellent undergraduates than graduate students. The potential for pluralism, in other words, can be found at faith-based institutions almost in spite of themselves. Sometimes, nonetheless, religious colleges and universities will find themselves with highly ranked departments aggressively competing for prestige on the terrain established by secular institutions: Notre Dame's sociology department, for example, one of the best in the country, is widely regarded as a quantitative department. Still, if one wants to find a version of the academic culture which existed before the totalizing tendencies of recent years—one which has all the attractions of a skepticism toward academic pretension, as well as all the problems of a certain insecurity and insularity—then one must turn to faith-based colleges and universities.

No one knows whether religious institutions will continue to serve as a viable alternative to the dominant academic culture in America. There clearly are forces urging them not to do so. George Marsden has written about the pressures that follow when religious institutions opt to modernize and to join the academic mainstream.[11] But there are also threats from the other direction, ones which do not challenge the stature of these institutions as alternatives—quite the contrary, for they insist on their theological character—but may challenge their ability to be a *viable* alternative in an otherwise secular culture. Most prominent among them is the question of *Ex Corde Ecclesiae*, which seeks to strengthen the specifically Catholic character of American Catholic colleges and universities. But it is not just Catholic institutions that may be facing pressure to become more orthodox. All institutions of higher learning are dependent on their core constituencies for financial support. Public institutions have to worry about state legislatures. Elite private universities study the mores of suburban families with as much zeal as those families study the admissions processes of elite private universities. And the future of faith-based institutions will inevitably be linked to the nature of the faith-based communities they serve. Among Jews, therefore, Yeshiva University will respond to the resurgence of orthodoxy and ultraorthodoxy in ways that may strengthen the historic mission of the institution but which will also insure its isolation from the mainstream of American academic life. Even Brandeis University, which historically has been suspect among the most orthodox Jews, will find its character altered by the strength of religious traditionalism. Brandeis' secular orientation was at its strongest when assimilation and intermarriage marked the Jewish experience in America. Now when Jews can attend any university for which they can qualify, Brandeis, to carve out a market niche, needs to protect its reputation as a general university while appealing to those Jews in search of reaffirmations of their faith.

Protestant colleges also find themselves the beneficiaries of a return to religion in the secular culture. Parents dissatisfied with binge drinking, fraternities, and the peer pressure to which young people are so vulnerable are increasingly looking to evangelical colleges as an alternative. Campus life issues have an unpredictable relationship with curricular issues, but there can be little doubt that traditionalism in the office of Dean of Students will have an impact on faculty culture as well. Max Weber wrote about the paradox of success: John Wesley worried that Methodist piety would produce people so economically successful that they would lose their taste for Methodist piety.[12] In some ways, faith-based institutions face the opposite problem: they cannot be pious enough, at least in the eyes of their natural constituents, but responding to their piety can further isolate them from what passes for success in the academic culture. Religious colleges and universities do not face conflicts between their mission and the forces of modernization at only one time. These are ongoing tensions, and the next time they are resolved it may be more in the direction of faith than it was when Northwestern or Emory were making their decisions to join with the dominant secular culture.

Caught, as they always have been, between the forces of modernization and the attractions of faith, religious institutions face a future that no one can predict. Yet if there are to remain alternatives to the dominant secular culture, the future of those institutions is important to all students of higher education and not just those seeking to protect and preserve faith-based communities. I can envision three ways in which faith-based colleges and universities will respond to their present dilemma of choosing between pressures toward orthodoxy and fulfilling their potential for pluralism. I will call these rejectionism, parallelism, and opportunism. In the final section of this paper, I want to make an argument in favor of the last of them.

Three Responses

By rejectionism, I mean the option of joining with assertions of orthodoxy in an effort to return religious institutions to a position of instruction in the faith. There will be some, strongly committed to their faith, who will view pressures toward orthodoxy as positive developments and will feel obligated to encourage them. I wonder, however, whether rejectionism, whatever one's views about it, is even possible, at least for all those religious institutions which are not at the margins of American academic life. To have some sense of the viability of rejectionism, we all ought to watch with care the response of America's leading Catholic colleges and universities to *Ex Corde Ecclesiae.*

The response to this point has certainly not been one of universal praise. The Jesuit magazine *America* has called the latest draft of norms "unworkable and dangerous."[13] The president and former president of two of America's most prominent Catholic universities similarly found the document "positively dangerous" to Catholic institutions of higher education and warned of "havoc" if it were implemented.[14] From the perspective of someone like myself, who is not Catholic but who admires much of the scholarship at Catholic universities, the bishops' recommendations as written appear to make it impossible for Catholic colleges to preserve their character as it has evolved over the past three or four decades, making the price of rejectionism high indeed. But this is a matter that clearly will have to be worked out between the bishops and the presidents, trustees, and theology faculty of Catholic universities, and one can only hope that whatever resolution finally emerges, it is one that respects the pluralism these institutions have embodied. The great fear, by contrast, at least on my part, would be one in which these colleges were tempted to return to orthodoxy.

If there were such a rejection of modernity in favor of faith, it would certainly not be the first time. The American academic environment has always been capacious enough to include at least a few institutions which reject much of the world around them, such as Grove City College in Pennsylvania which consistently turned down federal funding as a way of avoiding what it considered to be intrusive federal regulation. One can easily imagine Protestant and perhaps some Jewish colleges responding to new pressures for orthodoxy by withdrawing from the world in ways familiar to us from the writings of Max Weber.[15] But they are almost certain to be small in number, which means, for many institutions, the search for other alternatives.

A second possible response to the situation in which religious colleges and universities find themselves would be to protect what I will call parallelism. By parallelism I mean the existence of more than one kind of academic culture within an institution, but structured in such a way that these various subcultures have little in common with each other but instead operate as if they were on parallel tracks. The temptations of parallelism can be found among those committed to a particular version of what George Marsden has called "the outrageous idea of Christian scholarship."[16] I have in mind the version that finds attractive the development of various kinds of "perspectivism" in the contemporary university. Not displeased to witness the collapse of Enlightenment projects based on the unity of knowledge, such scholars, while not necessarily attracted to feminism or multiculturalism, argue that such movements are correct to emphasize the partiality of knowledge in the contemporary world. Since the university acknowledges no one overriding truth, it follows that a Christian way of understanding the world constitutes a particular perspective which has just as much legitimacy as any other way of understanding the world.

The point I want to make about this attraction to perspectivism is not an epistemological one but a sociological one. Whether or not the philosophical claims undergirding perspectivism can be sustained, the concrete result of its appeal is to generate a series of academic subcultures each of which is committed to a particular approach but, because of its self-referential quality, has little to say to others who work from a different perspective. The issue, in a word, is not whether there are feminist or Christian ways of knowing, but whether there are feminist or Christian ways of granting tenure. For the creation of parallel subcultures within the university usually leads to a situation in which each subculture generates its own journals, its own circles of prestige, its own career paths, and, finally, its own claims to be the sole judge of those working within the parallel tradition.

When many parallel subcultures exist side by side in the contemporary university, the result is clearly not rejectionist. Advocates of particular points of view, including Christian points of view, accept rather than dismiss the forms and functions of the contemporary university: they emphasize the importance of the academic vocation, are committed to scholarship, and try to influence national debates about subjects of importance to them. But while such approaches are not rejectionist, neither are they pluralist. One does not, from a position of parallelism, enter the fray of academic debate prepared to have one's first assumptions open to scrutiny of others. Interaction with others outside one's perspective is not so much a situation of give-and-take as it is a kind of, at best, peaceful coexistence. Ways of knowing are not dissimilar from ways of life. And if ways of life are at stake, then the impulse of parallelism is defensive and protectionist. Parallelism survives by a kind of mutual suspicion. Its approach is not so much to welcome other points of view as to encourage a situation of academic laissez-faire which allows one point of view to exist so long as it agrees not to challenge the existence of other points of view.

Catholic universities have become homes for many types of parallel subcultures. It may make sense, therefore, for those responding to such pressures as *Ex Corde* to react by emphasizing the importance of parallelism to such institutions; indeed *Ex Corde* itself, with its proposed way of treating theology departments at Catholic colleges and universities in a way different from other departments, seems to endorse one version of parallelism. It may be that parallelism is an attraction in Catholic colleges because such colleges have always been to some degree parallel to other academic institutions in America. Not so long ago, after all, Catholic universities embodied a conservative alternative to the dominant liberal culture of the American academy, and one that was therefore attractive to dissenters seeking a place in a general system of higher education to which they felt marginal.

Yet this situation is no longer the case. Many religious institutions have willingly joined a national academic culture which has committed itself to such notions as academic freedom and hiring through merit. In some cases, Catholic commitments to liberalism go much further; indeed the position of the Catholic bishops on both domestic and foreign policy, with the exception of abortion, is closer to the left end of the contemporary political spectrum than to the right. The dilemma facing Catholic colleges and universities is that forms of parallelism have been essential to their growth into institutions of national prominence. They could rest at that point; after all, there is enough parallelism in secular research universities, usually embodied in feminist and multicultural perspectives, to enable Catholic colleges and universities to claim equality with them. But why should equality necessarily be enough?

There is, I believe, a third option facing Catholic colleges and universities as they struggle with the latest stage in the never-ending quest for the proper identity. I will call this option, opportunism. I intend this term to be taken positively. Secular institutions, I have argued in this paper, are committed in theory to pluralism but rarely practice it; members of departments, whatever their orientation, usually like to hire people exactly like themselves and universities like to compare themselves to other universities like themselves. Religious institutions, by contrast, are not pluralistic in theory but have been forced by circumstances to have a potential for pluralism in practice. By opportunism I mean an effort to try to fill that potential.

This is not an opportunity all such institutions will welcome. Surely many, if not most, religious institutions have a greater obligation to the life of their faith than they do to the reform of American higher education. The fact that the leading secular universities have in many cases developed their own forms of dogma, complete with strict professions of the faith, suspicion of outsiders, and arcane rituals is no reason why religious institutions, whose purposes are generally not pluralistic, should fill the resulting gap. Since appeals to live by one's principles are hard to resist, moreover, there are many reasons to believe that an atmosphere emphasizing greater religious orthodoxy is not one that would result in a search to fulfill pluralist potential.

Still, I think it would be a sad day for higher education if the lack of pluralism in the secular culture were matched by a lack of pluralism in the religious culture. Should that occur, we would indeed have a culture war in higher education, one in which the certain loser would be those, including myself, who think that culture wars of all kinds are far less preferable than efforts to live side by side with cultural and moral differences. But I do not think I would be the only one whose interests would not be served by such a situation. Should it come to pass that secular universities will continue down one path while faith-based colleges continue down another, both will be harmed.

I am not one of those writers prone to find fault with the modern research university. In my experience, faculty who pursue an active research agenda are often among the most stimulating and worthwhile teachers, while those who have given up on research all too often have given up on teaching—and service to their communities—as well. Nor do I join with those critics of the research university, from the right or from the left, who mock its scholarship and consider its way of doing business as little more than serving the needs of a tenured, and out of touch, professorate. But not everything in the contemporary university is as good as it can be. In particular, undergraduate education is often given less consideration in tenure decision than work with graduate students, even as the tuition of the undergraduates pays for the whole thing. There is, moreover, a failure of too much academic research, particularly in the humanistic disciplines, to speak to important issues facing our culture with which all citizens, including even professors, ought to be concerned. Finally, I find considerable truth in the arguments of David Damrosch, who uncovers in the mores of the contemporary university a kind of isolation, one that in turn can breed an atmosphere of resentment and irresponsibility.[17]

An engagement with religious traditions, as well as a willingness to live side by side with religious institutions, can, I believe, serve as a partial corrective to some of these tendencies. (I say partial because, suspicious of overzealous efforts to root out wrongdoing, I think some of them will never, and probably ought never, be changed). One gift that religion can offer the humanities and social sciences is memory. All too much academic research, I believe, is committed to innovation for the sake of innovation, as if it will inevitably be the case that the newest ideas are the best ideas. This may well be true in the sciences, but when the history of sociological (or economic or political) thought is viewed as a curiosity of little relevance to what contemporary social scientists are doing, the results are often as trivial as they are arrogant. One of the enduring lessons I take from the Lilly Seminar on Religion and Higher Education is Mark Noll's comment that the Christian has an affinity with history, for his religion is a historical religion. Academics who knew more about the histories of their disciplines—let alone the histories of their universities—would be less likely to exaggerate their own innovations.

In addition, religious scholars and religious institutions can help prevent the academy from insulting itself against the larger questions of meaning and purpose within which it exists. In theory, America's tradition of separation of church and state ought to lead religious institutions to a withdrawal from society, while America's other great tradition of land-grant universities ought to lead secular institutions to an engagement and involvement with the social problems of the day. Yet in some ways the reverse has taken place. Big Ten universities, in emphasizing a highly professional and scientific model of academic success, prize detachment, while religious institutions, arising out of a need to define for themselves what kinds of institutions they are, are constantly reworking mission statements in an effort to emphasize their relevance to the society around them. One could, of course, argue that for the university, mission statements are inappropriate; the university ought to do what it does rather than try to articulate what it does. But I think that if research universities worried more about what kinds of goals they have, they would be more likely to look favorably on research with public relevance, emphasize their commitments to undergraduate students, and even try to make a place for public intellectuals as well as for scholars.

Any benefits which might flow to secular universities from greater respect for people and institutions committed to their faith are more than matched by the gains which religious institutions would obtain from engaging with secular universities on their own terms. For whatever they are worth, I offer my personal impressions of the faith-based scholarship and commentary with which I have become familiar through my involvement with the Lilly Seminar. The most striking characteristic of this work is its oscillation. One voice in which religious scholarship speaks is an insecure voice, as if those who are engaged in such work feel a need to prove that they really do belong in the academy after all. Despite our faith, this message reads, we do pretty good work and you, the non-religious folk presumed to sit in judgment over us, really ought to recognize this. Yet, on other occasions, religious scholars speak out of a sense of superiority, that because of their communities of faith, they have managed to avoid the ills plaguing everyone else in academic life, especially the isolation, competitiveness, and lack of purpose they see around them. One advantage of the opportunistic response I am advocating might be to tone down both attitudes: to give faith-based scholarship enough security so that it feels less need for a defensive stance and to give it enough respect for what happens in the secular university to recognize how much academics of all persuasions have in common.

An even greater benefit which might flow to religious based institutions of higher education, if they took advantage of the opportunity to fulfill the pluralist potential they have been given, would be the avoidance of self-referentialism. A by-product of the paucity of pluralism in secular universities, I have argued, is the proliferation of academic subcommunities: whatever their other differences, postmodernists, rational choice theorists, Straussians, feminists, and critical race theorists tend to judge each other but to resist judgment from others. (Indeed one can foresee, if it has not already occurred, each of these subcommunities breaking up into sub-subcommunities, each with its own standards and prerogatives.) Despite, or perhaps because of, this sense of being a persecuted minority that can be found among religious scholars, a place can be made at the academic table for them. They would then become one more academic interest-group complete with their own journals, prestige circles, and professional associations.

This is a tendency that ought to be resisted for the same reason that postmodernists should not be allowed to be the sole evaluators of other postmodernists. In the social sciences (and to a lesser degree the humanities), an earlier generation's striving for objectivity has lost its legitimacy. There is something of value in that loss, for the notion that human beings could be studied without taking into account that human life is in significant measure moral and value-preferring proved to be naïve indeed. But one can also go too far in the other direction, as various Foucauldians have with their tiresome repetition that knowledge is political, a half-truth which in turn becomes the rationale for engagement in scholarship that is rarely tested against the criticism that comes from people outside the circle of like-minded believers. Given a history of religious sectarianism, there are certainly built-in tendencies for religious scholars to erect walls around their own work, to distrust the views of outsiders, and to use their work to reaffirm their faith. I leave it to others to wrestle with the complicated issue of how they balance their faith-commitments with their commitments to truth. But so long as truth is part of the equation at all, they will suffer from a lack of exposure to criticism which comes from uncomfortable, sometimes even unwanted, sources. The lack of such criticism, I believe, is what gives so much trendy academic work its character as seemingly daring yet bloodless, unorthodox yet thoroughly predictable, and politically motivated without political content. It would be a terrible shame if the religious scholarship I have come to admire and respect were to duplicate, in form if not in content, work like that.

There is strong reason to believe that what Christopher Jencks and David Riesman in 1968 called "the academic revolution" is over. Those who know that book will recall that its title was not meant to refer to the student rebellions of the period but to a transformation of the university in which faculty professionalism would become the model of academic organization. Jencks and Riesman wrote their book with a strong commitment to the kind of academic pluralism I have been advocating, which explains why they spent so much time on women's colleges, black colleges, and religious institutions. The authors were not very hopeful about the prospects for Protestant institutions, noting in passing that such colleges could only survive by opposing the world of capitalist rationality which Protestantism did so much to create. In writing about Catholic higher education, about which they had more sympathy, Riesman and Jencks wrote that "there is as yet no American Catholic university that manages to fuse academic professionalism with concern for questions of ultimate social and moral importance,"[18] a goal, they believed, such institutions should seek to reach.

One can argue about whether religious institutions of all types ever did combine professionalism with ultimate questions in the way Jencks and Riesman hoped that Catholic institutions would. My sense is that while the task of balancing these competing goods is enormously difficult and sometimes impossible, faith-based institutions have done at least as well as, if not better than, secular institutions. The question now is whether they will continue along those lines or will move either in the direction of copying secular universities or in the direction of returning to their religious roots. Oddly enough, both of the latter directions, however opposite from each other, share the fact that neither is as pluralistic as the continuing struggle to reconcile objectives that work at cross-purposes.

Notes

1. This chapter has also been published in *Religion, Scholarship, & Higher Education: Perspectives, Models, and Future Prospects*, ed. Andrea Sterk (Notre Dame, Ind.: University of Notre Dame Press, 2002), 22-39.

2. Isaiah Berlin, *The Proper Study of Mankind: An Anthology of Essays* (New York: Farrar, Strauss, and Giroux, 1998), and Michael Ignatieff, *Isaiah Berlin: A Life* (New York: Metropolitan Books, 1998).

3. Ignatieff, *Isaiah Berlin,* 221-43.

4. Berlin, *Proper Study,* 121.

5. Berlin, *Proper Study,* 156.

6. Berlin, *Proper Study,* 149.

7. An extensive critique of rational choice theory is contained in Donald P. Green and Ian Shapiro, *Pathologies of Rational Choice Theory: A Critique of Applications in Political Science* (New Haven, Conn.: Yale University Press, 1994).

8. My own participation in the radical caucus within political science is described in Alan Wolfe and Marvin Surkin, eds., *An End to Political Science: The Caucus Papers* (New York: Basic Books, 1970).

9. Alan Wolfe, "Books versus Journals: Two Ways of Publishing Sociology," *Sociological Forum* 5 (September 1990): 477-89.

10. Rodney Stark, *The Rise of Christianity: A Sociologist Reconsiders History* (Princeton, N.J.: Princeton University Press, 1996).

11. George M. Marsden, *The Soul of the American University: From Protestant Establishment to Established Nonbelief* (New York: Oxford University Press, 1994). See also Philip Gleason, *Contending with Modernity: Catholic Higher Education in the Twentieth Century* (New York: Oxford University Press, 1995).

12. Max Weber, *The Protestant Ethic and the Spirit of Capitalism* (London: Allen and Unwin, 1976), 175.

13. *America,* November 14, 1998.

14. J. Donald Monan, S.J., and Edward A. Malloy, C.S.C., "Ex Corde Ecclesiae Creates an Impasse," *America,* January 30, 1999.

15. Max Weber, "Religious Rejections of the World and Their Directions," in *From Max Weber: Essays in Sociology,* ed. Hans Gerth and C. Wright Mills (New York: Oxford University Press, 1946), 323-59.

16. George M. Marsden, *The Outrageous Idea of Christian Scholarship* (New York: Oxford University Press, 1997).

17. David Damrosch, *We Scholars: Changing the Culture of the University* (Cambridge, Mass.: Harvard University Press, 1995).

18. Christopher Jencks and David Riesman, *The Academic Revolution* (Garden City, N.Y.: Doubleday, 1968), 405.

Chapter 2

Neo-Calvinist Social Thought and Civic Education

Kevin Pybas

Within contemporary liberal political thought today the debate over educational authority generally centers on the issue of school choice. Broadly speaking, the issue of school choice is a debate about the justice of the state's monopolization of public education funds. Put another way, if education is a public good requiring the support of all taxpayers, does it necessarily follow that nongovernmental schools should generally be precluded from sharing in public funds? While the U.S. Supreme Court has recently declared that properly drafted voucher programs do not violate the United States Constitution, a more difficult objection to the use of public funds in nongovernmental schools is the claim that a unitary scheme of public education is required in order to ensure a peaceful liberal civic order.[1] Although there are important differences among commentators who advance this position, the general argument is that a unitary scheme of public education is necessary to inculcate those liberal values that promote civic unity.[2] Writers who take this view are "unitary" in their orientation in that they believe that civic education must be carried out primarily through tax-supported governmental schools. Unitary liberals, as I shall call those who insist upon the necessity of a unitary scheme of civic education, do not oppose private or nongovernmental schools per se, but believe it appropriate that little or no tax dollars be permitted to flow to such schools. They also believe that the existence of such schools should be conditioned on the ability of the state to require these school to teach liberal civic values. Some unitary liberals argue further that religion, especially fundamentalist Christianity, is a divisive force in need of taming. In this view, the state's monopolization of public education funds is necessary also so that children from families with strongly held religious beliefs will be drawn into the public schools where they can be educated away from inherited beliefs and toward liberal democratic civic values.[3]

Neo-Calvinist social thought, a neglected yet important tradition with liberalism, rejects the notion that social unity depends on a unitary scheme of education. The neo-Calvinist commentators under consideration, principally Rockne M. McCarthy, Donald Oppewal, Walfred Peterson, Gordon Spykman,[4] William A. Harper,[5] and James W. Skillen,[6] are what I shall call "pluralist liberals." Of course, all liberals tend to be pluralists in some sense or another. I am using the term here in a very specific way, namely, to characterize a group of contemporary liberals who reject a "unitary" approach to education and, instead, advocate a plurality of alternatives.[7] The neo-Calvinist position is, briefly, that public justice requires that the state treat its citizens fairly and equitably in their actual social and cultural diversity. This means that the state's funding only of schools it owns and controls while denying support for schools it does not own and whose underlying moral and philosophic commitments differ from what is deemed acceptable by the state is unjust. The state's attempt, moreover, to draw a sharp distinction between sectarian and supposedly nonsectarian beliefs is itself a deeply sectarian position that cannot withstand close scrutiny. In order to do justice to the diversity of moral and philosophic commitments represented in the polity, the state must fund a diversity of educational opportunities. The neo-Calvinists do not limit the state's role in education to collecting taxes and distributing proceeds therefrom. In order to guard against fraud and to promote good citizenship, the state may establish health and safety codes, attendance and antiracism requirements, and even academic standards. The state may not regulate in any of these areas, however, in a way that interferes with or undermines the inner life or particular mission of a given school.

In what follows, I lay out the foundations and important concepts of neo-Calvinist social thought and then discuss how the writers under consideration apply them to education.

The Religious Nature of All Beliefs

The educational pluralism of the neo-Calvinists is born of a larger view of social pluralism that derives from modern Dutch Calvinist thought. Critical to the coherence of the Dutch Calvinist tradition is the understanding that human beings are deeply and inescapably religious, whether an individual makes an expressly religious confession or not. This argument is both a descriptive and functional one. The neo-Calvinists argue that all belief, including guiding beliefs about such things as physics, mathematics, biology, economics—and science in general—are religious in character. Roy Clouser argues that a belief is a religious belief if "it is a belief in something(s) or other as divine, or it is a belief how humans come to stand in proper relation to the divine" where "'divine' means having the status of not depending on anything else."[8] In other words, a belief that something is self-existent is a religious belief, as is a belief about how human beings ought to orient themselves to that which is self-existent.

According to Clouser, then, belief in God is not the only type of belief that is religious in nature. Belief which replaces God "with something believed to be the nondependent reality on which all else depends" is no less religious in character than belief in God.[9] Clouser's point is that at the heart of all theories, practices, and institutions are core beliefs that are inescapably religious, beliefs which have as their foundation some idea about the "nondependent reality on which all else depends." Religious neutrality is thus not humanly possibly. All moral, legal, and political arguments about the right ordering of society, therefore, including that notion that public life must be nonreligious or committed to some idea of a common civic religion, are at their core religious arguments. To state the point another way, all worldviews and ideologies are expressions of religious belief. Marxism, pragmatism, humanism, and evolutionary materialism, for example, are no less religious at their core than are Christianity, Judaism, Islam, and other self-professed religions. The neo-Calvinists' insistence that all belief is fundamentally religious leads them to reject modern distinctions, evident in the political thought of Thomas Jefferson and other Enlightenment thinkers and enshrined especially in First Amendment religion clause case law, between sectarian and so called nonsectarian beliefs. Because all belief is fundamentally religious, all belief is at the same time sectarian in one way or another. In other words, all belief systems or worldviews, whether explicitly religious or not, arise from commitments that go beyond reason.

Structural Pluralism or "Sphere Sovereignty"

According to the neo-Calvinists, "sphere sovereignty" is a term that describes the Biblical account of the plural structure of society. The neo-Calvinists reject both the individualistic idea that atomistic individuals are the locus of authority and meaning in society and the collectivist notion that the aggregate whole or the solidarity of mankind has exclusive claim as the only social structure where ultimate value and meaning resides. The neo-Calvinists hold, instead, that our existence as human beings is defined by membership in a plurality of social relationships. Society is composed of "multiple social structures [which] are real and meaningful. Social entities, such as family, school, church, business corporations, and state, all have ontological standing." Society is not merely a collection of atomistic individuals, nor is it a seamless whole. It is complex and differentiated, comprised of multiple relationships, associations, or institutions, each with its own identity and responsibilities.[10]

The neo-Calvinists maintain that while John Calvin (1509-1564) and Johannes Althusius (1557-1638), second- and third-generation Protestant Reformers, laid important groundwork in the development of the concept of sphere sovereignty, the idea finds its clearest expression in the work of Abraham Kuyper (1837-1920), a Dutch Calvinist thinker and politician. Indeed it is Kuyper, a theologian, journalist, and prime minister of his country, among other things, who first uses the term "sphere sovereignty" to describe the divine normativity of the plurality of associations that make up society. As McCarthy and associates note, Kuyper lived during a time of increased governmental centralization, not only in his own Netherlands, but across much of Europe. The modern state's intrusion into more and more areas of life, Kuyper believed, came at the expense of the plurality of associations in society. Kuyper, building on the thought of Calvin and Althusius, among others, argued that social justice requires recognition of the fact "that there exist in life as many spheres as there are constellations in the sky, and that the scope of each sphere has been unerringly delineated by a unique principle, as its focal-point, namely, the apostolic injunction, 'each in its own order.'"[11] Kuyper's point is, as Skillen and McCarthy note, that the many spheres of life—family, church, education, politics, art, science, and others—are rooted in the structure of creation and that "each sphere of life should be free of direct control by any other so that each can learn obedience to God's special ordinances for its own domain."[12] Each sphere of life has its own structural norms that are to guide activities in that sphere. In each sphere individuals must be free to respond to the creational ordinances given for that activity. Kuyper writes:

> Family, business, science, art, and so forth are all social spheres which do not owe their existence to the State, and do not derive the law of their life from the superiority of the state, but obey a higher authority within their own bosom, an authority which rules by the grace of God, just as the sovereignty of the State does.[13]

Justice depends on the state observing the natural boundaries between its rightful sphere and the other spheres of society.

If the state may not intrude upon the activities that rightfully belong to another sphere of life, what, then, lies within the proper domain of the state? Kuyper writes that all the spheres of life

> interlock like cogwheels, and precisely in acting upon one another and in meshing with one another, they produce the rich, multifaceted variety of human society. But this also brings with it the danger that one sphere in life may break in upon another like a jerky cogwheel that shears off one cog after another until the operation of the entire machine is disrupted. This danger constitutes the rationale for still another sphere of authority, that of the state. The state must make it possible for the various spheres, insofar as they manifest themselves externally, to interact appropriately, and to keep each sphere within its proper limits. And since personal life may be suppressed by the group in which one lives, the state must protect the individual from the tyranny of his own group.[14]

The role of the state then is to ensure public justice, to "see to it that the cogwheels operate as they are meant to." It does this, first, by not assuming authority unto itself that rightly belongs to another social sphere. Second, it must see to it that the various spheres of society respect their own legitimate or creational limits. The state accomplishes this by seeing to it that one sphere of life does not impose itself on another and by preventing the different spheres from tyrannizing over individuals within them. For one nonstate sphere to try to exert influence over another nonstate sphere is as much a violation of God's creational norms as it is for the state to try to claim all authority unto itself. It would be a mistake, for example, to try to introduce the ordinances given for guiding life in the world of business into the world of art. The sphere of business is not the sphere of art is not the sphere of science is not the sphere of family and so on. Each sphere is ruled internally by sphere-specific ordinances from God. The role of the state is to "protect . . . the individual and define . . . the mutual relationships among the visible spheres."[15]

It might seem that the state, as the sphere charged by God with protecting the mutual relationships among the various spheres, stands above or is superior to all other spheres, but Kuyper denies this. The state does overarch the other spheres, so it is in a sense higher. But in contrast to collectivism, for example, its high position is due not to it being the whole of which the nonstate spheres are but mere parts. The state, in other words, is not coextensive with society. The state is one among other social spheres, but with a distinctive responsibility for administering justice in the whole of society. As Skillen and McCarthy note, "For Kuyper, the state takes its place not *above* all other spheres, but rather next to them. Its high and overarching position is due not to a natural hierarchy but to the state's peculiar character as *public* authority."[16] The responsibility of the state as public authority is to see that life in and among the many spheres of life abide by the creational ordinances. As public authority, the state "may not adopt its own will or choice as the standard, but is bound by the decision of a higher will, as expressed in the nature and purpose of these spheres."[17] The role of the state is, by the lights of God's creational ordinances, to ensure and promote public justice and to protect the rights of all social spheres and individuals within them.

Biblical Origins of Social Differentiation

According to neo-Calvinist social thought, then, society is composed of multiple social spheres, each with its own creational integrity. Within each sphere, distinctive creational ordinances guide its internal activities and restrict its authority to encroach upon the internal life of other spheres. But how does society come to be differentiated into distinct spheres? How do we know that society is indeed naturally differentiated and not a monolithic whole? Might not the plural structure of society be artificial, a result merely of human convention? If divinely or naturally ordained, how may we identify the various creational spheres of social life? The neo-Calvinist's response to these questions rests on a view of God's revelation in creation and scripture. According to the neo-Calvinists, before the Fall, life was a unity. Though human beings (Adam and Eve) were given different tasks, society was undifferentiated. The neo-Calvinists continue that basically all of life in its many dimensions was but one, an undifferentiated unity in complete communion with God. The wholeness of social life, however, was lost with the Fall. Sin fragmented and polarized society. The unfolding history of mankind could no longer be one with the creational design. Undifferentiated life gave way to a broken, clearly differentiated one.

The fact that social life was originally undifferentiated does not mean, McCarthy and associates argue, that the different aspects or spheres of life were not also present at the beginning. The various dimensions of life were indeed part of the creational design, but they have come into greater visibility and increasing clarity through historical practice. In the creational narrative of Genesis, we see different tasks being performed. There is "marrying . . . family living (Adam, Eve, Cain, Abel, and Seth), working (tilling the soil), learning (naming creatures after their kind), governing (guarding the garden), and worshiping (walking with God in the cool of the day)."[18] This account of how the differentiated nature of social life has its origin in the creational design does not suggest, the neo-Calvinists argue, a Thomist-like natural teleology, whereby there is a movement from potentiality toward completion or perfection. The Fall means, to be sure, that life can no longer be experienced in unadulterated unity with God, that social life is indeed fragmented and polarized. Even though the institutional forms of differentiated social life—families, the state, the church, schools, occupations, and so forth—come into view only after the Fall, the ordinances upon which they are based were established by God in the creation order. It is creation itself, therefore, and not sin, that accounts for the differentiated tasks to which human beings attend, for the separate and distinct spheres of life.[19]

The neo-Calvinists maintain further that the creation narrative does not exhaustively list the distinct, sovereign spheres of human activity. Nor, they contend, may an exhaustive list be found in scripture itself. While every social sphere has its origin in the creation order, history, read in light of God's revelation (creation and scripture), provides a record of the distinct spheres of human activity gaining greater clarity. McCarthy and coauthors write:

> History is the record of faithful and unfaithful responses to the creation order within various human communities. The structures *for* society take on concrete form in the structures *of* society. As we allow the biblical narrative to enlighten this unfolding process of historical differentiation, we see these nuclear tasks, originally clustered in a highly unified way around the family, gradually coming to their own in more sharply focused, highly specialized ways, each with its own structure and function.[20]

As history is "the record of faithful and unfaithful responses to the creation order," differentiation did not unfold in a consistent, even manner. Human beings frequently resist the creational mandates. Still, McCarthy and his coauthors maintain, we see in the historical narratives of the Bible, however inconsistently and sporadically, the disclosure of separate and distinct spheres of social activity, each guided by its own creational ordinances or norms.

The Progressive Revelation of Creational
Ordinances and Their Applications in Human History

As we have seen, the neo-Calvinists trace the plural structure of society to the ordinances of God. These ordinances, and not autonomous human desires or impulses, account for the differentiation of social life into different spheres of activity and are the authoritative foundation of all human life.[21] Genuine human flourishing depends on subjection to these divine laws. Human life is neither self-directed nor governed by material laws discoverable in nature through observation and reason. Even if one should hold that the laws governing the physical world are moved by material causes, this says nothing about the laws governing political or social life. "We are dealing with people," Kuyper writes, "thus, with spiritual beings. It follows that the laws which govern the political life of the nations are of a moral nature, and moral laws are inconceivable apart from a personal will as the source from which they issue."[22] Those who argue that the laws of the polity are discoverable by observation and reason alone are thus mistaken, not about the existence of discernible laws governing human affairs, but about the source of those laws and how they are known.

That observation and reason are not in themselves sufficient to discern God's ordinances does not mean that scientific observations are unimportant. Indeed the creational ordinances

> reveal themselves spontaneously in life. In the very process of painting
> and sketching and performing and sculpting our artists discovered the
> laws for the artistic enterprise. . . . The same is true of the laws which
> govern our thinking, the laws which govern commerce, and the laws
> which govern industry. We learn to know the laws of thought by
> thinking. By doing business we discover the art of commerce. Industry
> blazes its own path. The same is true for political life.[23]

Kuyper's point is that the ordinances that govern human affairs were woven into or made part of human nature at its creation. "Life comes first; afterward reflection on that life." In other words, man thinks, acts, does, then afterward discovers the laws of thought, of action, of doing, even as these laws are embedded in human nature from creation. Kuyper admits that this portrait of human life does not accord with our experience, as we commonly interpret it. Because of sin, because of its distorting effect, the idea that the laws for human affairs would progressively reveal themselves in history as humans progressed and developed is a "rarefied abstraction." The Fall means that our lives and experiences betray the creational design. "Pathology alone," Kuyper writes, "can never lead to knowledge of healthy life." What is more, our powers of observation and understanding are distorted as well. Sin means that man is no longer able to read aright the creational design. Human beings are thus doubly handicapped. The existence of sin means both that there is no undistorted life to observe and that our powers of observation are untrustworthy. Kuyper's point is that political theory, if it is not to lead us astray, must take into account the reality of sin.

The fact that sin distorts our lives and our understanding does not mean, however, that we forego observation of and reflection upon our experiences and seek simply to model political life on the Old Testament example of Israel. This view, Kuyper asserts, is itself unbiblical. Those who would seek to model the polity on the example of Israel mistakenly view political life as lying outside of the creational order; in other words, they believe that the state exists only as a result of sin. If this were true, it would be impossible to discern the creational ordinances in our nature and experiences. But on the neo-Calvinistic account, as we have seen, all of God's ordinances, including those for political life, were interwoven in human nature at creation. Political life thus does not lie outside of human nature. Our experiences, therefore, are not irrelevant to the right ordering of the polity. Two additional reasons counsel against modeling the polity after the ancient Hebrews. First, if the ordinances for political life lie outside of human nature and instead are revealed only in the scriptural account of the Jewish state, one could not expect to find any meaningful wisdom or insight in those polities unfamiliar with scripture. According to Kuyper, the examples of antiquity prove this thesis wrong. The wise laws and insightful statesmen and philosophers of the ancient states demonstrate that the ordinances of God were indeed planted in the breast of man at creation. Secondly, God's revelation to man, Kuyper argues, consists of both scripture and creation. Sin did not end the unfolding of the revelation begun at creation. Rather, even after sin, the creational revelation continues in "nature, human life, and history." The creational ordinances thus continue to display themselves in human actions, in human relationships and associations, in work and leisure. Scripture was given not because sin brought an end to the original revelation but because sin distorted life and our ability to draw accurate observations about our experiences. "What life itself, distorted and derailed by sin, could no longer reveal," Kuyper writes, "God in his love made known in his Word, also for our political life."[24] Knowledge of God's ordinances then depends not on special revelation but on natural or common revelation. Reading creation through the lens of scripture reorients human beings to the creational design that is now partially obscured by sin. Scripture "reveals to us the ground rules, the primary relationships, the principles that govern man's life together and his relationship to the most holy God."[25] Still, all human beings participate in the unfolding of history and, quite apart from biblical knowledge or an awareness that they may to some degree be living in accord with God's ordinances, do in fact bear witness, in greater and lesser proportions, to the ordinances.

That God reveals himself in history, in the lives of people and nations, as well as in scripture, means that one can neither "patch together civil laws from Bible texts" nor "supply a handbook for Christian political theory that is valid for all nations and all times."[26] In other words, although the Bible, the neo-Calvinists say, speaks to the whole of human existence, it is not an encyclopedia of revealed truths that can be applied in a cookbook-like manner to every conceivable situation. Instead, the Bible contains God's revelation for man in the form of the creational ordinances, whose practical application is not necessarily immediately obvious. This is not to say, however, that the "principles that govern man's life together and his relationship to God" are not eternal and universal. Rather, the principles or ordinances are unchanging, authoritative for all people at all times. The application of these principles, however, may vary. How, then, may these ordinances be identified and applied? In explaining how man can acquire knowledge of God's ordinances, Kuyper argues that what is fundamental is the "relationship one posits between God's life and the human world."[27] For Kuyper, God's ordinances come to light by a "mutual inter-penetration" of the unchanging principles of scripture *and* the scientific study of peoples and nations. The example of Christ is instructive, Kuyper argues. "The divine does not just hover above us," he writes, "nor just position itself beside the human, but it enters into human life, just as sin did, in order to permeate it and ennoble it."[28] A political philosophy that attempts to derive the ordinances for life from scripture without paying attention to the life and history of a nation is as inadequate as a philosophy that looks only at experience and ignores scripture.

In expounding how we come to know and apply God's creational ordinances, and what they mean for our lives, Kuyper emphasizes the importance of humanity's struggle for freedom and progress. Freedom is an unchanging biblical principle "because God's Word desires a moral, not a violent triumph of the good."[29] Scripture also reveals an impulse in human beings and nations toward progress, toward a fixed goal—that is, toward the kingdom of peace and righteousness. An additional principal that must be considered, Kuyper argues, is that happiness and human flourishing depend on faithful responses to these general principles. While these principles or creational ordinances are universal and unchanging, their application cannot be considered in the abstract. One must know something about life of the nation one seeks to apply the principles to. "What the application of these principles to contemporary issues should be," Kuyper writes,

> how they ought to be adapted to the nature of various times and peoples,
> what kind of expression they should find in the laws and decisions of
> government, must be regulated so exclusively by the phenomena of life
> that Holy Scripture does not even opt for any single form of
> government, and allows Christian constitutional law to consider a

> monarchy as well as a commonwealth, an aristocratic republic as well
> as a democratic federation.[30]

The point to stress here is that, according to Kuyper, liberal society can rest on biblical principles. Liberal society can be an appropriate expression of the creational ordinances. Put another way, adherence to biblical principles does not require a theocratic state. For Kuyper, the political arrangements appropriate for a specific nation depends on the interpenetration of scripture and the particularities of that nation, as revealed by close study of its history, its economic, political, and social life, and the habits, sentiments, and temperament of a people—in short, by study of all those features which give a nation its peculiar character. It is important to remember, Kuyper adds, that nations differ from each other and are constantly changing, even if slowly. One therefore cannot dismiss

> the differences among nations and the changing times. Each nation . . .
> has its own character, and in the course of time [one] finds a perpetual
> fluctuation of circumstance. These facts demand attention. [One] wishes
> not to be speculative or doctrinaire, but historical, because reality
> constrains [one] to be so.[31]

Christian political philosophy is thus neither static nor composed solely on the claims of scripture. But neither is it relativistic, grounded as it is in certain biblical principles.

Kuyper's account of creational ordinances and how they are known has important implications for statesmanship. The Christian statesman begins with fixed general principles, then

> knowing what man is, knowing what a nation is and the purpose of the
> nations, knowing the source of justice and authority, knowing too where
> the claim to freedom and progress derives its impulse, he possesses the
> compass that points the way across the tossing sea even when there is
> no land in sight.[32]

The Christian statesman, in other words, takes as his starting point God's sovereignty over all creation, the reality that God is the author of justice, that He reigns over men and nations, that genuine human flourishing depends on faithfulness to God and His ordinances. Absorption of these principles into his very being constitutes for the Christian statesman the "compass" which is to guide him in applying the ordinances to concrete situations. God's ordinances are thus to be given actual expression, not in a formulaic fashion, "but from that faith which takes up the Word of God into itself." The Christian statesman thus has great flexibility in deciding how, at any given time and place, the biblical principles apply. Once principles are formulated, they are to be clarified and sharpened as times and situations change. The needs of the present generation are not the same as the needs of past generations, nor will they be the same as those of future generations.

Though the general principles of scripture are unchanging, authoritative as they are at all times and for all people, as circumstances change, as different demands and needs arise, as the sentiments and habits of a nation change, so too should the application of the general principles change. In short, it is impossible to articulate a biblically informed public policy that is valid for all people at all times.

Applications of Sphere Sovereignty in Liberal Democratic Society: "Confessional Pluralism"

Closely related to structural pluralism is confessional pluralism. Confessional pluralism is, for the neo-Calvinists, an extension of the concept of sphere sovereignty to the circumstances of heterogeneous, secular liberal society.[33] Confessional pluralism is both an acknowledgment of the diverse belief commitments men and women have in liberal democratic society such as exists in the United States and a call for fair and equitable protection of the different commitments. We saw that under the principle of sphere sovereignty the state is not competent to define or dictate the activities of other social spheres. Recall that the state's role in society is to promote public justice. This requires that it not claim authority for itself over that which belongs to another sphere of life. It means also that the state must ensure that each sphere of society honors its own creational limits. That is, a critical role for the state is to ensure that one sphere does not infringe upon the rights and responsibilities of another sphere.[34] By this account of the responsibilities of the state, then, it lacks competency to define or dictate what philosophic and religious commitments individuals and groups ought to have and it violates its trust as the institution of public justice when it attempts to do so. Alternatively stated, the state violates its creational mandate as the sphere or institution charged with promoting public justice when it attempts to establish acceptable or orthodox beliefs for all of society. Implicated here, of course, in our own context, is the state's obligations under the First Amendment to the U.S. Constitution. According to the neo-Calvinists, public justice requires equal treatment of the religious freedom of all citizens,

> not because every religion is presumed to be equally correct or true on theological or ecclesiastical grounds but because government's competence to establish public justice coupled with its incompetence to define and enforce religious orthodoxy leads to a *civic-moral* conclusion that there should be fair and equitable confessional pluralism.[35]

This means more than simply that the private expression of religion ought to be safeguarded. Religion, the neo-Calvinists argue, cannot be confined to or confounded with institutional places of worship. Religious believers express themselves not only within the confines of churches, synagogues, and mosques, for example, but also outside of formal places of worship. Religious diversity expresses itself in the whole of society; therefore, genuine religious freedom means more than the right to worship during a chosen hour as one sees fit. In other words, religious diversity is not something that exists only inside houses of worship. The religious character of the citizenry is as diverse outside the formal gathering places where believers meet as it is inside them. "Believers of different stripes," Skillen writes, "may be obligated by their faith to rear their children in specific ways, to eat different kinds of food, to pursue their occupations in a certain manner, and to exercise their responsibilities distinctively in a variety of professions such as medicine, law, and even politics itself."[36] The neo-Calvinists contend that the Enlightenment project has sought to deny or suppress the reality that religious belief has a heterogeneous public character. It encourages heterogeneous private religious expression, but insists that all public expression of religion be homogeneous and of the civic variety. Confessional pluralism acknowledges the diversity of public religious expression and insists that the state, as the instrument of public justice, must protect the public and private expressions of religious belief of all its citizens. This means, for example, that the state's monopolization of public education funds violates the integrity not only of structural pluralism by ignoring the rights of families and schools but also of the religious freedom (confessional pluralism) of parents and children whose religious convictions lead them to seek an education different than that offered and permitted in government schools.

Sphere Sovereignty, the State, and Education

We have seen that, according to the neo-Calvinist tradition, God at the creation established governing and education or learning as separate and distinct human activities, each endowed with its own sovereignty and with its own creational integrity. This means that the state has responsibility for public justice and for protecting and promoting human flourishing in the various spheres of life—families, schools, churches, work, and countless other organizations and voluntary associations—that God has ordained for human beings. The creational mandate for the state is to see to it that each sphere of life interacts appropriately with all other spheres and that the rights of individuals within each sphere are protected. The neo-Calvinist view of schooling, on the other hand, is that it is an extension of child rearing. "Since children are not merely citizens, not simply wards of the state," McCarthy and associates write, "then their life in families must be recognized and nurtured in a way that harmonizes formal school education with family life."[37] Schooling is the primary means by which children are prepared for adulthood. It involves training in substantive academic subjects, moral instruction, training for employment, and training for citizenship. The neo-Calvinists contend further that in most circumstances parents are more likely to look out for the interests of their children than is the state. Schooling is thus primarily, though not exclusively, an extension of parental responsibility. In the neo-Calvinist account, then, "insofar as families have different views of life and different expectations for their children's future they ought to be free to choose schooling that is consonant with their religiously deep convictions as well as their civic obligations."[38]

Since the development of the common school in the mid-nineteenth century, a dominant view has been that one of its chief responsibilities is civic training.[39] According to advocates of common or public schooling, the state must inculcate in children values that tend to ensure the durability of liberal democracy. Common schools, it is argued, are necessary for the formation of a common civic culture; they enable society to overcome divisive moral and religious divisions in public life. While religious beliefs are classified as sectarian and confined to the private sphere, the moral instruction provided by the public schools is said to be is nonsectarian and common. Neo-Calvinist pluralism rejects the argument that civic education must be provided in public schools with a strictly secular setting for the sake of social unity. The neo-Calvinists maintain that "a common civic life no more depends on or requires uniform, government-run schools for all children than it depends on or requires an established church."[40] The neo-Calvinists argue that theirs is not a privatization argument. They insist that the state, as the agent of public justice, should fund *all* elementary and secondary education by means of public taxation. Allegiance to a liberal civic order, the neo-Calvinists maintain, depends not on the state, through the public schools, inculcating a common set of values in all children, but rather on laws that treat all citizens evenhandedly. "Only laws that treat all citizens fairly in their actual social and cultural diversity (the *pluribus*)," Skillen writes, "will be able to carry the moral force necessary to bind people together legally as citizens in a single republic (the *unum*)." A common polity, Skillen continues, "maintains the support of its citizens insofar as they are convinced that its laws treat them all fairly. It does not require the political imposition of a common educational or political ideology. It requires the just treatment of personal and social diversity."[41]

Believing as they do that all belief is sectarian in nature, the neo-Calvinists insist that the equitable funding of all schools would not violate the Establishment Clause of the First Amendment. Recall that for the neo-Calvinists, all beliefs, whether explicitly religious or not, rest on commitments that go beyond reason. Religious neutrality is not humanly possible—all human beings are deeply and inescapably religious. At the core of all moral, philosophical, political, even scientific, arguments are religious beliefs. Secular worldviews and ideologies are no less religious in character than are the beliefs of self-professed religions. Not only are so-called secular beliefs religious in character but they function in the same way as self-professed religious beliefs. That is, like the foundational presuppositions of religious beliefs, those of so-called secular beliefs likewise provide comprehensive orientations and beliefs from which all moral reasoning springs. The idea that self-professed religious belief is deeply sectarian while other belief is not is a myth, a vestige of the Enlightenment. It is wholly arbitrary, therefore, from the standpoint of public policy, to draw sharp distinctions between self-professed religious belief and ostensibly nonreligious belief. The neo-Calvinists thus maintain that the current school funding arrangement itself violates the Establishment Clause in that one faith or belief system is established at the expense of others. The neo-Calvinists' claim is not that there is a single ideological establishment across all public schools. Indeed, they note that "the dominant ideology and pedagogy might be highly Protestant in some parts of the country, thoroughly secularist in another part, or highly eclectic somewhere else."[42] The point, rather, is that a single belief system is established in each local school, whether it be Protestant, secular, or other. The present arrangement thus discriminates against parents who want an education for their children that is different from that which can be had in the local public school.

The neo-Calvinists insist that theirs is not a case of special pleading for Christians. They argue that the education of all children should be publicly funded, irrespective of the moral and religious commitments they and their parents have. Their argument is that the educational options families have should reflect the rich moral and religious diversity of our nation. All schools would share equally in public funds, whether organized around the teachings of self-professed religions such as Judaism, Christianity, and Islam, for example, or centered on humanist, Marxist, libertarian, or other ideologies. Fair and equal treatment of the diversity of moral and religious commitments in the American polity, the neo-Calvinists argue, would strengthen the common commitment of all citizens to the civic order. As things stand, the state's attempt to foster a common civic religion by drawing sharp distinctions between sectarian and supposedly nonsectarian beliefs divides rather unifies. Families whose moral commitments, theistic or otherwise, differ from what is deemed acceptable by the state are thus forced to educate their children at their own expense while still supporting the local common school through tax contributions. In a nation of diverse religious and moral commitments, the establishment of a moral orthodoxy in public education generates strife, the very thing supporters of the common school want to overcome. The solution, the neo-Calvinists argue, is to disestablish the common schools. In other words, just as the equitable treatment of diverse religious beliefs required the disestablishment of state churches in the early nineteenth century, equitable treatment of the diverse beliefs about schooling requires the disestablishment of state schools and the establishment of a tax-supported pluralistic school system.

In essence, the call for disestablishment, for public funding of all schools, whether the state owns and operates them or not, is a call for redefinition of the meaning of "public" schools. The criterion by which a school should be judged to be public, the neo-Calvinists argue, is not whether it is owned, financed, and managed by the state, but whether it serves a public function, i.e., whether it prepares children for adulthood by means of moral instruction, training for citizenship, and training for employment. On this score, nongovernmental schools contribute significantly to the public good and are therefore just as "public" in character as state-owned schools.[43] The criterion for funding then is whether the school is a genuine school, which thereby contributes to the public good, and not some fraudulent institution claiming to be a school.

To guard against fraud, the neo-Calvinists recommend the establishment of nongovernmental accreditation organizations along the lines that exist for institutions of higher education.[44] These accreditation agencies could establish criteria to ensure the health and safety of school children and to distinguish genuine schools from fraudulent ones. The accreditation agency would then inform the governmental agency charged with distributing public education funds of those schools entitled to such funds. The accreditation criteria could not be employed, however, in a manner that undermines the particular identity and mission of a given school. In other words, it might be an appropriate condition for accreditation that standardized exams be administered in English, history, civics, mathematics, and science, that teachers be certified, and that compulsory attendance laws and laws stipulating the number of days schools must be in session be enacted. It would be inappropriate, however, for the accrediting agency or the state to dictate how the subject matters must be taught. In calling for disestablishment of the public schools, the neo-Calvinists thus do not maintain that the state has no interest in civic education. The neo-Calvinists insist, rather, that the state's interest in civic training can be satisfied without it owning and controlling the schools and without it dictating how academic subjects are to be taught. The neo-Calvinists do not attempt to specify what form a common civics curriculum should take, but they insist that all schools should have a voice in deciding that curriculum. No school, in other words, should have standards it had no part in creating imposed on it. All affected parties must have a voice in establishing the criteria by which schools are deemed entitled to public funds.

While acknowledging the persistence of racial discrimination in America, the neo-Calvinists maintain that requiring all schools to be racially balanced would violate the principle of confessional pluralism. According to the neo-Calvinists, "Confessional or ideological identity, not racial identity, should qualify a student for acceptance in a school."[45] All schools should, in other words, have open enrollment. So long as the parents of a child expressed solidarity with the particular mission of a school, the school could not deny admission to the student based on his or her race. To be sure, this practice would result in some schools with racial imbalances. For example

> Some schools with an explicit religious confessional identity, such as Jewish day schools, are unable to meet racial balance quotas because of the relatively few minority race members in such a community. A school sponsored by a Black Muslim group represents the other side of the racial coin. The denial of [public funds] to either of them because of a failure to meet racial quotas is a denial of confessional pluralism in education.[46]

The point is that although schools receiving public funds would be required to accept students of all races so long as they and their parents agreed with the mission of the school, some schools will inevitably be populated predominantly if not entirely by one race due to the religious or confessional nature of the school. Allowing that racial imbalances will occur, the neo-Calvinists add, however, that the state, as the agency of public justice, is entitled to deny public funds to schools organized simply to promote racist ideologies.

Conclusion

One need not accept the theological foundations of neo-Calvinist social thought, as most Americans today surely do not, to acknowledge the fairness and equity in the pluralistic education scheme the neo-Calvinists propose. Were their recommendations heeded, no longer would dissenting parents and children have to suffer violations of conscience in order to partake directly of a public good they have helped to fund. A pluralistic education system, moreover, would no doubt go far toward ending the divisive political battles that ensue as one group of parents after another struggles, quite understandably, to see that the education their children receive is consonant with their own values and commitments. Those who advocate a unitary educational scheme would assuredly object that what the neo-Calvinists propose is a formula for social disunity. Besides, resources are limited and the liberal tradition has never regarded rights of conscience as absolute. Might it be, however, that advocates for a unitary educational system have it backward? Should not the state be obligated to present persuasive evidence that civic peace actually depends on the government monopolizing public educational funds? Should not the state be required to present compelling evidence demonstrating that social cohesion can be achieved only by collecting taxes from all families but distributing education funds therefrom to government schools only? What evidence is there, after all, to show that children educated in nongovernmental schools and at home do not become good citizens? The neo-Calvinist writings are important, too, in light of the deep suspicion, if not hostility, of many contemporary liberal theorists toward people of serious religious belief. When so many secular liberal theorists are of the opinion that firm religious beliefs inevitably lead to intolerance, if not also to outright racism and anti-Semitism, how ironic it is that the neo-Calvinists, who could not be more explicit about the comprehensiveness of their biblically centered faith and philosophy, turn out to be more genuinely liberal and accepting of diversity than their secular counterparts.

Notes

1. See *Zelman vs. Simmons-Harris*, 122 S. Ct. 2460 (2002).
2. See generally Amy Gutmann, *Democratic Education* (Princeton, N.J.: Princeton University Press, 1987); Amy Gutmann, "Undemocratic Education," in *Liberalism and the Moral Life*, ed. Nancy L. Rosenblum (Cambridge, Mass.: Harvard University Press, 1991);

Amy Gutmann, "Civic Education and Social Diversity," *Ethics* 105 (1995): 557; Stephen Macedo, "Liberal Civic Education and Religious Fundamentalism: The Case of *God v. John Rawls?*" *Ethics* 105 (1995): 468; Stephen Macedo, "Multiculturalism for the Religious Right? Defending Liberal Civic Education," *Journal of Philosophy of Education* 29 (1995): 223; Stephen Macedo, "Community, Diversity, and Civic Education: Toward a Liberal Political Science of Group Life," *Social Philosophy and Policy* 13 (1996): 240; Stephen Macedo, "Transformative Constitutionalism and the Case of Religion," *Political Theory* 26 (1998): 56; Stephen Macedo, *Diversity and Distrust: Civic Education in a Multicultural Democracy* (Cambridge, Mass.: Harvard University Press, 2000); William A. Galston, *Liberal Purposes* (New York: Cambridge University Press, 1991); and William A. Galston, "Two Concepts of Liberalism," *Ethics* 105 (1995): 516.

3. Gutmann and Macedo are representative of this view. They simply presume that Christian fundamentalists and others of serious religious belief threaten social cohesion. That is, they make no real showing that serious religious belief is incompatible with support for the civic order. There is an unfortunate tendency, too, as Stanley Fish notes, in many contemporary liberal political thinkers, of whom he includes Gutmann and Macedo, to categorize Christian fundamentalists as racists and anti-Semites. For many liberals, says Fish, these groups constitute a "an epistemological criminal class . . . an undifferentiated mix joined together by an obdurate refusal to 'listen to reason.'" "In liberal eyes," continues Fish, religious fundamentalists, be they Christian, Jewish, or Islamic, "are, or are very likely to be, racists." Stanley Fish, "Mission Impossible: Settling the Just Bounds between Church and State," *Columbia Law Journal* 97 (1997): 2255, 2283-84.

4. Rockne M. McCarthy, Donald Oppewal, Walfred Peterson, and Gordon Spykman, *Society, State, and Schools* (Grand Rapids, Mich.: Eerdmans, 1981).

5. Rockne M. McCarthy, James W. Skillen, and William A Harper, *Disestablishment a Second Time* (Grand Rapids, Mich.: Christian University Press, 1982).

6. James W. Skillen, "Educational Freedom with Justice," in *The School-Choice Controversy: What Is Constitutional?* ed. James W. Skillen (Grand Rapids, Mich.: Baker Books, 1993), and James W. Skillen, *Recharging the American Experiment: Principled Pluralism for Genuine Civic Community* (Grand Rapids, Mich.: Baker Books, 1994).

7. Though not my concern here, there are, of course, other traditions within liberalism that might be called pluralist, as I have used the term. For example, Stephen Arons makes policy arguments similar to those of the neo-Calvinists, though from a modified libertarian perspective in his *Compelling Belief: The Culture of American Schooling* (New York: McGraw-Hill, 1983) and *Short Route to Chaos: Conscience, Community, and the Re-Constitution of American Schooling* (Amherst: University of Massachusetts Press, 1997).

8. Roy Clouser, *The Myth of Religious Neutrality: An Essay on the Hidden Role of Religious Beliefs in Theories* (Notre Dame, Ind.: University of Notre Dame Press, 1991), 22-23.

9. Clouser, *The Myth of Religious Neutrality*, 18.

10. McCarthy et al., *Society, State, and Schools*, 15-30 (quote is from 18-19); James W. Skillen and Rockne M. McCarthy, *Political Order and the Plural Structure of Society* (Atlanta: Scholars Press, 1991), 2-3.

11. Abraham Kuyper, "Inaugural Address at the Opening of the Free University of Amsterdam," October 20, 1880, in Skillen and McCarthy, *Political Order*, 260, citing 1 Corinthians 15:23.

12. Skillen and McCarthy, *Political Order*, 241.

13. Abraham Kuyper, *Lectures on Calvinism* (Grand Rapids, Mich.: Eerdmans, 1931), 90, quoted in McCarthy et al., *Society, State, and Schools*, 49.

14. Kuyper, "Inaugural Address," 260.
15. Kuyper, "Inaugural Address," 260.
16. Skillen and McCarthy, *Political Order*, 398. Emphasis in original.
17. Kuyper, "Inaugural Address," 261.
18. McCarthy et al., *Society, State, and Schools*, 158.
19. McCarthy et al., *Society, State, and Schools*, 156-59. See also Skillen and McCarthy's discussion of Abraham Kuyper in their *Political Order*, 400-401.
20. McCarthy et al., *Society, State, and Schools*, 159. Emphasis in original.
21. The following discussion is drawn from Abraham Kuyper, "Selections from Newspaper Articles Written for *De Standaard*, October 16-November 7, 1873," in Skillen and McCarthy, *Political Order*, 242-57.
22. Kuyper, "Selections from Newspaper Articles," 245.
23. Kuyper, "Selections from Newspaper Articles," 245-46.
24. Kuyper, "Selections from Newspaper Articles," 250.
25. Kuyper, "Selections from Newspaper Articles," 250.
26. Kuyper, "Selections from Newspaper Articles," 251, 255.
27. Kuyper, "Selections from Newspaper Articles," 254.
28. Kuyper, "Selections from Newspaper Articles," 254.
29. Kuyper, "Selections from Newspaper Articles," 256.
30. Kuyper, "Selections from Newspaper Articles," 250.
31. Kuyper, "Selections from Newspaper Articles," 255.
32. Kuyper, "Selections from Newspaper Articles," 256.
33. It is not clear in the writings of the neo-Calvinists under consideration whether the idea of confessional pluralism is a twentieth-century development or has its origins in pre-twentieth-century interpreters of Calvin. McCarthy and coauthors note, in writing of Calvin, that "confessional pluralism had not yet come to expression in his thinking or in that of his contemporaries. They were still living too much in the shadow of a society shaped by the ideal of an enforced universal Christendom." McCarthy et al., *Society, State, and Schools*, 42.
34. Undeveloped in neo-Calvinist thought is reflection upon just how much diversity of views can be accommodated within a particular sphere of life. That is, the neo-Calvinists do not address the likelihood that in a generally secular liberal order such as exists in America, where few people are disposed to accept the neo-Calvinist worldview, there will be disagreement within a particular sphere as to what the creational ordinances are and what they require for that sphere.
35. Skillen, *Recharging the American Experiment*, 84. Emphasis in original.
36. Skillen, *Recharging the American Experiment*, 86.
37. McCarthy, Skillen, and Harper, *Disestablishment a Second Time*, 129.
38. Skillen, *Recharging the American Experiment*, 128-29.
39. See generally Charles Leslie Glenn, Jr., *The Myth of the Common School* (Amherst: University of Massachusetts Press, 1987), and Diane Ravitch, *The Great School Wars, New York City, 1805-1973: A History of the Public Schools as Battleground of Social Change* (New York: Basic Books, 1974).
40. Skillen, *Recharging the American Experiment*, 129. See also McCarthy et al., *Society, State, and Schools*, and McCarthy, Skillen, and Harper, *Disestablishment a Second Time*.
41. Skillen, *Recharging the American Experiment*, 90, 135.
42. Skillen, *Recharging the American Experiment*, 130.
43. See especially Rockne M. McCarthy, "A New Definition of 'Public' Education," in *The Blackboard Fumble*, ed. Ken Sidey (Wheaton, Ill.: Victor Books, 1989), 77.

44. The following discussion is drawn from McCarthy et al., *Society, State, and Schools*, 174-88; McCarthy, Skillen, and Harper, *Disestablishment a Second Time*, 124-35; and Skillen, *Recharging the American Experiment*, 125-36.

45. McCarthy et al., *Society, State, and Schools*, 187.

46. McCarthy et al., *Society, State, and Schools*, 187.

Chapter 3

The Principle of Subsidiarity
and the Agrarian Ideal

Joshua P. Hochschild

> It is an injustice and at the same time a grave evil and disturbance of
> right order to assign to a greater and higher association what lesser and
> subordinate organizations can do.
>
> —Pius XI, 1931

> Throw out the radio and take down the fiddle from the wall.
>
> —Andrew Nelson Lytle, 1930

There is a normative principle of social associations which has been articulated in various intellectual and religious traditions and is implicit in much classical and medieval political thought. According to this principle, smaller, more local, or "lower" human associations have proper social functions which should not be assumed by larger or "higher" associations. For ease of discussion, let us refer to this principle as it has been denominated by modern Catholic social thinkers, as "the principle of subsidiarity."

In discussions about religion, politics, and community, the principle of subsidiarity has been invoked most commonly as a basis for limited government.[1] However the principle is even more relevant to such discussions—especially with respect to the idea of "community"—than merely in terms of its immediate implications for government policies. Insofar as it recommends a pattern of organizing social life in general, and not just that part of social life which touches the state, the principle has implications for the choices of families, neighborhoods, and commercial enterprises, indeed for all social agents, individual and corporate.

The implication on which I wish to focus in this chapter is the responsibility of primary, local associations, especially families, to prevent their proper functions from being taken over by other social spheres, particularly by the sphere of the modern, technologically enabled market economy. This implication, I argue, can properly be described as "agrarian," insofar as the agrarian tradition has highlighted the value of relative self-sufficiency for such primary and local associations as family and community, and insofar as the agrarian tradition has opposed social forces such as capital markets and technological "progress" which can threaten a more "natural" social order.

The Principle of Subsidiarity and Limited Government

It is easy to see why the principle of subsidiarity has so far been considered mainly with respect to its immediate implications for the scope of government. To the extent that the principle has entered public discussions, it finds a natural home in considerations of political theory, where there are established debates about the appropriate degree of government intervention in social and economic matters.

Indeed, historically, the explicit articulation of the principle of subsidiarity has been prompted by a desire to respond to the increasing power of the state and the kinds of regimes that such power makes possible. In Roman Catholic circles, the history of the formulation and articulation of the principle of subsidiarity is usually traced to the first so-called social encyclical, *Rerum Novarum*, written by Leo XIII in 1891.[2] This encyclical addresses those "new things" which in the modern world were affecting "the condition of the working classes," and it consists largely of a condemnation and refutation of socialism. Though it does not yet mention by name a "principle of subsidiarity," it does seem to assume some such principle, especially in passages like the following:

> It is not right, as We have said, for either the citizen or the family to be absorbed by the State; it is proper that the individual and the family should be permitted to retain their freedom of action, so far as this is possible without jeopardizing the common good and without injuring anyone. (*Rerum Novarum*, §52)

This passage implies that certain activities are proper to lower associations and should not, at least under normal circumstances (where "the common good" is not "jeopardized"), be taken up by higher ones. But here the specific higher association being considered is the state, and Leo is warning that the state ought not to usurp functions which do not properly belong to it. Thus, the emphasis of *Rerum Novarum* is that states must avoid "unwarranted interference" (§48), and again that societies should "avoid unwarranted government intervention" (§64).

The principle of subsidiarity was more explicitly formulated in a social encyclical written on the fortieth anniversary of *Rerum Novarum*. Pius XI wrote *Quadragesimo Anno*, "on reconstruction of the social order," not against socialism but against liberal individualism and the more inhumane manifestations of capitalism; nonetheless, as in *Rerum Novarum*, one of the major concerns is the dangers of the centralization of power. It is with respect to this concern that the principle of subsidiarity begins to be formulated. The relevant passage is worth quoting at length:

> As history abundantly proves, it is true that on account of changed conditions many things which were done by small associations in former times cannot be done now save by large associations. Still, that most weighty principle, which cannot be set aside or changed, remains fixed and unshaken in social philosophy: Just as it is gravely wrong to take from individuals what they can accomplish by their own initiative and industry and give it to the community, so also it is an injustice and at the same time a grave evil and disturbance of right order to assign to a greater and higher association what lesser and subordinate organizations can do. For every social activity ought of its very nature to furnish help to the members of the body social, and never destroy and absorb them. (*Quadragesimo Anno*, §79)

Though formulated more generally here, the focus of this encyclical again is the restraint of the state. Indeed, like *Rerum Novarum*, *Quadragesimo Anno* begins with a discussion of the state. The influential German theologian Oswald von Nell-Breuning—who is said to have contributed to the composition of the encyclical—explained the reasoning of Pius XI: "The reason for beginning his discussion with the state is, characteristically enough, not the intention of having the state assume new responsibilities, but, on the contrary, to demand that it refrain from activities into which it has intruded or, in part, been forced."[3]

The principle of subsidiarity was revisited in another anniversary social encyclical, John Paul II's *Centesimus Annus* of 1991. There, even more than in *Quadragesimo Anno*, the emphasis of the principle is its demand for the restraint of higher associations. The following passage appears in a discussion of the proper relationship of the state to the economic order:

> The principle of subsidiarity must be respected: A community of a higher order should not interfere in the internal life of a community of a lower order, depriving the latter of its functions, but rather should support it in case of need and help to coordinate its activity with the activities of the rest of society, always with a view to the common good. (*Centesimus Annus*, §48)

It is this formulation of the principle which could be considered its official Roman Catholic formulation, as it is quoted in full in the *Catechism of the Catholic Church* (1994). There again the implications of the principle for government policy are emphasized, as is clear from the context that the *Catechism* gives to the quotation:

> Socialization also presents certain dangers. Excessive intervention by the state can threaten personal freedom and initiative. The teaching of the Church has elaborated the principle of subsidiarity, according to

which "a community of a higher order should not interfere in the
internal life of a community of a lower order. . . ." (*Catechism of the
Catholic Church*, ¶1883)

The *Catechism* stresses the implication of limited government again, saying: "The
principle of subsidiarity is opposed to all forms of collectivism. It sets limits for
state intervention" (¶1885).

Consistently, then, in the Roman Catholic Church, the principle of subsidiarity
has been offered as setting limits on the scope of government. It is perfectly
understandable that this is precisely how the principle has been received. In the
1986 pastoral letter "Economic Justice for All," the U.S. Catholic bishops wrote:

> The primary norm for determining the scope and limits of governmental
> intervention is the "principle of subsidiarity." . . . This principle states
> that, in order to protect basic justice, government should undertake only
> those initiatives which exceed the capacities of individuals or private
> groups acting independently. Government should not replace or destroy
> smaller communities and individual initiative. (*"Economic Justice for
> All,"* ¶124)

It should be no surprise, then, that to the extent that the principle of subsidiarity has
been invoked in discussions of political theory and political policy, it is the
implication of government restraint that has been most widely discussed.[4] As an
article by Christopher Wolfe makes clear, the primary relevance of the principle of
subsidiarity appears to be as a "ground of limited government"; as he argues,
"subsidiarity . . . is a more satisfactory foundation for ideas of limited government
than what the American tradition of political thought (drawn largely from Locke)
offers."[5]

Because of this (classical) "liberal" or "libertarian" implication, the principle of
subsidiarity has found a natural home in "neo-conservative" Catholic thought.
George Weigel has emphasized the libertarian implication of the principle,
explaining that it "tried to set clear boundaries to state power."[6] David Bosnich has
argued that "the principle is the bulwark of limited government and personal
freedom." According to Bosnich, its consistent application "would entail respect
for the mechanisms of the free market and opposition to state intervention." The
principle, he says, "conflicts with the passion for centralization and bureaucracy
characteristic of the Welfare State."[7] Adolpho Lindenberg, another Catholic
interested in defending free markets, has written:

> We believe that in order to better understand the limits of government
> action in the socioeconomic order, we must invoke the principle of
> subsidiarity. According to this principle, the state should take action and
> exercise a substitute function only when social sectors or business
> systems are too weak or are just getting under way, and are not equal to
> the task at hand. Such supplementary interventions must be as brief as

possible, so as to avoid removing permanently from society and business systems the functions which are properly theirs.[8]

In the same vein, Robert Sirico has written:

> The clear meaning of the subsidiarity principle is to limit the powers and responsibilities assumed by the higher orders of society. In nearly every occasion in which the principle has been invoked in the last one hundred years of official Catholic social teaching, it is in the context of limiting the uses of power.[9]

Sirico continues this trend, noting:

> The principle has found its political expression in the American concept of federalism, and, in Europe, the concept has become a critical part of the debate on the relations between nations and the central authority of the European Community. In these political contexts, the principle has been invoked by the partisans of limited government over centralized management of people, states, and nations.[10]

Stephen Krason, in a study which offers "an evaluation of contemporary American political ideologies in light of Catholic social teaching," has the principle of subsidiarity playing a central role in that evaluation, but primarily insofar as it implies restraints on government intervention. "The basic principle limiting the state," says Krason, "is subsidiarity."[11]

These representative discussions of the application of the principle of subsidiarity by Catholic social thinkers all make reference to that principle as it was developed explicitly in the recent history of Catholic teaching. However the principle of subsidiarity has had some expression in other religious traditions. A parallel to the Catholic formulation of the principle of subsidiarity is the principle of "sphere sovereignty" articulated by the Dutch Reformed theologian and statesman Abraham Kuyper (1837-1920).

Here again, we find that the emphasis of the principle is on limiting government. Kuyper discusses sphere sovereignty in his lecture on "Calvinism and Politics." Articulating different social spheres, Kuyper explains that they each have a proper degree of sovereignty, with which the sphere of government must not interfere. "In all these [social] spheres, the State-government cannot impose its laws, but it must reverence the innate law of life."[12]

Kuyper's notion of sphere sovereignty seems to be implicitly present in the political philosophy of another important Protestant political theorist, Johannes Althusius (1557-1638). Althusius structured his great work *Politica* (1603) to emphasize the primacy of local, more "natural" associations, beginning with the family.[13] Though his ultimate goal is to describe the commonwealth as a whole, Althusius is very clear that the government of a commonwealth must respect the authority and jurisdiction of the smaller, more local and natural, associations out of which it is constituted. It is no surprise, then, that Althusius's "design for a federal commonwealth" has been presented as an important theory limiting the scope of government.[14]

The Principle of Subsidiarity and the
Responsibility of Lower Associations

We have seen that in its historical articulation and application, the primary implication of the principle of subsidiarity has been what we might call libertarian, or, in the classical sense, liberal: the restraint of the state. But the principle of subsidiarity has broader implications, because the principle concerns all human associations; in all cases, not just in cases involving the state, it presumes the priority of the "lower" or more local association, and the responsibility of the "higher" association not to hinder, but only to help, the lower associations in their functions.

Indeed, the principle can be summarized thus: it is the function of higher associations to help lower associations fulfill their functions. This is why it is called the principle of *subsidiarity*; *subsidium* is Latin for "help" or "assistance."[15] This central notion of assistance is perhaps most clear in the language of *Quadragesimo Anno*: "Every social activity ought of its very nature to furnish help to the members of the body social, and never destroy and absorb them" (§79).

It is important to notice, then, that the principle of subsidiarity regulates human associations because it assumes something about the *relations* of the *functions* of different "levels" of associations. The principle assumes that there are different levels of associations and that each level of association has its proper functions. The fact that the principle of subsidiarity implies a specific limitation on state intervention only follows from a more general and immediate implication: *any* higher association must avoid unwarranted interference with the functions of a lower association. It is a weakness of the "libertarian" appropriation of the principle of subsidiarity that it tends to ignore the fact that the principle can be applied to all relations of associations, not just to cases where the state is one of the associations.

But there is a second, related weakness of the libertarian appropriation of the principle of subsidiarity: it tends to place the main burden of responsibility on the higher association—in this case, on the state—not to interfere with lower associations. However, inseparable from the burden of responsibility on higher associations not to take over the functions proper to lower associations, is the burden of responsibility on lower associations to keep proper functions from being taken over by higher associations. In order to abide by the principle of subsidiarity, not only do higher associations have to avoid usurping the functions of lower ones, but lower associations must avoid abdicating their functions to higher ones.

Indeed, even in an article which argues primarily for curbing government intervention, Sirico notes this burden of responsibility on lower associations. Of the principle of subsidiarity, he says, "Its implications are profound." After noting a first implication, that "it places limits on the rightful duties of the state," Sirico continues by saying that the principle

> imposes obligations on lower order institutions such as the community, church, family, and individual, and it obliges these lower orders to fulfill certain moral and practical functions essential to the functioning of a well-ordered and free society.[16]

Sirico insists that the main emphasis of the principle of subsidiarity is to limit the power of higher orders, but then he says, "It is also true, of course, that the lower orders are by no means relieved of their responsibilities."[17]

The mutual responsibility of the relative higher and lower associations is also clear in the summary of the principle of subsidiarity offered by Joseph Komonchak. Among the elements of the principle Komonchak elucidates are the following two:

> The principle of subsidiarity requires *positively* that all communities not only permit but enable and encourage individuals to exercise their own self-responsibility, and that larger communities do the same for smaller ones.... It requires *negatively* that communities not deprive individuals and smaller communities of their right to exercise their self-responsibility. Intervention, in other words, is only appropriate as "helping people help themselves."[18]

The burden of responsibility which belongs to the lower order is also implicit in the formulation of the principle of subsidiarity from *Quadragesimo Anno*: "It is an injustice and at the same time a grave evil and disturbance of right order to assign to a greater and higher association what lesser and subordinate organizations can do" (§79). This language equally prohibits higher associations from seizing the functions of the lower, and lower associations from ceding their functions to the higher.

Nell-Breuning makes it clear that the principle is concerned more generally with a natural social order than with the specific right of lower associations to be free from interference:

> As far as the activity of the individual and the smaller community is adequately efficient, it must not be replaced by the activity of higher social units. If, notwithstanding, this is done, a reversal of social order ensues, an offense against nature which, as experience teaches us, will meet with heavy penalties.[19]

Of course, the maintenance of the natural social order is just as much the responsibility of lower as higher associations. The emphasis on a natural order is also implicit in the etymology of "subsidiarity." As noted, the principle is denominated "subsidiarity" from *subsidium*, or "help"; if higher orders are limited to helping lower orders, it must be assumed that there are proper functions of the lower orders, functions which the higher orders may help the lower orders to perform.[20] If higher associations have a responsibility to "help" lower associations, then presumably the lower associations have a prior responsibility to perform their functions as best they can—higher associations cannot help lower associations which do not help themselves.

The emphasis on help or assistance is seen also in Kuyper's formulation of the principle of subsidiarity, even though it is not reflected in his title for the principle, "sphere sovereignty." According to Kuyper, though the state cannot "interfere" with other social spheres, it does have a responsibility to "cooperate" with the social spheres. Beyond what is required for its own maintenance, the state has the "right and duty," according to Kuyper, to assist the other spheres in the performance of their proper functions. This involves specifically the right and duty, in Kuyper's words, "whenever different spheres clash, to compel mutual regard for the boundary-lines of each" and "to defend individuals and the weak ones, in those spheres, against the abuse of power of the rest."[21]

As Kuyper's articulation of the principle of subsidiarity reflects the responsibility of the state to limit itself to *assistance*, so too does it reflect the responsibility of lower orders to help themselves. Kuyper states this responsibility directly:

> A people therefore which abandons to State Supremacy the rights of the family, or a University which abandons to it the rights of science, is just as guilty before God as a nation which lays its hands upon the rights of the magistrates. And thus the struggle for liberty is not only declared permissible, but is made a duty for each individual in his own sphere.[22]

The responsibility of lower associations to help themselves is made more clear once the principle of subsidiarity is understood within the context of the history of Western political philosophy which is supposed to be its home. For though it has been explicitly formulated only recently, the principle of subsidiarity is not supposed to be a new principle. As Sirico has put it, "Subsidiarity is not some new notion . . . ; rather it lies at the core of the Western concept of the free and virtuous order."[23] Another writer, emphasizing the long pedigree of the principle of subsidiarity, has said that it is "neither a theological nor even really a philosophical principle, but a piece of congealed historical wisdom."[24] John Finnis is among those who have traced its theoretical origins to Plato and Aristotle.[25] Indeed, we have already seen how the principle of subsidiarity was implicit in Althusius's approach to politics. The general structure of Althusius's *Politica*, moving from the primary, most local and natural, association—the family—up through different, progressively less local and less natural associations, parallels the structure of the beginning of Aristotle's *Politics*.

Indeed, any history of the principle of subsidiarity must place it in the tradition of classical philosophy, with its explicitly teleological approach to government.[26] According to Thomas Kohler, "The principle of subsidiarity insists that the state and all other forms of community exist for the individual."[27] As Nell-Breuning wrote in commenting on *Quadragesimo Anno*, "Let us remember that Leo XIII never tired of repeating that all social life and, therefore, of course, all economy, emanates from the individual."[28] Johannes Messner, writing on the principle of subsidiarity, argued that it cannot be separated from the view that "society must be organized around man, his ends, and the vital tasks of his self-fulfillment."[29] As Benjamin Llamzon put it, "Subsidiarity, of course, stands four-square with the priority of the individual over the state."[30]

The priority of the individual is a central insistence of classical political philosophy;[31] Llamzon finds it in Thomas Aquinas, whom he calls "the foundational thinker for subsidiarity as it appeared in *Quadragesimo Anno*."[32] Althusius quotes Aquinas on the function of government: "To govern is to lead what is governed to its appropriate end."[33] Dante summarizes this fundamental element of classical thought in his *Monarchia*: "Citizens do not exist for the sake of consuls, nor the people for the sake of the king, but on the contrary the consuls exist for the sake of the citizens and the king for the sake of the people."[34]

Indeed, it would be fair to say that the principle of subsidiarity is as much an anthropological principle as a social one.[35] Its foundation is a certain view of man, namely of man as an essentially political animal, whose primary political needs are best satisfied by the communities of association closest to him. Thus, the tradition of political philosophy in which the principle resides emphasizes the functions of individuals and the lower orders of association which serve them. Aristotle, for instance, in discussing political organization, first discusses the functions of marriage, and the household broadly speaking, as satisfying the individual's most basic and direct social and economic needs.

Yet despite giving priority to the individual, it should not be inferred that either the principle of subsidiarity or the classical tradition of political philosophy to which it is traced implies a strict individualism which cannot regard social associations as real, natural, and irreducible. The ability of a social association to serve its members in fact depends on that association's being a real social unit with its own proper functions. Not only the individual but the family and every other relatively local social sphere has real and natural functions which must be respected. Indeed, higher levels of association serve not only individuals but lower levels of association, and for higher spheres to be expected to serve lower ones, those lower ones must respect the reality of their own proper functions and their responsibility to carry them out. It is for this reason that, just as strongly as the principle of subsidiarity forbids higher associations from assuming the functions of lower associations, it also forbids lower associations from surrendering their functions to higher associations.

The Economic Sphere and the Family

While historical circumstances make it perfectly understandable why the principle of subsidiarity has been considered primarily in terms of its implications for state intervention, and especially for state intervention in economic matters, it should now be clear that the principle has implications for all levels of social association and that between any two levels of social association there are reciprocal burdens of responsibility: higher associations should not "interfere" with lower ones, and lower ones have a duty to perform their proper functions without relying on higher ones.

The responsibility of lower associations not to surrender their proper functions to higher associations has been partially obscured by the fact that in the context of established debates it is reasonable and proper to emphasize the libertarian implication of the principle of subsidiarity, namely, that governments not interfere in lower associations. This libertarian implication fits especially conveniently with classical liberalism's defense of free markets and praise for the functions of the market economy. The usefulness of the principle of subsidiarity for this agenda is clear, and of course a central contention of this agenda must be granted: advances in technology and the growth of the industrial commerce have brought great advantages to individuals and families.[36] Nonetheless, material prosperity is not the only social effect of economic and technological advance. It would be irresponsible to ignore the extent to which the lower levels of social order have changed in order to accommodate the scale and institutional forms in which the "advanced" economies of "developed" industrial (or postindustrial) societies manifest themselves.

One of the intended effects of economic and technological advance is the possibility that social functions can be performed with greater ease or efficiency. But such apparent progress often entails that the performance of a particular social function becomes dependent on forms of technology, or on economic and social institutions, from which they were formerly independent. As a result of technological innovation and economic development, such lower associations as families, neighborhoods, and towns can become tempted (and sometimes even required) to rely on higher associations—either particular business organizations, specific industries, or the sphere of commerce generally—for what was once provided by, and considered the responsibility and function of, lower and more local associations.

Again, it needs to be reiterated that the market economy and technological progress have brought undeniable material benefits; and of course the economic sphere can be understood as one of the beneficial "mediating institutions" between the individual and state, acting as a check on the trend toward centralization and consolidation of political power.[37] Nonetheless, a social sphere which is capable of "mediating" between higher and lower associations must take care to maintain its proper, subsidiary relation to lower associations. Whatever can act as a "mediating institution" is itself capable of usurping the proper function of lower associations. Specifically, the technologically enabled market economy is a social "sphere" which has historically been capable of taking over social functions previously reserved for lower associations.

These are facts which have been ignored or downplayed by those who exploit the libertarian implication of the principle of subsidiarity in the context of the defense of free market capitalism; there the principle of subsidiarity is invoked to limit state intervention, and any criticism of the market is assumed to be at least implicitly a call for state intervention. But it is certainly not necessarily socialist or statist to notice that a high percentage of the citizens of advanced Western countries today are dependent on large business corporations; after all, much of this dependence is encouraged by government, in the form of subsidies, contracts, tax structure, and other regulations. Even those who use the principle of subsidiarity primarily in defense of a free market economy sometimes admit that "moral, social, and psychological abasement accompanied the technological and economic progress [of industrialization]."[38] Such an acknowledgment is an established part of Christian social criticism, including much that has been inspired by the "social encyclicals" discussed previously. Nonetheless, among those who have written about the principle of subsidiarity, Kohler is rare in noticing that the principle is violated by "the strong tendency of modern capitalism to overwhelm and eventually to dissolve the discrete, the local, the particular . . . the places where the habits of self-rule are practiced and learned."[39]

The most obvious association, or social sphere, which has suffered from this tendency is the family. Yet few writers have discussed the relevance of the principle of subsidiarity to the family or household. Those few writers who have considered the principle of subsidiarity with respect to the family have only treated how the principle can be applied *within* the family. Wolfe, for instance, cites as an illustrative "example" of subsidiarity the relationship between parents and children: though parents have greater competence to perform a task, they appropriately allow some tasks to be performed by children, for the sake of the children and the family as a whole.[40] But the principle of subsidiarity also applies to the relationships between the family and other social associations. This is recognized explicitly in the *Catechism of the Catholic Church*:

> The family must be helped and defended by appropriate social measures. Where families cannot fulfill their responsibilities, other social bodies have the duty of helping them and of supporting the institution of the family. Following the principle of subsidiarity, larger communities should take care not to usurp the family's prerogatives or interfere in its life. (¶2209)

One of the "larger communities" which should not "usurp the family's prerogatives or interfere in its life" is obviously the state; thus, as the *Catechism* discusses, the principle of subsidiarity forbids the state from usurping the functions of the family.

But besides the state there is another threatening "larger community." While it might be difficult to conceive of it as a "community," we have seen that it can and has been considered a "social sphere," indeed, as a social sphere with which the government ought not interfere: the sphere of the market economy.

The modern family, as an institution, is marked by its willingness to shift from what was once a dependence on its own resources and those of closely related local associations to dependence on large industries and distant economic forces. For the performance of many of their basic functions, families are now dependent on very removed social "associations": they depend for food on a food industry, for health on a health care industry, for entertainment on an entertainment industry; they depend for energy on an energy system, for transportation on a transportation system, and for education on an education system. This constitutes an extreme dependence on distant and higher social associations to perform the functions which have traditionally been considered the responsibility of more primary, local, and natural associations. Indeed, this historically rather recent dependence of households on a (government-subsidized) "global economy" constitutes perhaps the most widespread and easily recognizable violation of the principle of subsidiarity today.

The erosion of household functions was already noticed by Catholic social thinkers in connection with *Quadragesimo Anno*. Nell-Breuning discussed it in his commentary on that encyclical:

> Liberal Capitalism did not create the family but Liberal Capitalism did create conditions under which, for increasingly large numbers of people, the family life which human nature and the natural law demand has become almost an impossibility. The transfer to independent organizations of much of the economic production formerly carried on in the family was in large part necessary. This alone would not have endangered and supplanted the family for which enough economic activity remained. Even though the family now as a rule cannot be a productive unit, yet it still remains a consuming unit and, as such, still has ample economic purpose to form a strong bond to secure its unity, especially, if the family have some common fund of goods, or best of all their own homestead. Instead, the family has been allowed to fall to pieces as a consuming unit and indeed, in alarming degree, even as a center for human living.[41]

What Nell-Breuning recognized as "the plight of family life" which was one of "the by-products of industrialism" has not gone unnoticed by American social and political thinkers. Robert Nisbet famously argued that what precipitated the twentieth-century "quest for community" was precisely this transfer of functions from the family to economic and governmental spheres. What has not been as often noticed is that the principle of subsidiarity speaks directly to what Nisbet recognized as the modern "functional irrelevance" of primary associations like the family:[42] according to the principle, families have a responsibility not to give up their proper functions.

Now it must be admitted that Nisbet spoke as if the loss of the functions of primary associations were a fait accompli, the result of economic and political forces beyond the power of the primary associations;[43] at best, it seems, Nisbet hoped that small associations would develop new functions. It is not clear, however, that the loss of function is totally beyond the power of the primary associations; indeed, there could be a responsibility to try to revive some of the old functions. Though economic incentives sometimes work against them, there is no reason why families today cannot take more seriously the business of taking care of their members: caring for the elderly, educating the young, and growing, making, building, and preparing the various things that family members "consume." Not only is the family a level of social association at which violations of the principle of subsidiarity are widespread but, it is also the level at which it is most obvious how to set about corrective measures: families can take it upon themselves to change their habits and patterns of life.

Of course, the present attempt to apply the principle of subsidiarity to the relationship between the sphere of local, natural associations and the sphere of the modern, technologically enabled market economy may appear somewhat anachronistic in regarding the household, and communities of households, as social units with duties to perform particular functions for themselves. After all, the "economic sphere" which was criticized earlier for taking these functions away from more local associations is most often justified on the very basis of its ability to meet the needs of individuals, families, and local communities with great efficiency and flexibility. If the new social institution, the market economy of the industrial age, fulfills these social needs so well, then it may seem that individuals and families best fulfill their functions precisely by taking full advantage of it. At the extreme, it might seem that if families and communities existed precisely in order to meet the needs of individuals, and if these needs are now met by new, modern social institutions, then the traditional, local associations are neither necessary nor even possible; any attempt, it can and has been argued, to treat households, neighborhoods, and villages as the primary or "natural" loci of various economic and social functions is not just anachronistic but nostalgic.

But the appearance of anachronism here highlights the radical nature of the principle of subsidiarity and its implications of responsibility discussed above. For while the principle of subsidiarity is usually explicated in terms of levels of social functions, if the principle is to have the normative force that it is intended to have, those functions cannot be understood simply in terms of the satisfaction of needs but in terms of the fulfillment of duties. The principle of subsidiarity is primarily about social roles, not resources; it is not a matter of the efficient distribution of power, but of the just distribution of authority. John Finnis characterizes the principle of subsidiarity as "a principle of justice";[44] it could also be described as a principle of jurisdiction.[45]

Moreover, the classical and religious traditions out of which the principle of subsidiarity emerges all insist that there are certain kinds of social associations, most obviously the family, which are natural and primary. The principle of subsidiarity does not require that certain functions be carried out by the lowest level of association, whatever those levels of association may be; rather, it requires that certain functions need to be carried out by particular forms of association. Within some prudential bounds, the principle of subsidiarity must allow for social change; but if the principle is to have any sense, there must also be some limit to the sort of social change it can accommodate—there must be some associations the existence and function of which are non-negotiable. If a new social order threatens to assume functions which had been the rights and duties of those particular "natural" forms of association, then that constitutes not a morally neutral evolution of social forms but a violation of the rights and duties of particular social associations and a violation of the principle of subsidiarity.

The Principle of Subsidiarity and the Agrarian Ideal

There are numerous traditions of social thought which share in varying degrees this general ideal of a locally distributed and natural social order, with or without the more specific criticism of economic and technological forces which threaten that ideal. In the United States, the ideal has been expressed partially and vaguely under such names as federalism, republicanism, and civic humanism.[46] Earlier in this century, it was expressed more explicitly by some Catholic thinkers—including G. K. Chesterton, Hilaire Belloc, and Dorothy Day—under the name distributism (or distributivism).[47] More commonly in European thought it is represented by some related social theories critical of widespread individualistic capitalism, under such banners as syndicalism, solidarism, and corporatism.[48] The ideal is even arguably an element in some forms of populism and, most prominently in contemporary discussions of American political theory, in communitarianism.[49] A fruitful historical consideration of the principle of subsidiarity could consider each of these traditions to be at least partial embodiments of the social insight which the principle tries to express.[50] In this final section I want to consider just one tradition which I think yields especially valuable connections to the principle of subsidiarity, namely, the tradition of agrarianism.

Richard Hofstadter has given an outline of the "component themes" of the American agrarian ideal as it appeared in the eighteenth and nineteenth centuries:

> Its hero was the yeoman farmer, its central conception the notion that he
> is the ideal man and the ideal citizen. Unstinted praise of the special
> virtues of the farmer and the special values of rural life was coupled
> with the assertion that agriculture, as a calling uniquely productive and
> uniquely important to society, had a special right to the concern and
> protection of government. The yeoman, who owned a small farm and

worked it with the aid of his family, was the incarnation of the simple, honest, independent, healthy happy human being. Because he lived in close communion with the beneficent nature, his life was believed to have a wholesomeness and integrity impossible for the depraved populations of cities. His well-being was not merely physical, it was moral; it was not merely personal, it was the central source of civic virtue; it was not merely secular but religious, for God had made the land and called man to cultivate it. Since the yeoman was believed to be both happy and honest, and since he had a secure propertied stake in society in the form of his own land, he was held to be the best and most reliable sort of citizen.[51]

Significantly, Hofstadter describes agrarianism in the past tense; indeed, he refers not to "agrarianism" but rather always to "the agrarian myth"—a myth, he insists, created by aristocrats for their political convenience and long ago defeated in the face of developing "commercial realities." But Hofstadter's dismissal of agrarianism as a "myth" is a rhetorical evasion of both the descriptive and prescriptive content of agrarian thought; the fact remains that agrarianism constitutes both a reasonable portrayal of the ordering of past societies and an earnest political philosophy which attempts to account for the justice of that order.

Indeed, the relevant elements of this agrarian philosophy are evident from Hofstadter's summary. Here it is important to note that the farmer is not so much important for the fact of his producing agricultural crops as for the kinds of virtues and habits thought to be typical of farming as a way of life—virtues and habits not only of the individual farmer but of all members of the kinds of households and communities in which farming is possible. The farmer thus represents not so much a particular career as a general ethical and political type. This agrarian type is independent, that is, relatively self-sufficient, not subservient to larger political and social forces; to the extent that he depends on anyone or anything, he is dependent on nature and on the members of his household and immediate community. The agrarian type is resourceful; in part because of his relative independence, he must rely on his own talents and his own resources to provide what he needs. The agrarian type is wholesome, living in harmony with nature, both benefitting from and contributing to the health of the land; moreover, he is politically wholesome, as he is tangibly invested in his own freedom and responsibility and the political order which makes them possible.

The connection between the principle of subsidiarity and the agrarian type just sketched should be clear: agrarians desire the widespread distribution of power, maintain that essential social and economic functions should take place at the most local and primary levels of association, and regard the consolidation and centralization of power as destructive not only of patterns of life but of political principle.

The agrarian resistance to consolidation of power has been partially obscured by an unjustified association of agrarianism with particular policies of economic planning. Though historically some agrarian political reforms, and agrarian thought in general, have been traced to socialist origins,[52] the American tradition of agrarian thought has explicitly opposed the consolidation and centralization of political power. The historian Forrest McDonald, who has identified "agrarian republicanism" as one of the important species of American thought which influenced the Founding, makes it clear that the agrarian republicans were far from socialists; according to McDonald, they emphasized the political benefits of widespread and distributed ownership and use of land.[53] Indeed, far from desiring a planned economy, McDonald finds that among those who influenced the Founding, the agrarian republicans were "the one group that came closest to accepting [Adam] Smith's doctrines [in the *Wealth of Nations*] in their entirety."[54]

The agrarian opposition to centralization is well illustrated by Thomas Jefferson, probably the most prominent early American thinker with whom agrarianism can be easily associated.[55] On several occasions Jefferson spoke of the yeoman farmer as the exemplar of moral integrity and the foundation of political stability.[56] Jefferson is very clear that his preference for an agrarian population is connected to a conviction that dependence on higher social associations is politically unhealthy. This conviction is well captured in a famous passage from Jefferson's *Autobiography*:

> But it is not by the consolidation, or concentration of powers, but by their distribution, that good government is effected. Were not this great country already divided into states, that division must be made, that each might do for itself what concerns itself directly, and what it can so much better do than a distant authority. Every state again is divided into counties, each to take care of what lies within its local bounds; each county again into townships or wards, to manage minute details; and every ward into farms, to be governed each by its individual proprietor. Were we directed from Washington when to sow, and when to reap, we should soon want bread. It is by this partition of cares, descending in gradation from general to particular, that the mass of human affairs may be best managed for the good and prosperity of all.[57]

This passage, about the maximally local distribution of political power, is particularly apt in illustrating the connection between the principle of subsidiarity and agrarian thought. But it was not only political power of which Jefferson preferred distribution rather than consolidation; he was also concerned with economic power. Jefferson's opposition to economic centralization is inseparable from his praise of the yeoman farmer, as is clear from his arguments that agriculture is a better basis for an economy than manufacture and commerce because it leaves men more independent and responsible.[58]

Agrarian opposition to the consolidation of economic power is even more evident in the language of late nineteenth- and early twentieth-century agrarianism, most notably in the writings of the "Southern Agrarians." In words that reveal the affinity of their position with the principle of subsidiarity, economist William Campbell has noted that "the Southern Agrarian tradition stressed that functions and responsibilities be lodged in the person and the family first, the broad range of community and voluntary organizations second, and the state last."[59] The enemy of these agrarians, indeed that in opposition to which they tended to define their agrarianism, was "industrialism," construed as the concentration of economic power in large-scale commercial endeavors.[60] By identifying its enemy as industrialism, the agrarian critic was condemning particular forms of social organization for violating a more natural order and specifically for resulting in the transfer of functions formerly performed by family and community to more distant social associations. Thus, in the context of agrarianism, the term "industrialism" can be understood as a counterpart to "statism"; just as "statism" is the term for inordinate dependence on the state, the agrarians' pejorative "industrialism" expresses a judgment of inordinate dependence on the social sphere of commerce and manufacture. In this light, this representative strain of agrarian thought is easily understood as an attempt to articulate social relationships—between families, communities, and larger economic forces—which observe the principle of subsidiarity.

It must be emphasized that only in the context of a judgment about the proper ordering of social functions can traditional agrarian attitudes, otherwise dismissed as the products of mere nostalgia or romanticism, be understood as expressions of coherent political principle. Agrarian critiques of technology and of the market economy, like the critique of "industry," are all based on the observation that certain social forces often lauded as instruments and signs of "progress" in fact play a role in redistributing political power and social functions away from the household and community. Agrarian use of such terms as "markets," "technology," and "industry" may be imprecise, but their intended sense is clear: they are meant to identify those social forces which tend to reduce the independence and self-sufficiency of families and communities, seducing men into greater and greater economic and social dependence.

Precisely because they constitute a theory of just social order, such agrarian criticisms have long appealed beyond the population of actual farmers, to all those who judge themselves to be, or wish to be, invested in local associations.[61] A general resistance to economic consolidation as much as political consolidation has been evident in a wide variety of loosely agrarian movements. In the last several decades, the agrarian sensibility is easily linked to a variety of movements, recognized by such catchphrases as "small is beautiful," "back to the land," "sustainable living," and "homesteading." Of disparate character, and always difficult to categorize as politically "right" or "left," such movements share an apprehension of the benefits of living in relative self-sufficiency apart from the large-scale institutions of modern commercial society. Thus, at least incidentally, and sometimes by conscious intention, these essentially agrarian movements are alike in advocating the restoration of "natural" functions to individuals and "primary" associations, in particular the functions of the family or household, which have increasingly been absorbed, not so much by the state as by the sphere of "the economy."[62]

By emphasizing resistance to the consolidation of economic functions, we do not mean to ignore the significant cultural implications of agrarianism. While in its earlier forms agrarianism emphasized the economic and political threats of industrialism, it should be evident from what has been said that agrarianism has come to encompass a general attitude toward all social goods. Thus, the agrarian argues that the household and community are not only the proper places for "employment" and the production of sustenance but also for providing education, entertainment, and fellowship; these should not be transferred to the realm of commerce and industry. This interest in broader, cultural self-sufficiency is especially evident, for instance, in the famous slogan from *I'll Take My Stand*: "Throw out the radio and take down the fiddle from the wall,"[63] an extreme localist imperative that could be deduced directly from the principle of subsidiarity.

The cultural implications of the agrarian view also help explain why the essays of a more recent agrarian writer, Wendell Berry, have had such broad appeal. Though often explicitly concerned with industrialism and its impact on agriculture and the environment, Berry's essays make clear that the agrarian opposition to economic consolidation is not just a matter of economic or environmental health but also of artistic, physiological, political, and even spiritual health. Though it is a central observation of his that "people have been seduced or forced into dependence on the industrial economy,"[64] Berry makes it clear that resistance to this consolidation is not a matter of large-scale political policy or economic planning; rather, it is a matter of individuals, families, and small communities having the courage to make responsible choices.

Berry has been influenced by the Amish tradition, which provides an extreme but useful example of what it would mean to consistently apply the principle of subsidiarity to the household and its economic relations. For the Amish, the household is the primary locus of production, not just of consumption; and to the extent that an Amish family is not completely independent and self-sufficient, it relies on neighboring households, joined together in a community, to provide the support that it needs. The Amish resistance to what others consider the staples of modern technology, though it varies in degree, is not based on a belief that technology itself is evil, but on the observation that by limiting their use of technology, men may limit their dependence on the institutions for which they cannot be responsible. As much as possible, the technology the Amish do use can be built and maintained by themselves. More than any other Westerners, the Amish have succeeded in living a life in which the most basic social needs of the household and local community are supplied by the household and community. For them, the family has experienced no slide into "functional irrelevance." That the Amish live this way by choice, not by necessity, is itself evidence that the movement of social functions to higher and higher levels of association is not an inevitable consequence of the putatively inexorable logic of technological development. Not only in "undeveloped" nations but even in "developed" nations, social functions can be carried out at the local, primary level without being seized by, or ceded to, higher levels.

The influence of the Amish tradition, and its consonance with the principle of subsidiarity, is evident in the words of another contemporary agrarian, Gene Logsdon, who in several books has promoted "cottage farming." According to Logsdon, modern technology and consumerism have paved the way for "economic dictatorship," manifested in man's enslavement to centralized economic power. In response, Logsdon advocates an agrarian "home-based society," emphasizing first the household production of food: "If the economic dictators use technology to gain a monopoly in the food business, as they are absolutely trying to do, then I will use technology to show how a society of garden farmers can start a new home economy that will confound the dictators." But again, as for most agrarians, Logsdon's interest in this is not only the production of food but also the balance of power, the just distribution of social functions. It is clearly a sense of political justice that is behind his claim that "to decentralize the marketplace" will make possible a "return to a more democratic and therefore healthful economy."[65]

This agrarian criticism of modern society evokes precisely the sense of political justice that the principle of subsidiarity is meant to express.[66] Indeed, both the principle of subsidiarity and agrarianism can be understood as attempts to defend the justice of social functions "naturally" ordered through traditional human associations, in the face of "artificial" forces which would redistribute those functions to different, or entirely new, social associations. We could as easily say that the agrarian ideal follows from the principle of subsidiarity as we could say that the principle of subsidiarity embodies the theory of just social order which agrarian thought always strives to articulate. According to both, just social order involves the widespread, local distribution of primary social functions; higher associations have a responsibility not to absorb the functions of lower associations, and lower associations have a responsibility not to abdicate their functions to higher associations.

One final connection between agrarianism and the principle of subsidiarity is worth observing. As the example of Hofstadter makes clear, the fact that agrarianism has been historically formulated in reaction to social and economic change has made it easy for critics to dismiss it as a nostalgic or romantic "myth." Nonetheless, like the principle of subsidiarity, it makes sense that agrarianism was not articulated explicitly until a social order once thought natural came to be threatened. For most of human history, agrarianism as a way of life was unavoidable; agrarianism as a social philosophy was not necessary, nor even really possible, until the agrarian way of life needed some justification in the face of an alternative. Like the principle of subsidiarity, agrarianism was taken for granted and tacitly understood as a basis of sound social order; we should not be surprised that it was not explicitly formulated except as a response to political and economic changes facilitated by technological innovations which threatened that order.[67]

Conclusion

In this chapter I have argued that the principle of subsidiarity needs to be understood as more than a basis for the limitation of state power. The principle of subsidiarity must be applied consistently to all social associations, and the responsibility of lower social associations to perform their proper functions without abdicating them to higher associations is just as important as the responsibility of higher associations not to interfere with lower ones. In modern society, where higher social spheres, facilitated by technological advance and large-scale commerce, take up functions once recognized as belonging to the household and its immediate community, the principle of subsidiarity can be understood as having implications which are appropriately identified as "agrarian," insofar as the agrarian tradition has criticized the centralization and consolidation of economic power and held up as a political ideal the relative self-sufficiency and independence of the household. In sum, I have argued that agrarianism and the principle of subsidiarity are expressions of the same normative social principle.

In light of this argument, I hope that the appropriation of the principle of subsidiarity by classical liberals and defenders of free markets is seen to be at the very least incomplete, as it applies the principle only to the state's relation to lower associations like the economy and ignores the applications of the principle that are far more morally burdensome on individuals, families, and local communities. Furthermore, insofar as the classical liberal appropriation of the principle implies an uncritical attitude toward the power of market forces and technological advance, it is not only incomplete but seriously misleading. While on some level modern liberal institutions and especially the market economy both grow out of and contribute to human freedom, it is irresponsible to ignore the extent to which they have changed patterns of living, primarily by arrogating the social functions of more primary and natural levels of association. Unchecked by the resolve of responsible individuals, families, and communities, the modern market economy is not morally neutral; it tends to violate the principle of subsidiarity.

It is important for Catholic social thinkers, and social thinkers generally, to apprehend that the principle of subsidiarity supplements and even criticizes classical liberalism more than it simply supports it.[68] However, this does not necessarily mean that the agrarian implication of the principle of subsidiarity is strictly at odds with the more commonly noted libertarian implication. As we have seen, agrarianism does not recommend a restriction of market freedom by statist policies. Historically, agrarians have been opposed to all consolidation of power, including state power. Not only has this been true since the eighteenth-century agrarians' appreciation of Adam Smith's economic theories, and the more recent Southern Agrarian position that industrialism, more than agrarianism, depends on the active support of government intervention[69]—an interest in limited government has been a feature of agrarian societies even before the development of modern agrarian theory.[70]

Unfortunately, in the context of current discussions of political and social theory, there are some important theoretical obstacles to a fuller appreciation of agrarianism. One such obstacle is the entrenched prejudice that agrarianism is economically naive. Apparently forgetting the physiocrats and their influence on Adam Smith, some defenders of classical liberalism have charged that agrarianism undervalues human creativity,[71] or that it misunderstands the possibility of increasing wealth.[72] But the "cultivator of the soil" is necessarily clever and resourceful, and he certainly knows how to produce, or rather help nature to produce, wealth where there was none before. Nobody who has studied agrarian thought, or who grasps the very idea of a yeoman farmer, should claim that agrarianism fails to comprehend the role of human effort and creativity in producing wealth.[73]

Yet another theoretical obstacle to a fuller appreciation of agrarian thought is the metaphysical anthropology usually assumed by the dominant tradition of social and political thought, classical liberalism. We have seen that the principle of subsidiarity respects the primacy of the individual but also respects the integrity of "natural" social associations, associations which have real unity precisely because they have proper social functions. Classical liberalism, and in particular that version of it which is usually marshaled in the defense of free markets, often takes the form of a strict, atomistic individualism, according to which only individuals are the bearers of moral status. This reductionism is plainly incompatible with the principle of subsidiarity, which assigns a moral status, complete with duties, responsibilities, and rights, to every level of social association. Agrarian Richard Weaver wrote of "two types of American individualism": the more familiar, atomistic type Weaver associated with the industrial North and Henry David Thoreau; a second type he called "'social bond' individualism," which for Weaver was exemplified by the agrarian South and John Randolph of Roanoke. Describing Randolph, Weaver wrote: "As a defender of the dignity and autonomy of the smaller unit, he was constantly fighting the battle for local rights."[74] It is this "social bond" individualism that is required both by agrarianism and by the principle of subsidiarity.

But surely the most important obstacle to an appreciation of the agrarian implications of the principle of subsidiarity is not theoretical but practical. In today's world, what can it mean to insist that a normative principle of social association has agrarian implications? Have not "commercial realities" superseded agrarian social arrangements? Is not any call for a revival of agrarianism a call to "unmake history"?[75] Are we suggesting that the only way to observe the principle of subsidiarity—that principle of just social order—is for the majority of families to start farming plots of land?

It must be admitted that if justice required that we all be farmers, then justice would be beyond our immediate grasp. But political justice depends not only on abstract principles but also on prudential application of those principles to particular circumstances. In present circumstances, it is not practical to recommend that all people become farmers. This does not mean, however, that the agrarian ideal cannot be pursued in some degree. Pursuing the agrarian ideal by degree would not only, nor even primarily, entail altering the legal structure to provide incentives for different, more agrarian patterns of life, or disincentives for participation in large-scale industry. Without any government prompting, individuals and families can take steps to decrease their dependence on the technologically enabled market economy. While such steps are burdensome ones which we tend to consider matters of personal and private choice, we have seen that they follow from a consistent application of the principle of subsidiarity, and as such they are the province of political theory. Alternatively used to bolster faith in government and faith in the market economy, in our time it is certainly appropriate for political theory to help inspire the kind of courage necessary for people to make difficult choices for the health of their families and local communities, by articulating the virtues of what have long been held up as the stronghold of a free society: productive and independent households.

Notes

1. See, for instance, Christopher Wolfe, "Subsidiarity: The 'Other' Ground of Limited Government," in *Catholicism, Liberalism, and Communitarianism: The Catholic Intellectual Tradition and the Moral Foundations of Democracy*, ed. Kenneth L. Grasso, Gerard V. Bradley, and Robert P. Hunt (Lanham, Md.: Rowman & Littlefield, 1995).

2. European theologians, especially in Germany, had already theorized about the principle of subsidiarity; for a summary of this intellectual history and references, see Thomas C. Kohler, "In Praise of Little Platoons," in *Building the Free Society: Democracy, Capitalism, and Catholic Social Teaching*, ed. George Weigel and Robert Royal (Grand Rapids, Mich.: William B. Eerdmans, 1993), 35; cf. Michael Novak, *Catholic Social Thought and Liberal Institutions (Freedom with Justice)*, 2d ed. (New Brunswick, N.J.: Transaction, 1989), 110ff.

3. Oswald von Nell-Breuning, *Reorganization of Social Economy: The Social Encyclical Developed and Explained* (New York: Bruce Publishing, 1936), 201.

4. This is more true in America than in Europe. In Europe, the discussions of "federalism" also emphasize another dimension of the principle of subsidiarity, namely, that according to it the exercise of higher, centralized power is permissible in those circumstances where lower associations could not perform a desired function. So while in America the principle of subsidiarity is more likely to be invoked by conservatives and classical liberals, in Europe the principle of subsidiarity has been useful, in Thomas C. Kohler's words, as a "cloak" for the "*libido dominandi*" of bureaucrats." Thomas C. Kohler, "Lessons from the Social Charter: State, Corporation, and the Meaning of Subsidiarity," *University of Toronto Law Journal* 43 (1993): 627.

5. Wolfe, "Subsidiarity," 81.

6. George Weigel, *Soul of the World: Notes on the Future of Public Catholicism* (Grand Rapids, Mich.: Ethics and Public Policy Center/William B. Eerdmans, 1996), 110.

7. David Bosnich, "The Principle of Subsidiarity," *Religion and Liberty* 6, no. 4 (July/August 1996): 9-10.

8. Adopho Lindenberg, *The Free Market in a Christian Society*, trans. Donna H. Sandin (Montreal: St. Antoninus Institute for Catholic Education in Business, 1999), 165-66.

9. Robert A. Sirico, "Subsidiarity, Society, and Entitlements: Understanding and Application," *Notre Dame Journal of Law, Ethics and Public Policy* 11 [issue 2, Symposium on Entitlements] (1997): 557.

10. Sirico, "Subsidiarity," 549.

11. Stephen M. Krason, *Liberalism, Conservatism, and Catholicism: An Evaluation of Contemporary American Political Ideologies in Light of Catholic Social Teaching*, rev. ed. (St. Louis: Catholic Central Verein of America, 1994), 44. Examples of the principle of subsidiarity invoked as a principle of limited government could be multiplied and are by no means only to be found within the past decade; cf. the description of the principle of subsidiarity in Benjamin S. Llamzon, "Subsidiarity: The Term, Its Metaphysics and Use," *Aquinas* 21 (1978): 44: "The ethico-political principle that the state should not take over and do what its smaller communities can do by themselves."

12. Abraham Kuyper, *Calvinism: Six Stone Foundation Lectures* (Grand Rapids, Mich.: William B. Eerdmans, 1943), 96. The lectures were originally delivered at Princeton Theological Seminary in 1898 and first published as *Lectures on Calvinism* (Amsterdam: Hoocker and Wormser, 1898); they provide a distillation of Kuyper's *Ons Programme* (Our program), 1878.

13. The connection between Althusius and the principle of subsidiarity has been noted in Donald W. Livingston, "The Founding and the Enlightenment: Two Theories of Sovereignty," in *Vital Remnants: America's Founding and the Western Tradition*, ed. Gary L. Gregg II (Wilmington, Del.: ISI Books, 1999), 248.

14. Daniel J. Elazar, "Althusius' Grand Design for a Federal Commonwealth," in Johannes Althusius, *Politica*, trans. Frederick S. Carney (Indianapolis, Ind.: Liberty Fund, 1995), xxxv-xlvi.

15. In this context, "subsidiarity" does not necessarily have connotations of "secondariness" or "subordination," except insofar as what is ordained to help another is secondary or subordinate to that which it is ordained to help.

16. Sirico, "Subsidiarity," 549.

17. Sirico, "Subsidiarity," 557.

18. Quoted in Kohler, "In Praise of Little Platoons," 36.

19. Nell-Breuning, *Reorganization of Social Economy*, 208.

20. Cf. John Finnis, *Natural Law and Natural Rights* (Oxford: Clarendon Press, 1980), 146: The principle of subsidiarity "affirms that the proper function of association is to help the participants of the association to help themselves."

21. Kuyper, *Calvinism*, 97.

22. Kuyper, *Calvinism*, 98-99.

23. Sirico, "Subsidiarity," 549.

24. John Coleman, "Development of Church Social Teaching," in *Readings in Moral Theology No. 5: Official Catholic Social Teaching*, 183, quoted in Kohler, "In Praise of Little Platoons," 35.

25. Finnis, *Natural Law and Natural Rights*, 144-46. Cf. Johannes Messner, "Freedom as a Principle of Social Order: An Essay in the Substance of Subsidiary Function," *Modern Schoolman* 28 (1951): 108.

26. "Every state is a community of some kind, and every community is established with a view to some good." Aristotle, *Politics* I, i.

27. Kohler, "Lessons from the Social Charter," 615.

28. Nell-Breuning, *Reorganization of Social Economy*, 206.

29. Messner, "Freedom as a Principle," 106.

30. Llamzon, "Subsidiarity," 49.

31. The priority of the individual must not be confused with a point which is sometimes taken to be its contradiction, namely, the priority of the political community. When, for instance, Aristotle (*Politics* I, ii) says that the state is prior to the individual, this does not contradict, but in fact follows from, the fact that the state exists to serve the individual, specifically by fulfilling the individual's greatest social needs; the political community is prior in the sense that the individual is incomplete without it. In other words, that man is a political animal means that he is intended by nature to be a part of a political whole; the political community is thus prior to the individual in the sense that the whole is prior to the parts, but the individual is prior in the sense that it is his nature, human nature, which determines the need for, and form of, the political community by which that nature is fulfilled, and no political community is good which is not good for individual people.

32. Llamzon, "Subsidiarity," 45.

33. Thomas Aquinas, *On Princely Government*, I, 13 and 14; quoted by Althusius, *Politica* I, §13.

34. "Non enim cives propter consules nec gens propter regem, sed e converso consules propter cives et rex propter gentem." Dante, *Monarchia*, I, xii. Cf. Joseph Komonchak, who lists as the first element of the principle of subsidiarity "the priority of the person as the origin and purpose of society: *civitas propter cives, non cives propter civitatem*," quoted in Kohler, "In Praise of Little Platoons," 36.

35. Kohler, "In Praise of Little Platoons," 42; Kohler, "Lessons from the Social Charter," 615ff.; Nell-Breuning, *Reorganization of Social Economy*, 206ff.

36. *Centesimus Annus* grants the benefits of free economy and connects it to subsidiarity (summarizing *Rerum Novarum*): "The State must contribute to the achievement of [social] goals . . . indirectly and according to the principle of subsidiarity, by creating favorable conditions for the free exercise of economic activity, which will lead to abundant opportunities for employment and sources of wealth" (§15).

37. Cf. Weigel, *Soul of the World*, 110; Lindenberg, *The Free Market*, 198.

38. Lindenberg, *The Free Market*, 97.

39. Kohler, "Lessons from the Social Charter," 627.

40. Wolfe, "Subsidiarity," 91-92. Gregory Beabout also discusses relationships of freedom and authority between parents and children in "The Principle of Subsidiarity and Freedom in the Family, Church, Market, and Government," *Journal of Markets and Morality* 1 (1998): 130-41.

41. Nell-Breuning, *Reorganization of Social Economy*, 326-27.

42. Robert Nisbet, *The Quest for Community: A Study in the Ethics of Order and Freedom* (Oxford: Oxford University Press, 1953), 49.

43. Indeed, this attitude of resignation appears to be expressed in words already quoted from two important sources: *Quadragesimo Anno*, §79 ("As history abundantly proves, it is true that on account of changed conditions many things which were done by small associations in former times cannot be done now save by large associations"); and Nell-Breuning, *Reorganization of Social Economy*, 326 ("The transfer to independent organizations of much of the economic production formerly carried on in the family was in large part necessary").

44. Finnis, *Natural Law and Natural Rights*, 144.

45. Cf. Messner, "Freedom as a Principle," 107: "As often as the limitations of the powers and rights of social authority or the fundamental claims and rights of the human person were discussed it was in substance always the principle of subsidiarity function that was in question."

46. For example, George W. Carey treats American federalism as an expression of the

principle of subsidiarity in his "Constitution and Community," in *Community and Tradition: Conservative Perspectives on the American Experience*, ed. George W. Carey and Bruce Frohnen (Lanham, Md.: Rowman & Littlefield, 1998), 63-84, esp. 73-75.

47. The connection between distributivism and the principle of subsidiarity has been explored by John C. Médaille in "'Power to the People' Can Only Mean Property to the People," *New Oxford Review* (January 2000): 27-34. See also Dermot Quinn, "Defending Distributism," letter to the editor, *First Things* 55 (August/September 1995): 2, to which compare Richard John Neuhaus, "Chesterton and the Thereness of It," *First Things* 97 (November 1999): 87: "The impulse of distributism, one might suggest, is to work out more fully the economic implications of the doctrine of subsidiarity."

48. Solidarism and corporatism are discussed in Kohler, "In Praise of Little Platoons," 37-39. Solidarism deserves a more serious treatment than is offered by Michael Novak, who dismisses it for its "conservative" belief in the value of "traditional" and "natural" associations (Novak, *Catholic Social Thought*, 118-20). Says Novak, "Although solidarism praises mediating structures, associations, and the principle of subsidiarity (according to which no larger social body ought to do what a smaller body can do for itself), it fails to grasp the indispensable role of liberal institutions in limiting the power of the state" (121). We might respond that while Novak praises mediating structures, associations, and the principle of subsidiarity, he fails to grasp the role of liberal institutions in taking over the functions of more natural and local associations.

49. Jean Bethke Elshtain has found the principle of subsidiarity valuable as pointing toward a more or less communitarian "third way": "Subsidiarity is a theory of and for civil society that refuses stark alternatives between individualism and collectivism." Jean Bethke Elshtain, "Catholic Social Thought, the City, and Liberal America," in *Catholicism, Liberalism, and Communitarianism*, ed. Grasso et al. (Lanham, Md.: Rowman & Littlefield, 1995), 106. Thomas Kohler has also noticed connections between the principle of subsidiarity and communitarianism: "The subsidiarity principle obviously has much to say to many who would identify themselves as communitarians, and much of the communitarian platform itself appears to draw from the social magisterium and the insights that subsidiarity principle offers." However, Kohler identifies a limitation of the communitarian appropriation of the principle. "The understanding of the human person that grounds, orients, and illuminates this principle, however, is its most significant insight. . . . If the communitarian project is to prosper, it will have to confront unflinchingly and adequately the [metaphysical] question of our personhood. Failure to do so would make the movement's prescriptions irrelevant—or worse." Kohler, "In Praise of Little Platoons," 45. In fact, while supposedly favoring the local, the communitarian position tends to invoke the principle of subsidiarity in *favor* of state programs and other government intervention; cf. Robert N. Bellah et al., *The Good Society* (New York: Alfred A. Knopf, 1992), 262-63. Thus Bruce Frohnen can criticize communitarians for ignoring the principle of subsidiarity in advocating "civic virtue" and dedication to national, as opposed to local, goals; Bruce Frohnen, *The New Communitarians and the Crisis of Modern Liberalism* (Lawrence: University Press of Kansas, 1996), esp. 215-18. A further criticism worth noting is that, though the communitarian invocation of the principle of subsidiarity contradicts the classical liberal interest in limited government, it does essentially reinforce the unwarranted tendency to talk about the principle solely in terms of its implications for the state.

50. A fruitful historical consideration of the principle of subsidiarity could also consider two individuals whose thought has obvious affinity with the principle: Alexis de Tocqueville and Edmund Burke. The connection to Tocqueville has already been made explicitly in Wolfe, "Subsidiarity," 89-91. Though it does not mention the principle of subsidiarity by

name, a relevant treatment of Tocqueville is Darcy Wudel, "Tocqueville on Associations and Association," in *Tocqueville's Defense of Human Liberty: Current Essays*, ed. Peter Augustine Lawler and Joseph Alulis (New York: Garland, 1993). As indicated by its title, the connection of Burke to the principle of subsidiarity is suggested in Kohler, "In Praise of Little Platoons," 43.

51. Richard Hofstadter, *The Age of Reform: From Bryan to F.D.R.* (New York: Vintage Books, 1955), 24-25.

52. Thomas P. Govan, "Agrarian and Agrarianism: A Study in the Use and Abuse of Words," *Journal of Southern History* 30 (1964): 35-47; Arthur E. Bestor, Jr., "The Evolution of the Socialist Vocabulary," *Journal of the History of Ideas* 9 (1948): 259-302.

53. Forrest McDonald, *Novus Ordo Seclorum: The Intellectual Origins of the Constitution* (Lawrence: University Press of Kansas, 1985), 70-77.

54. McDonald, *Novus Ordo Seclorum*, 128.

55. For a description of, and more references to, early American agrarianism, see Bruce S. Thornton, "Founders as Farmers: The Greek Georgic Tradition and the Founders," in *Vital Remnants*, 33-69.

56. E.g., "Cultivators of the earth are the most valuable citizens. They are the most vigorous, the most independent, the most virtuous, and they are tied to their country, and wedded to its liberty and interests, by the most lasting bonds." Letter to John Jay, August 23, 1785, in *The Life and Selected Writings of Thomas Jefferson*, ed. Adrienne Koch and William Peden (New York: Modern Library, 1944), 377.

57. *The Autobiography of Thomas Jefferson*, in *The Life and Selected Writings of Thomas Jefferson*, 84-85.

58. E.g., "Those who labor in the earth are the chosen people of God, if ever He had a chosen people, whose breasts He has made His peculiar deposit for substantial and genuine virtue.... Corruption of morals in the mass of cultivators is a phenomenon of which no age nor nation has furnished an example. It is the mark of those who, not looking up to heaven, to their own soil and industry, as does the husbandman, for their subsistence, depend for it on casualties and caprice of customers. Dependence begets subservience and venality, suffocates the germ of virtue, and prepares fit tools for the designs of ambition. This, the natural progress and consequence of the arts, has sometimes perhaps been retarded by accidental circumstances; but, generally speaking, the proportion which the aggregate of the other classes of citizens bears in any State to that of its husbandmen, is the proportion of its unsound to its healthy parts.... The mobs of great cities add just so much to the support of pure government, as sores do to the strength of the human body. It is the manners and spirit of a people which preserve a republic in vigor. A degeneracy in these is a canker which soon eats to the heart of its laws and constitution." *Notes on the State of Virginia*, Query 19, in *The Life and Selected Writings of Thomas Jefferson*, 280-81.

59. William Campbell, "Introduction," in Wilhelm Roepke, *The Social Crisis of Our Time* (New Brunswick, N.J.: Transaction, 1992), xvi.

60. The most obvious example is the agrarian manifesto of the "Twelve Southerners," *I'll Take My Stand: The South and the Agrarian Tradition* (New York: Harper and Brothers, 1930). In this volume, the essential opposition between agrarianism and industrialism is ubiquitous but is spelled out in the initial pages, "Introduction: A Statement of Principles." The sequel volume—Herbert Agar and Allen Tate, eds., *Who Owns America? A New Declaration of Independence* (Boston: Houghton Mifflin, 1936)—which includes essays by two British distributists, makes it even more clear that the main interest of these agrarians was not sectionalism or pride in Southern culture, but political and economic principle:

specifically, it was a call for the decentralization of power, for widespread small proprietorship as an antidote to plutocracy and collectivism.

61. As Christopher Lasch has written, "Instead of regarding populism itself as a purely agrarian impulse, we now have to regard the agrarian version of populism as part of a broader movement that appealed to small producers of all kinds. Artisans and even many shopkeepers shared with farmers the fear that the new order threatened their working conditions, their communities, their ability to pass on both their technical skills and their moral economy to their offspring. In the nineteenth century, 'agrarianism' served as a generic term for popular radicalism, and this usage reminds us that opposition to monopolists, middlemen, public creditors, mechanization, and the erosion of craftsmanship by the division of labor was by no means confined to those who worked the soil." Christopher Lasch, *The True and Only Heaven: Progress and Its Critics* (New York: W. W. Norton, 1991), 217.

62. Two recent works treat twentieth-century and recent "new" agrarian thought: Allan Carlson, *The New Agrarian Mind: The Movement toward Decentralist Thought in Twentieth-Century America* (New Brunswick, N.J.: Transaction, 2000), and Eric T. Freyfogle, ed., *The New Agrarianism: Land, Culture, and the Community of Life* (Washington: Island Press, 2001).

63. Andrew Nelson Lytle, "The Hind Tit," in *I'll Take My Stand*, 244.

64. Wendell Berry, "Out of Your Car, Off Your Horse," in Wendell Berry, *Sex, Economy, Freedom and Community* (New York: Pantheon Books, 1993), 22.

65. Gene Logsdon, "Seeking Personal Freedom in a Money Dictatorship: An Address to the Second Luddite Congress," in *The Plain Reader*, ed. Scott Savage (New York: Ballantine, 1998), 6-9.

66. The influence of Logsdon, Berry, and the Amish tradition are all evident in a recent agrarian movement advocating "plain living," according to which relative independence from the modern industrial economy is a matter not only of environmental, psychological, and bodily health but also of economic and political justice; the Center for Plain Living (60805 Pidgeon Pt., Barnesville, Ohio 43713) published a now-defunct quarterly journal, *Plain: The Magazine of Life, Land and Spirit. The Plain Reader*, cited above, is an anthology drawn from this magazine.

67. "What is at once striking is that this principle of natural law emerged so late: Why did so basic a principle not need to be formulated sooner? This can be understood if we accept the view that its formulation is a reaction against the characteristic developments of *modern* society, that is, that the idea of subsidiarity is not problematic in traditional societies." Franz-Xavier Kaufmann, "The Principle of Subsidiarity Viewed by the Sociology of Organizations," *Jurist* 48 (1988): 279. Cf. Donald Davidson and Theresa Sherrer Davidson, "Regionalism," *Modern Age* 37 (1995): 104: "Historically considered, regionalism does not emerge as a theory of culture and government until the modern nation-state, using economics as a tool of power, achieves the capability to enforce upon all citizens, regardless of their inclinations, whatever degree of cultural uniformity is deemed necessary for the national welfare."

68. Cf. Kenneth Grasso, "Beyond Liberalism: Human Dignity, the Free Society, and the Second Vatican Council," in *Catholicism, Liberalism, and Communitarianism*, 27-58. For a sophisticated *theological* criticism of the neoconservative appropriation of the principle of subsidiarity and the social teaching of *Centesimus Annus*, see David L. Schindler, *Heart of the World, Center of the Church: Communio Ecclesiology, Liberalism, and Liberation* (Grand Rapids, Mich.: William B. Eerdmans, 1996), especially chap. 2, "Neoconservative Economics and the Church's 'Authentic Theology of Integral Human Liberation,'" 114-42.

69. Frank Lawrence Owsley, "The Irrepressible Conflict," in *I'll Take My Stand*, 74-75, 86, 88.

70. Victor Davis Hanson has argued that the rise of the Greek *polis*, which is usually credited as the foundation of Western political ideals, is merely an "epiphenomenon" of a widespread, agrarian way of life, which is itself responsible for our inherited conceptions of democracy, private property, constitutional government, liberty, and equality. Victor Davis Hanson, *The Other Greeks: The Family Farm and the Agrarian Roots of Western Civilization* (New York: Free Press, 1995).

71. Michael Novak has asserted that "agrarian habits of thought . . . undervalue the creativity of managers, inventors, and persons of commerce [and] undervalue the creativity of the individual." Novak, *Catholic Social Thought*, 121.

72. Gregory Gronbacher, speaking of distributism, says that it advocates an "agrarian" society, charging that its "primary error . . . lay in its understanding of the economy as a zero-sum game, where wealth was seen as a static, non-reproducible entity. . . . [This] hindered the emergence of an adequate understanding of human capital and productivity." Gregory M. A. Gronbacher, "The Need for Economic Personalism," *Journal of Markets and Morality* 1 (1998): 17. (This article was reprinted as "Economic Personalism: A New Paradigm for a Humane Economy," in *Centesimus Annus: Assessment and Perspectives for the Future of Catholic Social Doctrine*, ed. John-Peter Pham [Vatican City: Libreria Editrice Vaticana, 1998].)

73. An important economist who has appreciated agrarian thought is Wilhelm Roepke. See especially his *Moral Foundations of Civil Society* (London: William Hodge, 1948).

74. Richard M. Weaver, "Two Types of American Individualism," in *The Southern Essays of Richard M. Weaver*, ed. George M. Curtis III and James J. Thompson, Jr. (Indianapolis, Ind.: Liberty Press, 1987), 82. (Reprinted from *Modern Age* 7 [1963]: 119-34.)

75. Speaking of the Southern Agrarians, Clinton Rossiter raised the questions: "How sincerely do these men believe in the embattled cause of Southern Agrarianism? What are they actually prepared to do in behalf of the way of life they cherish so deeply? Do they want to unmake history, and do they think they can?" Clinton Rossiter, *Conservatism in America* (London: William Heinemann, 1955), 206.

The author extends thanks to Gerard Bradley, Thomas Kohler, William Campbell, Eric Enlow, Mark Shiffman, Cory Andrews, Zachary Calo, Adam Hochschild, and Paige Hochschild for reading and commenting on earlier drafts of this chapter.

Chapter 4

The Varieties of Democratic Experience

Michael Bailey

Will politics in the future be an arena for important thought and fundamental choice, or will the fundamental political choices already have been settled for us? Alexis de Tocqueville tells us, following Jean-Jacques Rousseau, that political history has a direction. He also tells us, following George Hegel, that equality of some form or another is its end or goal. More recently Francis Fukuyama has confirmed that history's end has arrived. Taking his cue from Fukuyama, journalist Jonathan Rauch, an astute observer of American politics, has argued that government's "overall scope and shape are no longer negotiable. They have evolved to a state from which they cannot, if you will, unevolve."[1] If Fukuyama and Rauch are correct, politics of the future will look much like it does today—only more so. Politics will be a diminished and largely administrative affair because the most profound political question—regime choice—will be, or perhaps already has been, resolved.

The demise of the Soviet Union signaled the end not only of communism but of all alternatives to liberal democracy. Stragglers to liberal democracy like the Republic of Cuba and the Democratic People's Republic of Korea may still embrace communism, but they are brittle regimes whose names, everyone knows, are prophetic. Only Islamic theocracy remains as an alternative to democracy around the globe. But even these regimes, as many Muslim scholars readily admit, are but rearguard efforts to preserve a vestige of Islam's glorious past. Unlike communism, Islamic theocracy holds little to no intellectual lure within established democracies, so no serious threat to democracy exists anywhere. John Locke once said, referring to the state of nature, that "in the beginning all the world was America." He might have as well added, "and will become so again."

Democracy's apparent global triumph has sparked joy *and* wistfulness. Joy for obvious and powerful reasons, but wistfulness because, with the conclusion of the Cold War, the last battle to marry courage with political philosophy has come to a close. One needs neither political courage nor political philosophy when one's political and intellectual opponents have all been buried. Or, at least, so goes the argument. In contrast to this view, here I contend that this wistfulness is misguided. Without taking sides in the end-of-history debate, I stress Tocqueville's insight that important, though less than fully comprehensive, political battles will continue to characterize our time. This holds true even assuming that liberal democracy, in some variety, has triumphed. Tocqueville invited his readers to develop a "new political science" whose job it would be to educate democracy.[2] The hard work of developing and employing a new science of politics, however, makes sense only if there is much to be gained or lost through political thought and action. In other words, Tocqueville's insight is that political philosophy still matters. Democracy naturally stresses equality and justice, but these values alone do not recommend it. At stake in choosing among the varieties of equality open to our age is not just freedom but the potentiality of humanity itself. That Tocqueville was not consistently optimistic about the future should not cloud our thinking that the choices we face are inevitable or, worse, trivial.

My argument in this chapter is threefold. First, I argue that the adoption of democracy as a regime choice does not exhaust a citizenry's fundamental political choices. There are a variety of liberal democracies, and the differences between them are far from trivial. I examine three issues in particular that shape the character of a democratic regime: moral neutrality; the comprehensiveness of liberalism; and liberal statism. Second, I argue that a good deal of contemporary liberal thought—and much of contemporary democratic practice—is largely mistaken in its answers to these questions. My critique of contemporary liberalism is chiefly polemical. I wish not to resolve the questions I pose but to demonstrate, through a critique of prevailing liberal wisdom, that there is still space open about the meaning and purpose of democracy. My third goal is to offer strategies for curbing the excesses of contemporary democratic politics. These strategies do not constitute a coherent political ideology, but my purpose in introducing them is not to provide an alternative to liberal democracy but to reinvigorate political debate within that perspective. Disagreement among proponents of the respective strategies in fact serves my purpose.

Will the Real Liberal Democracy Please Stand Up?

So triumphant is liberal democracy that citizens today see older warrants for political legitimacy—divine authority, virtue, birth, and so on—as insane or, more patronizingly, simply confused. But what distinguishes liberal democracy from these older rejected views? In its every variety, liberal democracy focuses on the political ideals of equality and liberty, together with an understanding of how to support these ideals through institutions, customs, and habits. To argue about politics in the twenty-first century therefore is to argue about the relative worth of liberty and equality, their grounding, and the best means to secure them. As narrow as this debate may seem from an extended historical perspective, it does not mean that all fundamental debates are closed. Indeed, seen from one perspective, *the* most fundamental political choice is indeed still open to us. After all, the ancients remind us that regimes can be subdivided in *two* ways: by the number of rulers and by the ends for which they rule. The former point is of secondary importance, and it is *this* point which has been settled conclusively. Liberal democracy would have the many rule. For which purposes the many shall rule, however, is very much up for debate, for liberal democrats disagree upon this point. All liberals are for liberty and equality, but they disagree about the meaning of these terms as well their authority in various spheres of society. This disagreement opens up space for a variety of democratic regimes, from good to disastrous.

To understand the breadth and variety of democratic liberalism, one need only look at how classical liberalism, the liberalism of Thomas Jefferson and other American Founders, differs from contemporary liberalism, the liberalism of John Rawls, Bruce Ackerman, and Ronald Dworkin. Apart from Thomas Paine, Jefferson was the most relentless liberal democrat of the Founding. Jefferson's democratic ideals shaped our America's understanding of who we are and, through this understanding, our actions. The theory implicit in the Declaration of Independence, Jefferson's archetypal liberal democratic document, suggests that rights come from nature, which is given to us by "nature's God." Though government is not natural, freedom is. We are naturally free because we are moral agents who are born equal, which is to say without natural authority to rule over others. In the absence of natural rulers, all political rule is artificial. The primary political question for Jefferson, then, is how to legitimate political rule, which is necessary to remedy the insecurity of anarchy, without doing violence to our natural liberty. Jefferson's answer, following John Locke, was that legitimate political rule comes from the consent of the governed and government's protection of the people's God-given rights. Jefferson's liberalism therefore attempts to put government in the service both of nature (through the observance of natural rights) and autonomy (through the consent of the governed).

Politics here is not a necessary activity for the flourishing of the soul; its benefits are utilitarian. Because government's purpose is practical, it follows that the best form of government is learned through experience, not reason. Jefferson does not state in the Declaration of Independence which form of government is best. Rather, he says, "it is the Right of the people to alter or to abolish [government], and to institute new Government, laying its foundation on such principles and organizing its powers in such form, as to them shall seem most likely to effect their Safety and Happiness." The Declaration of Independence is *liberal* because it holds that the purpose of government is to protect our rights. It is *democratic* not because it sets forth a blueprint of representative democracy but because it is the people who establish the *form* of political rule.

Contemporary liberals such as Rawls can admire much in the Declaration of Independence, but they can also find much to criticize. In particular, they may find the Declaration too foundational and insufficiently democratic. Too foundational because Jefferson's document grounds our equality and liberty in reference to "nature's God." Though it is unclear what this odd little phrase means, it seems to suggest, together with the reference to our "unalienable rights," that our rights are grounded in something more than preference or self-interest. Our rights are natural, which is to say they are subject to natural limits and are resistant to innovation or multiplication. Declaring something a right, such as a right to a well-paying job, does not make it so. Government therefore is limited in what it may do to us even in the name of rights, for the rights that deserve protection are prepolitical, not given by political fiat. In contrast, in the Rawlsian world our rights are largely conventional. One has a right to the basic goods of society, but these goods change all the time. They do not depend upon any understanding of God or nature but are reflective of our desire to be self-governing persons.

Nor would any contemporary liberal accept the Declaration of Independence's claim to be democratic. Jefferson's democracy is manifested most clearly in the social contract and in revolution, but the people may choose for themselves monarchical or aristocratic rulers. Jefferson's liberalism, in other words, still views democracy as a *choice*. In contrast, Rawls attempts to make liberal democracy intelligible from the inside, suggesting that liberal democracy is synonymous with reason itself.

In effect, Jefferson, the archetypal liberal democrat of the framing period, is insufficiently liberal and insufficiently democratic by contemporary standards. This means that political philosophy cannot be laid to rest just yet, for which set of ideals we embrace will inevitably shape how we see ourselves and, through this self-understanding, our capacity for greatness. I argue that all varieties of liberal democracy, not just the two discussed above, turn upon three pivotal questions: Is liberal democracy morally neutral? How comprehensive should liberal democracy be? What is the appropriate role of the state in liberal democracy? How one answers these questions has profound implications on the moral defensibility of liberal regimes, the development of community life, and the liberty which liberalism purports to protect. Put simply, and overbroadly, contemporary liberalism may be characterized as *neutral comprehensive statism*. This approach to politics, I will argue, is seductive but ultimately mistaken, and therefore I address three correctives to it championed by Tocqueville and others.

Moral Neutrality

Contemporary liberals characteristically attempt to ground political legitimacy in morally neutral discourse. The contemporary liberal desire for moral neutrality is a response to the permanent plurality of opinions about the good life.[3] People disagree about what is good and which virtues have primacy, and no degree of argumentation seems to bring consensus.[4] The contemporary liberal response to this feature of modernity is to relegate all questions of good to the private arena. Public dialogue is to take up only questions of right which are discoverable by transparent public reason. In this view, a polity must be neutral regarding notions of the good because the political endorsement of ways of life brings state coercion to bear upon unwilling citizens on contestable grounds. To preserve universal consent, the keystone concept for liberal legitimacy, argument is limited to areas where consensus is possible.

Liberal neutralists fear that by adopting a contestable conception of the good—meaning *any* conception of the good—the state will infringe upon individual autonomy. Neutrality is here motivated by the laudable goal of respecting the interests of the individual. In pursuit of this course, Bruce Ackerman argues that when two or more political discussants come to a disagreement, they should prescind their controversial beliefs from the discussion. By prescinding from points of disagreement, policy may be forged from agreement, brick by consensual brick. You believe X and I believe its opposite Y, but we can agree on Z, and from Z we have a basis to act together. As Ackerman words it, when we come to point of moral disagreement, we

> should simply say *nothing at all* about this disagreement and put the moral ideals that divide us off the conversational agenda of the liberal state. . . . Our mutual act of conversational restraint allows all of us to win a priceless advantage: none of us will be obliged to say something in liberal conversation that seems *affirmatively false*. We may instead use dialogue for pragmatically productive purposes: to identify normative premises all political participants find reasonable (or, at least, not unreasonable).[5]

The neutralist perspective, while honorable in its search for reasonable consensus, is confused. Persons disagree as much about justice as the good life, for there simply is no neutral stance by which to judge the moral universe. Even Ackerman himself violates neutrality in the name of neutrality. Like flypaper, the good is removed from the left hand, only to be stuck to the right. What Ackerman calls "a priceless advantage," autonomy, is simply a characteristic of the *good* life worthy of protection—and a contestable one at that. Autonomy as a good does not even appeal to all fellow liberals as priceless. For example, Robert Dahl, one of the most celebrated liberal political scientists of the last century, argues against making "autonomy . . . an absolute value to which all other ends should give way. Why should happiness, justice, personal freedom, equality, security and all other values yield to the supreme value of autonomy?"[6] After all, were autonomy the supreme value, could we justify prisons? Could we justify the state itself? Rigging the rules of dialogue to protect autonomy as an absolute value forces people in effect to adopt a stance that seems to many persons "affirmatively false." True neutrality would be silent not only about the choices one makes but also about *how* those disputes are solved, even if resolution was purchased through the barrel of a gun.

In fairness, contemporary liberal advocates of neutrality do capture some truth about how negotiation proceeds. Very often discussants do make progress by setting aside some points of contention. But there is no reason to call this process morally neutral. This is so for three reasons. One reason is that belief Z, the belief we can both agree upon, may be some supposition about the good. Another reason is that we may agree upon belief Z because we believe that agreement on this point secures for us some future good. Lastly, point Z may *appear* neutral but actually be shaped by background beliefs about the good. The very meaning of point Z, in other words, may be dramatically altered if pried from the larger moral framework which illuminates it from behind. J. Donald Moon develops this point: "Beliefs are not discrete objects like cats but bear 'internal' or conceptual relations to other beliefs. The meaning of a particular belief depends on its place in a system of beliefs, and abstracting the belief from the system may distort its sense. This is particularly true in political and moral matters."[7] To illustrate, whether or not one thinks evolution should be taught in public schools will depend upon how one argues for the fit of fossils, the existence of which no one disputes, into a broader theory of reality.

In short, issues of right cannot be entirely freed from conceptions of the good, as neutralists would have us believe. To know what people are due—the essence of justice—one has to have a conception of reward and penalty. Such conceptions, in turn, are central to discussions of the good. In *Walker v. The Superior Court of Sacramento County*, the California Court faced a problem of justice—what citizens are owed—that turned on conceptions of what a person is and what is good for them.[8] The specifics of the case cannot be addressed here, but in outline form the family in the case, the Walkers, were Christian Scientists who eschewed Western medicine to embrace prayer as the remedy for their sick and dying child. The Court in this case sanctioned government custody of the child for medical treatment. Despite the Court's rhetoric to the contrary, its decision ultimately was based on a contestable point of ontology, including a view of the good. As Fred Frohock argues, public reason itself was thrown into question here because the two contestants fought for rival conceptions of empirical reality born from competing ontological conceptions about what constitutes the good.[9] What counts as *real* medicine turns on how one views the person—whether persons are, fundamentally, material or spiritual. All this goes to say that whether a product of collective discussion, solitary deliberation, tarot cards, or tea leaves, political choice is inherently nonneutral. As Leo Strauss puts it: "All political action aims at either preservation or change. When desiring to preserve, we wish to prevent a change to the worse; when desiring to change, we wish to bring about something better. All political action is then guided by some thought of better and worse. But thought of better or worse implies thought of the good."[10] Therefore the attempt to make political choices in a neutral fashion terminates in vacuity or utter incoherence.

If the account above is true, then government's adoption or rejection of neutrality as a liberal goal has important political implications from the policy level to the regime level. Consider the relationship between church and state. If neutralism is a dead-end street, while church and state can be distinguished institutionally and functionally, they cannot be separated to the degree neutralists desire. In addition to separating ecclesiastical and political institutions, neutralists wish to keep religiously informed ideas out of the public sphere. Yet one's religious beliefs cannot help but inform one's political beliefs so long as politics remains a branch of ethics. The connection between the two may not be obvious, straightforward, predictable, or even helpful, but it cannot be avoided.

The high and impermeable wall between religion and politics has not been a historical constant among liberals. Indeed, in the early years of the republic, it was widely accepted that a robustly religious people was compatible with, or even necessary to, free liberal government. The American citizenry's broad commitment to Christian beliefs largely did not get in their way of embracing Jefferson's liberal paean, the Declaration of Independence. In his Farewell Address, George Washington warned his fellow citizens against "the supposition that morality can be maintained without religion."[11] Even the early drive to disestablish the church, for instance, James Madison's *Memorial and Remonstrance,* was motivated as much by religious as political considerations, appealing to both Baptists and Deists. Liberal democracy was also seen as good for religion. Tocqueville viewed the First Amendment as a chief cause of America's stunning religiosity. From Tocqueville's perspective, persons are naturally religious because they are self-conscious of their mortality and therefore miserable. Government cannot significantly promote the natural impulse toward religion, but it can mute it. By allowing the free exercise of religion, liberal regimes help protect those institutions that teach virtue and foster our full humanity.

In contrast to this older tradition, today's liberals too often operate upon the false dichotomy that the only alternative to neutrality is the imposition of an intolerant and comprehensive theory of the good upon the unwilling. But no regime can avoid imposition, the neutralists any more than the nonneutralists. The point is to minimize state imposition while maintaining civilization. Neutrality silences citizens on matters of the highest import, while simultaneously it "covertly presupposes one particular partisan type of account of justice, that of liberal individualism . . . so that its apparent neutrality is no more than an appearance."[12] Ironically, it is perfectly reasonable to think that society would, if it had the chance, endorse goods that are perfectly consistent with tolerance. As William Galston claims: "The good is a continuum, not a dichotomous choice. Some accounts are very constraining, others much more capacious. There is a vast—and vitally important—terrain between Plato and Ronald Dworkin."[13]

We should not confuse the disposing of neutrality with the rejection of the goals animating liberal neutralists. Liberals promote neutrality on grounds that it promotes peace, reasonableness, a limited state, and the justification of state power. Every acceptable regime will find these traits attractive and seek to protect them. Even tolerance, the engine behind contemporary liberalism, serves an invaluable role in the cause of multiple political purposes. It is necessary for the development of the moral and civic virtues, the creation of economic wealth, the maintenance of political stability, the protection and facilitation of talents, and the search for truth. But to ground tolerance and all other attributes of politics in moral neutrality is to cut off the branch on which we are sitting, for it makes it impossible to answer the question, *Why liberal democracy?*

Comprehensiveness

Tocqueville points out that humans desire to harmonize earth with heaven.[14] That is, we strive for what Abraham Kuyper calls the curse of modern life, uniformity of thought.[15] We desire a single set of regulating principles to govern every sphere of society and every relationship within those spheres. This creeping tendency toward uniformity is driven largely by the ruling political principles of society. This holds true for two reasons. First, only political institutions legitimately employ coercion to enforce their decisions. Therefore implicit in every regime, even liberal ones, is the felt but rarely acknowledged threat that all secondary institutions exist at the government's discretion. Second, because of its power and visibility, government uniquely honors persons and ideas. So long as the government has the respect of the people—and therefore the ability to confer honor—the principles and persons it champions gain favor in the public eye. Its ideals become society's ideals. Politics is, in short, society's architectonic activity.

To understand politics as architectonic, however, is not to understand it as totalitarian or even comprehensive. True, the political ideals and distribution of offices in a regime affect everything in society, but when political rule is constituted to preserve a differentiated society it fully *determines* very little. Tocqueville tells us that aristocratic societies in particular are able to circumscribe centralized political power. Because landed aristocrats do not owe their power, prestige, or wealth to the favor of the state, they are largely independent from political control, and this independence protects real diversity of thought and freedom of action. Indeed, political rulers in aristocracies are forced to leave important administrative details to the nobles. Aristocracy therefore serves as both an important check on state power and an important source of creative greatness. Aristocrats have the means, leisure, training, and unbounded pride to set for themselves enormously ambitious projects, and they worry little about mass opinion. As Tocqueville puts it, "In aristocratic societies, while there is a multitude of individuals who can do nothing on their own, there is also a small number of very rich and powerful men, each of whom can carry out great undertakings on his own."[16] Aristocratic societies, in short, purchase multiformity of thought at the price of injustice.

Liberal democratic societies, in contrast, purchase justice at the risk of uniformity. The tendency for individuals in a democracy is "to become so much alike that the particular features of each individual may soon be entirely lost in the common physiognomy."[17] All persons are equal and weak in a democracy, so the only strong and superior entity is the state, whose principles threaten to infuse all of society. Not all democratic regimes, however, suffer equally from the threat of comprehensiveness or uniformity. For instance, Tocqueville argued that America's greatness stemmed in part from the sharp distinction it drew between ecclesiastical and political authority. Tocqueville promoted the split between church and state not only because it purified religion but also because he believed heterodoxy of thought to be critical for human greatness. While democracy appeals to the needs of the body and the wallet, religion appeals to the needs of the soul. The creative tension between these two contrary impulses awakens thought and stirs anxieties that expand the imagination. And this expansion, in turn, helps benefit democratic politics itself. "Whatever elevates, enlarges, and expands the soul makes it more able to succeed even in those undertakings which are not the soul's concerns."[18] For this reason, Tocqueville worked feverishly to preserve the remaining vestiges of aristocracy within a democratic society.

The proper goal of the statesman in democratic societies is therefore to guard against equality's unchallenged reign in every aspect of life. Advanced equality leads to uniformity of thought, which ultimately enervates the soul, encourages the sacrifice of individuals to principle, and undermines the preconditions for human greatness. As Tocqueville describes it, as democracies become more equal, "each individual becomes more like his fellows, weaker, and smaller, and the habit grows of ceasing to think about the citizens and considering only the people. Individuals are forgotten, and the species alone counts."[19] The statesman is not to reject equality—indeed he must be "friends of equality"—but also must work against its excesses.[20] "All those who still appreciate the true nature of man's greatness should combine in the struggle" against the extreme manifestations of unity which "foster the pride and soothe the laziness of their minds."[21]

Tocqueville struggled to fight against comprehensive equality, but *Democracy in America* is a record of its growth. Today we see Tocqueville's fears coming true all the more. Slowly but steadily the twin liberal principles of consent and equality have come to reshape every institution of society in their image. At work is something like a reverse *Invasion of the Body Snatchers*. In the 1950s movie of that name, individuals were taken over by a collective organism as they slept. Persons who were snatched by the alien collectivity continued to share their victim's body, but the souls of their victims were destroyed in service to the collective identity. The ideological baggage of the film was blunt and obvious: if we are not awake to the dangers of communism, we will fall prey to it. Today the reverse holds more nearly true. Nearly every corporate body, whether the family, the church, the university, and even the government itself, is reconfigured under liberal thought as a collection of self-satisficing individuals. Normal human affections and bonds that were once thought to hold communities together are translated into various shades of self-interestedness. Moral discourse itself has changed, with the lexicon of pride, love, affection, responsibility, and duty dropped in favor of the liberal language of rights. Authority of every stripe is under attack as consent and autonomy become the only justifications for inequality. As a result of this change, children instinctively sense the weakness of their parents and teachers. Church denominations set aside scripture to be more inclusive. Organizations such as the Boy Scouts are reshaped according to the standards of government. Universities fret more over the diversity of their populations than the fact they have lost the nerve to teach truth. Gifted urban students coast in their studies for fear of being ostracized. The authority of equal individualism alone—the authority of liberalism—remains unchallenged. Democrats and Republicans today fight largely over *which* manifestation of possessive individualism, government or business, will have primacy.

When we consider Barry Shain's groundbreaking work on early American communities, the triumph of individual authority in America becomes all the more remarkable.[22] Shain tells us that the contemporary reading of America as a land of supreme individualism is a modern fable read into our founding. Shain originally sought to examine the individualistic strains of early American thought, but to his surprise he did not find them. Instead, he found diverse small Protestant communities of various levels of tolerance in which the character of the community was considered prior to the freedom of the individual. Citizens had freedom to choose the kind of life they led, but to do so they had to find the community that supported their views. Communities scattered throughout the land were like so many islands of intolerance. The change toward a uniform liberalism changed only *after* the American Revolution.

To their credit, some contemporary liberals, most notably John Rawls, have attempted to more finely delineate the claims of liberalism. This effort is born from the recognition that it is unrealistic in a pluralistic society such as our own for any comprehensive ideology to gain universal favor. Liberalism, therefore, must be confined to the political arena and not be made the standard for all of life. Private belief systems that contradict the claims of liberalism are acceptable so long as they do not bleed into the public arena. Rawls reasons that politics is the attempt to navigate a peaceful society in the face of serious disagreement about what is good and bad for persons. We need agree only on the just arrangement of fundamental political institutions.

Rawls' recognition of liberalism's limits is a definite improvement over the unapologetic democratic comprehensiveness of, say, John Dewey's thought. Still, Rawls' recognition of the limits of politics becomes less promising upon closer examination. The fundamental purpose of the public-private dichotomy for Rawls is not to prevent the spread of liberal principles into other spheres of life. Indeed, Rawls finds that prospect rewarding, though unlikely. Rather, the purpose of the private-public distinction is to insulate the political sphere from infection by nonliberal thought. Rawls reasons that since humans have no final purposes of concern to the statesman, discussion of final purposes should be prohibited from the public sphere. To an extent, then, Rawls hastens society's liberalization by declaring unworthy for political consideration all nonliberal ideas. Rawls insists that only those kinds of reasons open to everyone's assent, in principle at least, are allowable in political discourse. Secret or revealed knowledge is properly prohibited in the public arena. Granting him this, one might have thought that Rawls would enter into a protracted investigation of how nonliberal traditions justify their stances. Do their justifications depend solely on secret or revealed knowledge? Does knowledge of the good, for the purposes of government, depend upon secret or revealed knowledge? Or, conversely, we might expect Rawls to investigate the extent to which liberal claims, such as the claim of our fundamental equality, are self-evident. In fact, he does neither. Instead, he takes for granted that *his* idea of justice is just such an area where agreement is possible—and *this* in the face of legions of detractors.

Rawls is not alone in his disqualification of his detractors to political debate. One prominent democratic theorist, for instance, champions political movements "concerned with peace, ecology, opposition to nuclear power, feminism, civil rights, community autonomy" as in keeping with communicative rationality, but lumps together conservative Christians with European neofascist parties as equally unacceptable reactions to modernity.[23] By excluding views contrary to his own from having a place at the table, this theorist promotes not diversity but uniformity of thought. Despotism comes in a variety of forms, from hard to soft, and any liberalism worth adopting must allow for nonliberal authority outside the political sphere and nonliberal arguments within it. Otherwise, we will fully realize what Tocqueville warned us of: a comprehensive statism couched in the language of individualism.

Statism

Liberalism was once, par excellence, the doctrine of state limits. While liberalism still confines government in important respects, the most remarkable change in liberal states during the last hundred years has been growth of the state. From the turn of the century to the Great Society, the chief sign of increased statism in the United States was the growth in the size of government. Government taxed more, appropriated more, and employed more people. Government did the same things it did before, but in larger scale. With only a few exceptions, even the New Deal programs expanded traditional state functions. Something quite different has occurred from the early seventies, however: Government did not grow larger; it became more intrusive. What is new is the scope and detail of social life subject to regulation. As Jonathan Rauch puts it:

> Today, there is nothing unusual about waking up one morning to find the government writing the rules of golf. The New York State Board of Law Examiners is required to give extra time on the bar exam to a woman who claims (contestedly) to have a reading disability. A group of gay municipal workers in Seattle is told it must include a hostile heterosexual man who outspokenly believes "biblical values." A television production company is ordered to pay a $5 million judgment

for refusing to cast a visibly pregnant woman in the role of a seductive vamp. The Supreme Court, in its majesty, decides when a coach may and may not smack a football player on the rump.[24]

The advent of state micromanagement is traceable to two closely linked reasons. First, the growth of government has followed the rise of comprehensive liberalism. As liberalism places more and more of social life under its regulative ideals, these ideals receive state backing. Ironically, then, statism follows inexorably from the multiplication of rights. Rights were once thought grounded in nature—and thus resistant to alteration or expansion—and were brought to bear *against* state action. But as liberalism has eroded the claims of nature through its celebration of personal autonomy, the explosion of rights was inevitable. Therefore today rights are a double-edged sword that both limit *and* expand the state. Every right warrants enforcement efforts, and as every sphere of life becomes more crowded with rights claims, the claims of justice *require* state involvement. For instance, as students have been accorded more rights, the state has become involved in the details of how, what, and when teachers teach and discipline their students. What is true of school is true also for the rest of society. The schoolmaster state that Tocqueville warned us of has arrived.

Liberal statism is also driven by the desire for security. Democracy's relentless desire for security stretches the state's realm of protection to almost limitless ends. The thirst for safety is closely linked to liberalism's device for legitimacy, the social contract, which links governmental action with consent. Since contemporary liberals do not ground government in nature, the only legitimate purpose of the state is that it protects individuals from harm. What kinds of harms warrant government intervention, of course, will depend upon a people's (read: theorist's) risk comfort and taste for liberty. Social contract theory is, in other words, particularly prone to tendentiousness. Nearly any state, from authoritarian to libertarian, can be rationalized by depicting the state of nature in various shades of brutality. For Locke, government was feared as much as the "inconveniences" of anarchy and so only harms done to the body or one's property were thought to warrant government action. Rawls, in contrast, views rights as claims to the basic goods of society—he takes them as given—which are necessary for self-esteem. He extends political action to the redistribution of wealth by depicting those in the original position—the conceptual launching point for contract—as acquisitive and risk averse. Ironically, in their moral forgetfulness, risk aversion, and acquisitiveness, parties to Rawls' contract nearly mirror parties in Thomas Hobbes' social contract. Though both Rawls and Hobbes open space for an expansive state, they do not draw the same conclusions about the limits of the state. Hobbes is more fearlessly consistent than Rawls because he does not take the social world as given. He also realizes that genuine risk aversion would make *any* form of government acceptable, free or otherwise, so long as it delivers one from the deprivations of anarchy.

In its search for security, liberalism is a middle-class affair aimed at making already comfortable lives more comfortable without risk. Calling a legislative proposal risky puts its defenders on the defensive. Invoking the "slippery slope" argument against it all but hammers the last nail in its coffin. Examples of crying risk abound in public life. Public prayers that should insult us for their vacuity and blandness are struck down by the Supreme Court for the risk they pose to the feelings of unbelievers. School choice is barred because it cannot be shown ahead of time that absolutely no child would receive a worse education. Whereas classical liberalism relegated harm to individuals and individual actors, modern liberals attempt to make entire *systems* risk-free. As Theodore Lowi, a fan of liberalism, has argued, "Liberalism came to a point where it considered itself *responsible* for every injury, every harm, and every potential cause thereof."[25] It goes without saying that such a position makes state action in every sphere of life inevitable.

In practice, liberalism is also a bohemian affair aimed at preserving diversity of lifestyles. Chic society has embraced the least attractive feature of Rawls' program—the moral equivalence of all life plans—while abandoning his admirable admission that sacrifice is a necessary component of justice. John Stuart Mill celebrated eccentricity because he believed genuine diversity of thought and lifestyle to be fertile soil for the development of genius and the advancement of society. Today's society, in contrast, views diversity as a commodity to be tasted or worn like a garment for a time. Differences in lifestyles represent personal choice and are acceptable because they are considered harmless. The state therefore is put to the service of promoting diversity of lifestyles even where claims of merit have to be put aside.

The problems with statism are many, but three problems relevant to liberal democracy stand out. To begin with, statism leads inevitably to rule by experts. The attempt to monitor and manage all aspects of life requires a scientific approach to administration. It requires scientists and other experts to make decisions about the economy, the family, the environment, immigration, and every other matter. Legislation is often written by bureaucrats or interest groups and frequently contains a heavy scientific component beyond the capacity of legislators to understand. Legislation is read by few legislators; cue-taking on votes is rampant. The sprawling complexity of statism today therefore seriously inhibits deliberation, both inside and outside of Congress. Citizens today feel alienated from their government because they do not understand what their government is doing and why it is doing it.

Second, statism in the American setting is conservative in the worst sense of the word. Government was once a progressive engine put to the use of bettering society. From the thirties to the early seventies the government employed millions of people, trained millions more, and taxed billions of dollars in a genuinely compassionate attempt to make society more decent and just. Programs were tried and discarded when they failed. A discursive process of trial-and-error fit and refit program to problem. Liberal aspirations ran high, but incrementalism was accepted as a means to accomplish society's goals. The point, as Franklin Roosevelt made clear during the Great Depression, was to keep trying until something worked. While this approach leaves much to be desired as rule of law, it was admirable in its honesty and pragmatic willingness to accept a program's failure. Today, no one can seriously call government flexible. Arguably, the most striking feature of politics today is the extent to which politicians and interest groups work hand in hand to protect the political status quo. Killing a program, *any* program, no matter how small, wasteful, or obsolete, is next to impossible. New programs spawn new interest groups motivated to protect their new benefits, and all interest groups invoke the liberal rhetoric of rights. No group claims special breaks; they want only to be treated fairly. What results is what Rauch calls demosclerosis, the clogging of the arteries of government.

A third danger of statism is its stifling effect on individual initiative. Much has been said of this point—liberals largely concede it—and we will not belabor it here. We need only remind ourselves of Tocqueville's insight that the chief problem with statism is not economic malaise but the malaise of souls. As Rousseau reminds us, once freedom is lost, it is difficult to recapture. Once the state feeds us, comforts us, tells us how to raise and educate our children, and provides for our happiness, it is difficult to break the habit. At risk in our dependence upon the government is the capacity for self-discovery or philosophy. It is through the act of doing things ourselves that we discover our talents, our limits, and our need for others.

Tocqueville's Correctives

This account of contemporary liberal thought and practice has been critical. Contemporary liberalism abstracts too much from nature, leaving self-interested and autonomous beings unfit for citizenship or virtue. It claims ethical neutrality while surreptitiously privileging some modes of life over others. It systematically appropriates all of social life as its own, jeopardizing genuine pluralism within and between social spheres. It depends too heavily on the state to solve social problems by striving for a perfectly safe and nicely diverse society. Still, to criticize *one* interpretation of liberal democracy is not to criticize liberal democracy altogether. Compared broadly to other regime types, liberal democracy is surely the most just regime and, arguably, simply the best. Its front-and-center placement of the individual, its limitations on the scope of government in religion, its commitment to freedom, and, yes, its encouragement of material progress are all great benefits to humanity. Of course, it also has its shortcomings. The political goal, of course, is to keep much of the good while minimizing and correcting for, where possible, its deficiencies. This was the strategy of Tocqueville, who saw democracy as inevitable but not altogether beyond human control. By warding off the worst tendencies of democracy, Tocqueville hoped to educate it. Here we will briefly examine three such strategies to correct for the worse tendencies of liberal democracy. Each of these were employed by Tocqueville and have continued to play an important role today. Our goal here is not to reflect Tocqueville's thought precisely but to learn from his political science.

Preserving the Moral Legacy of the Past

Liberal thought and its institutional props have gained progress over the decades, but not uniformly or without dissent. At the forefront of the counterattack against liberalism is an army of conservative think tanks, organizations, and political groups who have targeted a host of liberal policies. Perhaps to use the term "army" is misleading, for an army suggests a hierarchy of unified control. In fact there is no single conservative position, and to an amazing degree conservatives have accepted the liberal agenda. Look as one may, no vast right-wing conspiracy will be uncovered. No serious conservative today, for instance, calls for monarchy or theocracy. Few conservatives challenge liberals on the twin political goals of liberty and equality except as to their relative priority. Still, conservatives do not believe that liberty and equality fill up the entire moral universe, and they wish to conserve *some* vestigial remains of a preliberal and predemocratic world. Tocqueville understood this effort as the attempt to keep alive a portion of the moral heritage given to us by aristocratic life, especially the claims of community, virtue, and authority.

Conservatives suggest that by viewing persons as self-aggrandizing autonomous equals rather than as naturally social beings, liberalism erodes the preconditions for community. By stressing freedom over loyalty, justice over love, and security over honor, liberals make society, not community, their chief concern. Equality abhors distinctions, and therefore democratic society practically invites the diminution of institutions and persons, the building blocks of community. At its extreme, liberalism even throws into question why one should have *any* allegiance for this community over another. Time, energy, and affection are scarce, so my love of *this* community prevents me from loving other equally worthy communities. Liberal justice erases arbitrary distinctions, so the inexorable tendency of liberalism is to erode the love of home. Less allegiance to our local communities, in turn, puts more power in the hands of the national government, which is gifted at treating us equally.

In addition to community, conservatives speak endlessly—often shrilly—about virtue. This shrillness stems from the bankruptcy of our moral lexicon. As J. Budziszewski has said, "Our ancestors could hardly speak five connected sentences on a political topic without mentioning the virtues. Our own speech, though, is increasingly forgetful of . . . every virtue but one."[26] That virtue, *the* liberal virtue, is tolerance. Above all else, we are to tolerate *values* different from our own. Values are democratic because they are hardly distinguishable from preferences. In contrast, virtues, at least as seen by conservatives, presuppose moral realism. Here is where liberals and conservatives disagree most sharply. Contemporary liberals, following Kant, hold that the self is the source of all authority, while conservatives recognize authority that transcends the self.

Recognizing God's authority in the public sphere is an important symbolic gesture for many conservatives. In practice, however, conservatives do not rely exclusively, or even essentially, upon the claims of revealed religion in their public arguments any more than do liberals. Few fundamentalist conservatives can match former President Clinton in quoting scripture. Still, the desire to invoke God is not meaningless. One suspects that behind this desire is not the yearning for theocracy but a reaffirmation of authority itself. Authority is important for conservatives not only as a means of keeping order but also as something that demands recognition beyond the claims of the self. Without authoritative institutions and habits to encourage our sociability, Tocqueville feared that each citizen would isolate "himself from the mass of his fellows" to leave "the greater society to look after itself."[27] As a corrective to the democratic tendency toward individualism, Tocqueville champions religion because it encourages those natural affections of sociability. Similarly, he supports citizen involvement in politics because it teaches us responsibility and multiplies our cares beyond our small social circles.

What we wish to conserve from the past is, of course, open to debate. The concept that much warrants preservation, however, is not. With Tocqueville thoughtful liberals and conservatives should fight to preserve our heritage to the extent it promotes community, excellence, and self-reflection.

Promoting Liberal Virtues

Tocqueville understood the charms of democracy to be too great and the sins of aristocracy too unbearable to prevent a democratic future, but he feared that this change would mean the loss of fundamental human goods. Still, despite his recognition of aristocracy's finer points, Tocqueville was finally an uneasy liberal—uneasy and therefore nothing like contemporary liberals. Even more than protecting the vestigial remains of aristocracy, Tocqueville attempted to make democracy decent on its own terms. As he elegantly put it:

> All those who now wish to establish or secure the independence and dignity of their fellow men must show themselves friends of equality; and the only worthy means of appearing such is to be so; upon this depends the success of their holy enterprise. There is therefore no question of reconstructing an aristocratic society, but the need is to make freedom spring from that democratic society in which God has placed us.[28]

Today, a group of political philosophers, many of them students of the late Leo Strauss, are attempting to reshape liberalism from the inside out, making liberalism hospitable to virtue and philosophy. Writers in this tradition such as William

Galston, Peter Berkowitz, and David Walsh do not agree on all particulars, but they each emphasize that liberalism is not a neutral regime type, and as such privileges some ways of life, and some virtues, over others.[29] More importantly, they agree that liberal democracy cannot survive without a virtuous citizenry. Liberalism also depends upon a robust, though less than comprehensive, understanding of the human subject. The virtues necessary for democratic government, however, cannot be instantly summoned by government and depend upon institutions outside government for their cultivation. One of the chief tasks of these theorists, then, is to explore how to make the consequences of liberal politics consistent with its preconditions. They feel that by neglecting the habits and virtues that give health to democratic politics, contemporary liberals contribute to the sapping of liberal foundations.

Employing this approach to revivify liberal democracy means facing hard choices. To the extent that a comprehensive discussion of first principles or foundations of virtue is made the focus of liberalism, liberalism itself is placed in jeopardy. True, liberalism depends upon virtue, but liberalism is chiefly about freedom and equality. There is no prima facie reason to think that democratic regimes are best suited either for teaching virtue or for squeezing the most good out of existing virtue. Tocqueville feared, after all, that democracies tend toward mediocrity, not inspired virtue or grandiose viciousness. Too much focus on this point, however, may highlight the deficiencies of democracies and thereby undermine its legitimacy. Moreover, liberalism is not a comprehensive theory of the human good. Though it must recognize some goods, the liberal state is chiefly a means of adjudicating between *competing* views of the good. While virtue cannot be ignored, focusing on the promotion of virtue almost guarantees the disruption of democratic politics itself.

Ignoring the foundations of virtue, on the other hand, risks relativizing virtue to liberal regimes, reducing virtue to utility. This, in turn, risks undermining the foundations of liberalism. Why should we care if some habits are necessary to liberal democracy if we cannot be assured that either the habits we call virtues or the goals of liberalism are good simply? Tocqueville noticed that Americans think of virtue not as beautiful but as useful for promoting our self-interest. The American approach is fine so long as people really *are* virtuous, for then virtue coincides with the self-interest of the parties as they themselves understand it. If, on the other hand, people are vicious or even short-sighted, then virtue works at odds with self-interest as the parties understand it. At the end of the day, liberal government requires its citizens to follow virtue for its own sake.

One way of threading this needle is for governments to protect the teachers of virtue rather than to promote virtue itself. Advocates of virtue disagree about the role of the state in promoting virtue, but practically no one argues that the state is the chief or even the best teacher of virtue. Direct state inculcation of virtue is not only clumsy but poses serious risks to freedom. We need not agree on the state's role, however, to agree that teachers of virtue such as the family and churches deserve protection. Most importantly, we need not agree on *which* virtues should be taught in these institutions. For our purposes what is most important is that these institutions can be defended on strictly liberal grounds. Religious institutions, of course, are protected by the First Amendment, and regulation of the family falls almost exclusively under the Reserved Powers of the states. Protecting these institutions, then, is part and parcel of protecting freedom itself. Because families and churches are legally private, they can freely pursue the teaching of virtue on their own ontological grounds without threatening political liberalism.

Differentiating the Spheres of Society

If the preceding is true, the promotion of virtue necessary to the flourishing of liberal democracy depends upon the health of private institutions. In truth we have no way of knowing beforehand whether private institutions will do their important tasks well. Certainly government has few tools to encourage them, since active intervention in their affairs would not only violate their liberty but also jeopardize the government's claim to liberal impartiality. What we can be certain of, however, is that if nongovernmental institutions lose their nerve to train us into truth and virtue—that is, to teach us what is good—liberal democracy will quickly spiral downward to nihilism. Political liberalism therefore needs not only private institutions—it needs *nonliberal* institutions.

Liberal democracy therefore requires an account of the differentiated spheres of society. Because no single institution in a decent society exercises authority over every social task, each institution needs to develop different principles in keeping with its responsibilities. Most people implicitly recognize this to be true without being aware of it as a principle. We resent it when public schools teach our children questionable or false moral lessons. We are horrified when churches attempt to impose their theological agenda on the democratic process. We fear the commodification of our very lives, not limited to our sexual relations, our genetic code, our body parts, our children.

Regime design therefore must take into account the different responsibilities stemming from our various relationships. Liberalism, however, is horrible at making sense of our social nature. Religious thought, on the other hand, naturally focuses on human relationships. Not surprisingly, then, the most thoughtful recent work to integrate our social nature into a political theory of the limited duties of the state has emerged from that intellectual corner. In particular, the Catholic theory of subsidiarity and the neo-Calvinist theory of sphere sovereignty start not with the satisfaction of the autonomous self, as liberals typically do, but with our natural sociability. These theories, though far from identical, both attempt to marry liberal democracy's emphasis on justice, the political and legal equality of man, and the distinction between private and public, with a respect for our social nature and the differentiation of society. Both camps fear that the practical advantages of liberal democracy have become threatened over time by liberal theory's grotesque anthropology and lack of understanding of its own limits. What they fear above all is the threat that comprehensive liberalism poses to the dignity of the individual and the wondrous multiformity of life. Again, Tocqueville was prescient:

> Men think that the greatness of the idea of unity lies in means. God sees it in the end. It is for that reason that the idea of greatness leads to a thousand mean actions. To force all men to march in step toward the same goal—that is a human idea. To encourage endless variety of actions but to bring them about so that in a thousand different ways all tend toward the fulfillment of one great design—that is a God-given idea.[30]

The problem Tocqueville raises is how men are to avoid thinking like men and to begin thinking more like God. Liberals see the absurdity of the project and avoid it altogether. They are, of course, right in doing so. Right, that is, unless the only thing more dangerous than trying to read the mind of God is ignoring it altogether. With this counsel in mind, Catholics look with humility to God's natural order for guidance, and neo-Calvinists look to the ontology of creation as the foundation of their political theory. It must be emphasized that neither group wishes to establish a theocracy. Both subsidiarity and sphere sovereignty support confessional pluralism because they both clearly delineate between the *institutional* tasks of church and state. Indeed, one of the chief architects of sphere sovereignty has said that the "secularization of state and society is one of the most basic ideas of Calvinism."[31] The purpose of these theories is not to impose church creed on society, but to create a society in which church creed can be meaningful for those who pursue it.

Conclusion

Liberal democratic society has unleashed unimagined material progress. It has also made tremendous gains for justice and the production of wealth. These accomplishments are genuine blessings. Still, it is hard to argue that democracy has not diminished the soul when it has no need for souls. To expect that political principles will bring us happiness is foolish, but at least we can expect them to differentiate us from clever animals. Even today, then, at history's apparent end, there is a need for political philosophers to think about regime design in light of our understanding of God, nature, and the human person. At stake is our dignity.

Notes

1. Jonathan Rauch, *Government's End: Why Washington Stopped Working* (New York: Public Affairs, 1999), 193.

2. Alexis de Tocqueville, *Democracy in America*, trans. George Lawrence (New York: Harper Perennial, 1969), 12.

3. Influential "contemporary" liberals include the following scholars: John Rawls, *Political Liberalism* (New York: Columbia University Press, 1993); Bruce Ackerman, "Why Dialogue?" *Journal of Philosophy* 86, no. 1 (January 1989): 5-22 and *Social Justice in the Liberal State* (New Haven, Conn.: Yale University Press, 1980); Charles Larmore, *Patterns of Moral Complexity* (Cambridge: Cambridge University Press, 1987); Ronald Dworkin, "Liberalism," in *Public and Private Morality*, ed. Stuart Hampshire (Cambridge: Cambridge University Press, 1978), 113-43; Thomas Nagel, "Moral Conflict and Political Legitimacy," *Philosophy and Public Affairs* 17 (Summer 1982).

4. Many reasons have been offered for why consensus is elusive. The usual suspects are a plurality of incommensurable values, the essential contestability of political concepts, the finitude of the mind, moral vice, the indemonstrability of first principles, and the inherent ambiguity of language.

5. Ackerman, "Why Dialogue?" 16-17. For similar points, see Larmore, *Patterns of Moral Complexity*, and Stephen Macedo, "Liberal Civic Education and Religious Fundamentalism: The Case of *God v. John Rawls?*" *Ethics* 105 (April 1995): 474, 476.

6. Robert A. Dahl, *Democracy and Its Critics* (New Haven, Conn.: Yale University Press, 1989), 48.

7. J. Donald Moon, "Constrained Discourse and Public Life," *Political Theory* 19, no. 2 (May 1991): 213.

8. *Walker v. The Superior Court of Sacramento County,* 47 Cal. 3d 112 (1988).

9. Fred M. Frohock, "The Boundaries of Public Reason," paper presented at the Southern Political Science Association annual meeting, November 2-5, 1994, 8-11.

10. Leo Strauss, *An Introduction to Political Philosophy*, ed. Hilail Gildin (Detroit: Wayne State University Press, 1989), 3.

11. George Washington, "Farewell Address of 1796," in *From Many, One: Readings in American Political and Social Thought*, ed. Richard C. Sinopoli (Washington, D.C.: Georgetown University Press, 1997), 65.

12. Alasdair MacIntyre, *Whose Justice? Which Rationality?* (Notre Dame, Ind.: University of Notre Dame Press, 1988), 3-4.

13. William Galston, *Liberal Purposes: Goods, Virtues, and Diversity in the Liberal State* (Cambridge: Cambridge University Press, 1992), 9.

14. Tocqueville, *Democracy in America*, 287.

15. Abraham Kuyper, "Uniformity: The Curse of Modern Life," in *Abraham Kuyper: A Centennial Reader*, ed. James D. Bratt (Grand Rapids, Mich.: Paternoster Press, 1998).

16. Tocqueville, *Democracy in America*, 514.

17. Tocqueville, *Democracy in America*, 701.

18. Tocqueville, *Democracy in America*, 546-47.

19. Tocqueville, *Democracy in America*, 451.

20. Tocqueville, *Democracy in America*, 695.

21. Tocqueville, *Democracy in America*, 452.

22. Barry Alan Shain, *The Myth of American Individualism: The Protestant Origins of American Political Thought* (Princeton, N.J.: Princeton University Press, 1994).

23. John S. Dryzek, *Discursive Democracy: Politics, Policy, and Political Science* (Cambridge: Cambridge University Press, 1990), 49.

24. Jonathan Rauch, "Tunnel Vision," *National Journal*, <http://nationaljournal.com/-njstories/0919nj1.htm> (September 19, 1998).

25. Theodore Lowi, *The End of the Republican Era* (Norman: University of Oklahoma Press, 1995), 63.

26. J. Budziszewski, *True Tolerance: Liberalism and the Necessity of Judgment* (New Brunswick, N.J.: Transaction, 1992), xi.

27. Tocqueville, *Democracy in America*, 506.

28. Tocqueville, *Democracy in America*, 695.

29. For representative works, see Galston, *Liberal Purposes*; Peter Berkowitz, *Virtue and the Making of Liberalism* (Princeton, N.J.: Princeton University Press, 1999); and David Walsh, *The Growth of the Liberal Soul* (Columbia: University of Missouri Press, 1997).

30. Tocqueville, *Democracy in America*, 734-35.

31. Kuyper, "Common Grace," in *Abraham Kuyper: A Centennial Reader*, 197.

Chapter 5

The Changing Landscape of Religion and Politics in America: The 2000 Presidential Election

Beverly Gaddy

Dear friends, I am so full of gratitude at this moment. I ask you to allow me to let the spirit move me as it does to remember the words from Chronicles, which are to give thanks to God. To give thanks to God and declare his name and make his acts known to the people. To be glad of spirit. To sing to God and to make music to God, and most of all, to give glory and gratitude to God from whom all blessings truly do flow. Dear Lord, maker of all miracles, I thank you for bringing me to this extraordinary moment in my life.

—Sen. Joe Lieberman
(upon being introduced by Al Gore as the Democrat's candidate for vice president)

As all students of American religion know, separation of church and state is one thing, separation of religion and politics is something else altogether. Religion and politics flow back and forth in American civil society all the time—always have, always will. How could it be otherwise?

—Jean Bethke Elshtain

We are living in a secular society, but a spiritual culture.

—Pastor Al Winseman

The 2000 elections will be talked about and debated for decades to come. They revealed a nation evenly divided between Republicans and Democrats. Once the dust cleared from the agonizing recounts and court challenges, we ended up with a 50-50 split in the Senate, a narrow five-seat Republican advantage in the House, and an even split in party control of the state legislatures (with each party controlling seventeen state legislatures, divided control in fifteen states, and Nebraska's nonpartisan unicameral). But the real cliffhanger was the outcome of the presidential election, where it took five weeks and a 5-4 decision by the Supreme Court to decide a winner, the first time in our history the Supreme Court stepped in to decide the outcome of a presidential election. With 105.4 million popular votes cast, George W. Bush and Al Gore each won 48 percent—with Gore winning a plurality of only about one-third of a percent or 350,000 votes. The outcome hinged on which candidate would receive Florida's twenty-five electoral votes, which after five weeks of closely watched recounts and court battles were finally awarded to Bush by a margin of only 537 popular votes out of more than six million cast statewide. This gave Bush 271 electoral votes to Gore's 267—a presidential election won by only four electoral votes and one vote in the Supreme Court. This was the first election since 1888 in which the Electoral College winner failed to win the popular vote, and the second time in history that the son of a former president won the presidency.

Much can be said and has been said already about how this election was decided. But in the midst of the debate over chads, butterfly ballots, court decisions, and the Electoral College, something else of great cultural and political significance in this election has received scant attention. As we enter the new millennium, religion in the United States is undergoing a massive transformation. This transformation, along with changes in the political agenda over the past couple of decades, has altered our views toward the proper role of religion in American public life and politics. The religious landscape of the last four decades of the twentieth century—one of conservative evangelicalism in opposition to religious liberalism, a "culture wars" era—is melding into a different kind of spiritual terrain. The chasm that has separated theological conservatives from liberals since the fundamentalist-modernist split of the 1920s is narrowing as baby-boomer evangelicals and progressives alike place less emphasis on the particularistic doctrines which separated them, while seeking greater unity with other faith traditions and increased spiritual relevance in their lives. In the words of one scholar, "Boundaries separating one faith tradition from another that once seemed fixed are now often blurred; religious identities are malleable and multifaceted, often overlapping several traditions."[1] Observers of the religious landscape note that Americans' religious preferences today have become so diverse, so untraditional, and so fluid and malleable that it has become increasingly difficult to determine exactly what is meant by spirituality in the United States anymore. After his most recent survey of religion in the United States, George Gallup, Jr., concluded that Americans' religious preferences include a "mixed bag of traditional and experimental, mainstream and fringe, Christ-centered and syncrestic."[2]

This changing religious landscape was manifested in the 2000 presidential campaigns both in the openness of the candidates in discussing their faith and in the growing public acceptance of "God talk" in the public square. Three of the major party candidates in the 2000 presidential and vice-presidential campaigns made frequent references to their religious beliefs and claimed that their beliefs guide their policy positions or actions. Although Dick Cheney was more reticent to openly discuss his faith than were the other candidates on faith issues, he is a Methodist who would fit comfortably in the evangelical category, and his traditional religious beliefs may be a primary source of his conservative policy positions. The other candidates were freer in their religious expressions, readily discussing how their faith would guide them in their public roles. Gore, for example, a born-again Southern Baptist, stated that his favorite book is the Bible and that he frequently asks himself, "What would Jesus do?" Bush was forthcoming about his conversion experience, how Christ changed his life, and how his evangelical beliefs are such an important part of his life that they would naturally guide him in the decisions he would make as president. Asked in a debate in December 1999 who his favorite philosopher was, Bush responded, "Jesus Christ, because He changed my heart." At the time, Bush was ridiculed for his response, especially by those who thought he mentioned Christ because he was unable to name a philosopher.

But when Gore announced Sen. Joe Lieberman as his choice for running mate, the debate concerning the proper role of a candidate's personal faith in his or her public life received more sympathetic and prominent media attention. Like Bush, Lieberman, an Orthodox Jew, boldly discussed the importance of his faith in both his private and public life. In sharp contrast to the way Bush's remarks about Christ were received, when Lieberman observed in August 2000 that Americans needed "to renew the dedication of our nation and ourselves to God and God's purpose," and added, "We are children of the same awesome God," no one laughed. Although the Constitution "wisely separates church from state," he noted, there must be a place for faith in the nation's public life.[3] In defense of his position that his religious beliefs must play an important role in his public life, Lieberman explained, "My faith is important to my life, and I'm exercising my First Amendment freedom of religion to occasionally talk about it."[4]

Some critics of Lieberman's remarks, including the Anti-Defamation League, cast the issue in terms not of religious freedom but of the First Amendment guarantee of separation of church and state, suggesting that Lieberman had violated that principle. These critics may not have realized that American attitudes toward the role of religion in public life have changed enough in the past few years that Lieberman's remarks—and similar remarks made by other candidates in the presidential race—are more socially and politically acceptable today than they have been in nearly half a century.

There are a number of explanations that can account for this change. The first has been mentioned by a number of observers: the public's need to be reassured of a candidate's moral fitness for public life given the sting the public suffered by Bill Clinton's personal moral failings. Just as anger over Watergate and Gerald Ford's pardon of Richard Nixon prompted Americans in 1976 to elect as their president a Southern Baptist Sunday School teacher who promised to restore honesty to the

White House, so also public unease over the immoral behavior and political scandals of the Clinton administration, accompanied by the emergence and enduring presence of religious conservatives as a force in American politics, may have motivated greater sympathy for a more public role of religion in political life in 2000. *U.S. News* wrote of a "post-Clinton craving" for piety among our politicians.[5] Even the director of Americans United for the Separation of Church and State, Barry Lynn, admitted that personal scandals involving political leaders have prompted Americans to seek a fuller integration of moral values and public life, leading candidates to reveal not only their moral vision, but also the religious foundation that undergirds it.[6]

A second explanation may be that the peace and prosperity leading up to the 2000 elections, as well as the lack of sharp policy divisions between the major party candidates, left an opening for Americans to focus more attention upon candidates' character and the nation's moral direction. John C. Green, director of the Bliss Institute of Applied Politics at Akron University, posited that a "diminishing worry over economic and international threats and a growing concern over the turmoil of political scandals, high school shootings, and hate crimes" may help to account for this shift in attitudes. He noted that candidates "have sensed this disquiet, and want to respond to it" either by speaking of religious faith or talking about morality and values, as Bush did in speaking of "prosperity with a purpose."[7] Green commented that the last time America has seen a candidate so open in discussing his faith was nearly a century ago, with William Jennings Bryan.[8]

A third explanation for the more public role of religion in the United States is changes in the political agenda. Over the past three to four decades, social and moral issues have received increased political attention, activating religious organizations to respond to perceived assaults on traditional values. The prominence of issues such as abortion, school prayer, children's issues, and sexuality in the national political agenda has provoked political involvement by the religiously committed, "diminishing the divide" between religion and politics in the United States and intensifying the link between political attitudes and religious affiliation.[9]

A fourth explanation, and my central thesis, is that a change in the nature of religion in the United States has made faith more amenable to public life in our democracy. That Lieberman, Bush, and Gore (and to an extent Clinton before them) were able to publicly and confidently express their personal faith and defend a role for religion in public life provides additional evidence for a phenomenon already noted by sociologists of religion: the new millennium marks a broad and enduring shift in the American religious landscape. Spirituality in the United States has become more fluid, less particularistic, more pluralistic, more tolerant, and less confined to specific places and issues, allowing faith to more easily spill out into and find wider acceptance in everyday public life and dialogue.

The Past Four Decades: Removing God from Presidential Politics and Putting Him Back Again

"God talk" by presidential candidates has not always played so well with voters. Lieberman's remarks prompted some to recall the example set by John F. Kennedy, who sought to reassure voters in 1960 that his Roman Catholicism would not influence his presidential decision-making. In an address to the Greater Houston Ministerial Association on September 12, 1960, Kennedy emphasized the importance of the separation of church and state while downplaying his Catholicism, stating that what is important in the campaign is "not what kind of church I believe in, for that should be important only to me—but what kind of America I believe in." He steadfastly insisted that his faith would not influence his policy decisions: "Whatever issue may come before me as President. . . . I will make my decision . . . in accordance with . . . the national interest, and without regard to outside religious pressures or dictates. And no power or threat of punishment could cause me to decide otherwise." The model for presidents for the next four decades became one of being publicly quiescent about faith, even if privately devout. References consistent with America's "civil religion" were a noted exception.

In the 1976 presidential elections, as Americans sought a more moral alternative to an administration tainted by Watergate, corruption, and cover-ups, they elected the aforementioned president "born-again" Southern Baptist Sunday School teacher, Jimmy Carter. But America was not yet ripe for a large role for private faith in public life so, like JFK before him, Carter promised not to allow his religious beliefs to dictate his public policies. As a consequence, and in sharp contrast to those of many other presidents, including Clinton and George W. Bush, Carter's inaugural address was nearly bereft of religious allusions. As president, Carter employed only general "God talk," and faith only rarely and indirectly came up in presidential communication.

The return to a public acceptance of faith in the public square began with the 1980 elections. On August 22, 1980, Ronald Reagan promised 15,000 members of the Roundtable, a nondenominational evangelical group, that he would govern according to "old-time religion." Reagan successfully courted religious conservatives, and Carter, much more active in his church life than was Reagan, was never able to win those voters back. During both inaugurals, Reagan took the oath of office with his left hand on his mother's Bible, open to II Chronicles 7:14: "If my people which are called by my name, shall humble themselves, and pray, and seek my face, and turn from their wicked ways; then I will hear from heaven, and will forgive their sin, and will heal their land"—a passage often referenced by evangelicals in motivating the religiously committed to political action. Dwight Eisenhower had used the same passage in his two inaugurations.

Not only did Reagan win religious conservatives for the GOP but he also helped to mobilize them into an active political force. Aided by an intensification of the "culture wars" as theological conservatives felt increasingly threatened by the slide into moral relativism, symbolized by the *Roe v. Wade* decision in 1973 and a perceived erosion of moral traditionalism, evangelicals reentered the political sphere with a vengeance, resulting in a massive religious realignment of the American party system in the 1980s and first half of the 1990s, as religious conservatives became a core Republican constituency.

Clinton continued the trend toward a more liberal dose of religious rhetoric in his presidential role. A Southern Baptist, like Harry Truman and Carter before him, Clinton was a very visible churchgoer and quoter of scripture, and the media often caught him emerging from church, Bible in hand. But many religious conservatives were more persuaded of Clinton's religious commitment (or lack thereof) as evidenced by his many sins, and by his liberal social policies, than they were by his frequent demonstrations of piety.

The 1994 congressional elections were the high point of Religious Right influence, as evangelical voters overwhelmingly turned out in support of the GOP, helping to make Republicans the majority party in both houses of Congress for the first time in six decades. But four years later, with a Democratic president newly impeached by the Republican-majority House for moral transgressions, evangelicals—who were firmly in support of impeachment—were not joined by a sufficient number of other voters to confirm their support of Republicans at the ballot box. Against all expectations, the GOP lost seats in the House and Republicans who had run with strong Religious Right support lost important state races in the South and the Midwest. The elections were a huge disappointment for the Religious Right and triggered much "soul searching" among the movement's leaders.

A Retreat of the Religious Right? Or a Redefined Religious Voice in American Election?

In February 1999, Paul Weyrich, one of the founders of the Moral Majority, wrote a letter to constituents of his organization, the Free Congress Foundation, lamenting, "We probably have lost the culture war" and warning "we need some sort of quarantine."[10] Former Moral Majority staffers Ed Dobson and Cal Thomas, echoing Weyrich's concerns, published *Blinded by Might* shortly thereafter. They expressed concerns that conservative Christians had "failed to change America"—were "losing the battle"—because they had employed the "wrong weapons." The Religious Right had been "blinded by might"—they had allowed their lust for political power and policy success to distract them from their primary mission of saving lost souls for Jesus. Unlike Weyrich, however, Dobson and Thomas did not call for a retreat from politics—"Believers must be energetically engaged in politics—a way to show love for our neighbors."[11] It was a plea for a reassessment of the motives, mission, and tactics of the Religious Right.

The September 1999 edition of *Christianity Today* featured as its cover story a symposium by these three and others (Ralph Reed, Jerry Falwell, Don Eberly, James Dobson, and Chuck Colson) titled "Is the Religious Right Finished?" in which the issue of the "proper relationship between politics, culture, the church, and one's faith and social responsibility" were debated. Something of a consensus emerged from the exchange: religion in American politics is changing, and it is changing for the better. People of faith cannot retreat entirely from the public square—diverse voices of faith must continue to salt political discourse.

These events—the 1998 elections, followed closely by the 1999 calls for disengagement and retrenchment—have led observers to conclude that the Christian Right has retreated. While there are indeed some signs of a retreat by the Christian Right, there are also signs of increased influence of religious belief in electoral politics.

On the one hand, the Christian Coalition is not what it used to be. It has not recovered from the loss of Ralph Reed, who departed the organization following the 1996 elections to found his own political consulting business. Since Reed's departure, the Christian Coalition has suffered from declines in membership and revenues, including resignations of numerous chapter leaders across the nation.[12] It also lost its tax-exempt status in a ruling by the IRS. Another sign of Christian Right weakness is that Christian Right candidates in 1998 did not fare as well as more moderate GOP candidates.[13] Third, there are indications that issues such as education, economics, poverty, and foreign policy are replacing the more traditional socio-moral issues of abortion and gay rights as the most salient issues for evangelical voters, and it was fervency on the moral issues that energized Christian Right support.[14] Finally, there are also indications that evangelicals are becoming less yoked to the Republican party. For example, while 60 percent of evangelicals identified with the Republican party in 1998 (up from 56.3 percent in 1994), a recent survey of the National Association of Evangelicals suggested 38 percent would be open to voting for a Democrat.[15] Also, there has been a decline in the number of strong Republican identifiers—from 14.3 percent in 1994 to 9.2 percent in 1998.

But even if the Christian Right, the grassroots social movement, is losing strength, this certainly does not translate into waning support for the GOP from religious conservatives, that religious conservatives are any less likely to turn out to vote, or that religious belief is any less important in campaigns and elections. Mark Rozell made this point in an op-ed in the *Washington Post* during the 2000 primary season: "The core constituency of the Christian Right has comprised approximately one-sixth of the United States voting population [since the 1970s], regardless of particular movement organizations or presidential candidates. If the Christian Coalition closes shop tomorrow, these active voters will remain involved in politics. . . . Movement organizations may come and go, but the activists rarely disappear."[16]

Rozell was correct in his predictions. A survey conducted by the University of Akron's Ethics and Policy Center both prior to and immediately following the 2000 elections found that the religiously committed voted much as they had in previous elections, although some new patterns also emerged. Bush was widely supported by religiously committed white Christians (both Protestant and Catholic), led by evangelical Protestants (84 percent of observant white evangelicals voted for Bush) and joined by less religiously committed white Protestants (about 56 percent of whom voted for Bush). Together these religious groups made up three-quarters of Bush's vote total and thus were hugely significant in winning this closely fought election for Bush. Gore's support came primarily from members of minority religious groups, especially black Protestants, 96 percent of whom voted for Gore, but also secular voters, 65 percent of whom voted for Gore, and less-observant white Christians—six in ten Catholics with low levels of religious commitment and four in ten less-observant Protestants voted for Gore. In total, these groups made up three-quarters of Gore's electoral support.

Since religious commitment is strongly linked to expressed concern for the moral health of the nation, it is also noteworthy that the CBS News exit poll (November 7, 2000) found that six out of ten voters felt that the moral climate of the country was "seriously off the wrong track," and 62 percent of those who responded in this way voted for Bush. Only 39 percent said they felt the country was morally on the right track, and 70 percent of these voted for Gore. Nonetheless, only 44 percent of those voters who felt that the nation was on the "wrong track" morally responded that it was more important for a president to be a "moral leader" than it is for him to be a "good manager."[17]

Thus while the Christian Right as an organized movement may have been less visible in this election, the Christian Right as an electoral force remains potent. The religiously committed cannot be ignored as important voting blocs for the parties, and the candidates in the 2000 presidential election employed religious rhetoric and imagery in an effort to appeal to these voters. To neglect to do so would have meant certain defeat in this election, as John McCain and Bill Bradley belatedly learned in their failed attempts to capture their party's nomination. Yet the three candidates who most liberally sprinkled "God talk" in their campaigns—especially Bush and Lieberman—did not appear to do so merely in an attempt to win votes. They appear to be sincere in their faith, yet willing to strategically employ public expressions of their personal piety in an effort to demonstrate that they are candidates of faith and moral character and that their morality rooted in faith would genuinely guide their public actions. And they knew that American voters were ripe for such a message.

The Changing Nature of Religion in America

Secularization thesis—the reigning doctrine within the sociology of religion for the past four decades that claimed that religion's influence in society, institutions, and individual lives was declining in the face of scientific rationality—has been largely disproved. Modernity did not bring a diminished reliance upon spiritual matters. Quite the contrary, individuals in postmodern America overwhelmingly affirm their faith in God and reliance upon their faith in their everyday lives, and religion has emerged as a vital force not only in the United States but worldwide. In fact, there are indications that Americans today demonstrate *greater* religiosity than did Americans of the 1920s.[18] Polls show that religious belief in the United States remains unusually widespread, especially when compared with Europe. A Gallup survey, for example, reports that 96 percent of Americans express a belief in God, 90 percent pray to God, two-thirds claim membership in a religious congregation, and half claimed to have experienced the presence of God within the previous twenty-four-hour period. Eighty-four percent believe in the deity of Jesus Christ, 90 percent in heaven, and eight in ten in some kind of Judgment Day before God.[19] Of particular significance for American campaigns, 61 percent of all voters claim they attend religious services at least once or twice a month, with 45 percent attending weekly.[20]The great majority of these regular attendees votes Republican and cast their vote for the Bush-Cheney ticket in 2000.

Although religious belief is widespread in the United States, the character of spirituality is changing. The religious beliefs of Americans are becoming both more eclectic and in some ways more private, with growing numbers of Americans opting for the word "spiritual" rather than "religious" to describe their beliefs.[21] As Robert Wuthnow explains, "Growing numbers of Americans piece together their faith like a patchwork quilt. Spirituality has become a vastly complex quest in which each person seeks in his or her own way."[22] This change is widespread, affecting both those within traditional religious traditions and those who had long opted out of traditional religion. But as spirituality becomes more fluid and the lines separating faiths less defined, faith becomes more amenable to public life in a democracy. How? As Wuthnow explains, it is because "traditionally, the spiritual ideal has been to live a consistent, fully integrated life of piety, such that one's practice of spirituality becomes indistinguishable from the rest of one's life."[23] As traditional religion melds into *spirituality*, we observe both a wider diversity of faiths—including individualized blends of a variety of belief systems—and hopefully also an increased emphasis on spiritual practice, a focus that would naturally cause genuine private faith to spill out of the privatized realm into public life, leading to more widespread and diverse expressions of belief in public, and resulting in greater acceptance of faith in politics.

The contemporary spiritual landscape is also much more accepting of religious relativism. For example, Wade Clark Roof reports that 48 percent of respondents in his survey, including a quarter of Evangelicals, agreed with the statement "All the religions in the world are equally true and good."[24] A wider acceptance of the validity of diverse religious beliefs, plus greater religious pluralism, would naturally lead to greater tolerance for expressions from a multiplicity of religious voices in the public square. As William Swatos and Kevin Christiano explain, religious pluralism "undermines the element of absolute certainty. . . . The more one becomes aware of more and more religions competing in a marketplace-like setting, the harder it becomes to assert that any one religion contains all truth and that others must be all wrong."[25] Increased competition among denominations has indeed been linked to greater religious mobilization.[26] More importantly, as the percentage of seculars has greatly increased over the past four decades, the lines dividing various religious traditions have blurred—the divisions of any real consequence are not between religious traditions but between the religiously committed on the one side and seculars and the less committed on the other.[27] Thus Americans have become much less particularistic when it comes to faith in the public square and much more welcoming of expressions of "God talk" regardless of the content of the doctrine.

Shifting Public Opinion on the Role of Religion in Politics

Forty years ago, candidate expressions of personal piety would not have played well with the electorate. No more. Today, God talk resonates with a majority of United States voters. Polls in the 1960s showed that a majority of Americans did not feel it appropriate for a candidate to openly discuss his or her faith; in 2000 a majority believe it is appropriate.[28] According to a *Newsweek* poll released in September 2000, more than half of Americans want religion to play a greater role in public life, and nearly three-quarters have no objections to Lieberman publicly discussing his faith. This same poll found that 61 percent of registered voters think it is appropriate for candidates to discuss their religious beliefs,[29] and a 1999 Gallup Poll found that 52 percent are *more* likely to vote for a presidential candidate who talks about his personal relationship with Christ, whereas only 25 percent would be *less* likely to vote for such a candidate. John Green observed from his surveys that "a greater demand" exists for religious talk in political life these days, and there is also "a greater supply of it." He adds, "The public is more interested in values these days, particularly questions of morality, than they have been in the recent past."[30]

Public opinion polls during the 2000 campaign also showed widespread and growing support for a president with strong religious beliefs. A Pew Research Center poll released in September 2000 showed that 70 percent of Americans want a president with strong religious beliefs, although half admit to unease when presidents talk about how religious they are. It is important to note, however, that older Americans are much less comfortable with presidential candidates openly discussing their faith than are those of the baby-boom generation and younger, underscoring the fact that this growing ease with God talk is a product of a generational shift in American spiritual culture that emerged out of the changes wrought in American society in the 1960s and 1970s.

Americans' growing comfort with candidates engaging in God talk does not translate to widespread support for churches engaging in political dialogue, although there is growing support for churches becoming politically engaged, especially in the African American community. About half of the respondents in a recent Gallup poll said churches should express their views on politics, but two-thirds do not think it appropriate for clergy to talk about politics from the pulpit. Whereas a narrow majority of Americans in 1968 wanted churches to stay out of politics, that opposition had eroded by 1996, when a narrow majority said churches should freely express their views.

Another piece of evidence underscoring growing support for the role of religion in American elections is the fact that the image of evangelical Christians has improved significantly in recent years, just as the political visibility of the Christian Right has diminished. The Pew Center's September 2000 poll found that 63 percent of all respondents, and 60 percent of Democrats, now have a favorable view of evangelicals. Four years prior, only 41 percent of all respondents, and 27 percent of Democrats, had a favorable view of them.

Campaigning on Their Faith: Lieberman, Gore, and Bush

How did the candidates in the 2000 presidential elections respond to this shift in the religious landscape and in the growing public demand for morality and values in politics? Bush, Gore, and Lieberman were all willing to openly discuss their private faiths and called for an increased role for faith in public life.

Lieberman

Lieberman's faith, Modern Orthodox Judaism, is a hybrid of tradition and modernity. Unlike Orthodox Jews, who choose to live largely segregated lives in America, Modern Orthodox Jews seek to wed Orthodox Jewish beliefs, based on faithfulness to Jewish scripture, with the demands and diversity of contemporary life in the United States Lieberman's brand of Judaism encourages him to blend his faith with political life. It also views religious pluralism positively and nurtures the ideology of inclusion that undergirds it.

Gore's choice of Lieberman as his running mate was initially viewed as something of a political risk—professional politicians had believed that a Jew on a presidential ticket would be a political liability. But anti-Semitism has abated over the years, and Gore's pick of Lieberman was actually a shrewd political strategy. Not only did picking Lieberman provide Gore with moral armor—an attempt to infuse his campaign with genuine religious sentiment and moral uprightness, protecting it from the harmful effects of Clinton fatigue—but many religious conservatives were more attracted by Lieberman's devoutness than they were put off by doctrinal differences between Christianity and Judaism. In this age of growing ecumenicism and decreasing schism, what has become most important to religiously committed voters is not the content of one's religious doctrine as much as the intensity of one's religious commitment. Thus, putting Lieberman on the Democratic ticket was an attempt to purchase back for Democrats some of the religiously committed voters who had strayed to the Republican party these last couple of decades.

Lieberman probably employed more God talk than any of the other candidates. When he was introduced in Tennessee as Gore's vice-presidential pick on August 8, 2000, Lieberman even offered a prayer at the beginning of his speech:

> Dear friends, I am so full of gratitude at this moment. I ask you to allow me to let the spirit move me as it does to remember the words from Chronicles, which are to give thanks to God. To give thanks to God and declare his name and make his acts known to the people. To be glad of spirit. To sing to God and to make music to God, and most of all, to give glory and gratitude to God from whom all blessings truly do flow. Dear Lord, maker of all miracles, I thank you for bringing me to this extraordinary moment in my life.[31]

Lieberman's religious voice was one of the Progressive Left, however, and the prominence of this voice in itself marks a significant shift in religious influence in United States electoral politics. Although observers of contemporary political life have seen the intersection of religion and politics as largely a phenomenon of the religious right, those familiar with the history of religion and politics in America know that religious progressives joined religiously devout evangelicals in being potent forces in the abolition of slavery, the women's movement, prohibition, labor reforms, urban reform, and the civil rights movement. In the last few decades, however, the debate about religion in public life has primarily focused on the divisive standoff between religious conservatives and liberal secularists who remained hostile to public expressions of religiosity, with the presence of the Religious Left barely discernible. Lieberman's voice has aided the revitalization of the Religious Left, adding a rich balance in the focus of faith in this year's campaigns.

By reminding us that religious devotion is not necessarily tied to political conservatism, and drawing so much media attention to this, Lieberman helped to revive the political debate on religion in public life. Although deeply religious, Lieberman holds positions opposite to many religious conservatives. Thus he prominently demonstrated the truth that religiously committed citizens can disagree on important political issues that imply deeply held moral beliefs.

Gore

Both Bush and Gore were very open about their evangelical beliefs, arguing that it is appropriate for these beliefs to be publicly expressed and that it is appropriate for their faith to influence their public policies. They agreed, for example, that government should provide funding to faith-based organizations ministering to the poor and those in need of social services. One observer noted that religion in the 2000 campaigns "moved from being a polarizing force (mainly on the right) to being the latest version of 'mom and apple pie' politics. Religion became a weapon in the see-saw battle between Democrats and Republicans to capture the 'mainstream' flag."[32]But there were differences in the spiritual journeys of the two presidential candidates and in how they thought their faith should play out in their public role.

Al Gore, the Southern Baptist and former seminary student, considers himself a born-again Christian. He was somewhat less open about the importance of his faith to his public life than were Bush or Lieberman, although he did employ religious rhetoric and symbols more freely than have candidates in the past and he freely offered that his faith is "the most important thing in my life."[33] Saying that the purpose of life "is to glorify God," he added that he turns "to my faith as the bedrock of my approach to any important questions in my life."[34] Gore explained in an interview that he attended Vanderbilt Divinity School following a tour in Vietnam "to intensively explore the questions I had which seemed then and seem now to be the most important questions about what's the purpose of life, what's our relationship to the Creator, what's our spiritual obligation to one another." He claimed not to have found all these answers, but "thought I found better questions, and I found a process for living out better answers."[35]

In response to a question regarding candidates openly discussing their faith, Gore offered support for the separation of church and state, adding that a public official who discusses his faith in public has "an obligation to couple that expression . . . with an affirmation of tolerance and respect" for other faiths. He believes public officials "should be free and open about what our beliefs are"[36] and added that "we have gone too far in conveying the impression that those in public life are obligated to refrain from ever acknowledging that they have a spiritual life and that they have a set of core beliefs. . . . I freely acknowledge the role of faith in my life and the centrality of faith in my values system."[37]

Part of the Democratic strategy was to try to win back some of the white evangelical vote, an important voting bloc that makes up a quarter of all voters (up from 19 percent in 1986); nearly three in four of them voted for Bob Dole in 1996. In a survey by the Pew Center in September 2000, 56 percent of white evangelical Protestants stated that Republicans are the party most concerned with protecting religious values, as opposed to only 26 percent giving that honor to the Democrats. Thus, Gore's willingness to discuss his faith, as well as his choice of a religiously committed running mate, may have been part of the Gore team strategy to improve their appeal to people of faith. In response to a question regarding Gore's embrace of Bush's proposal for expanding federal funding to faith-based organizations, Gore policy adviser Elaine Kamarck claimed to the *Boston Globe*, "The Democratic Party is going to take back God this time." (It should be noted that more Democrats than Republicans or Independents favor funding for religious organizations: the Pew poll released in September 2000 reported that 61 percent of

Democrats are in favor of this proposal, as opposed to 46 percent of Republicans and 52 percent of Independents.)

Bush

Americans elected as their forty-third president a devout Methodist in the evangelical tradition. Bush is not timid in expressing his evangelical convictions, nor of having his religious beliefs influence his public policies. In fact it was Bush's ease in thinking and talking like an observant evangelical that brought him to the White House in this election.

The statistics bearing out this conclusion are unmistakable. Exit polls showed that 11.6 million Bush voters consider themselves part of the "religious right"—up significantly from the 10.6 million of this group who voted for Dole. The evangelical vote brought Bush victory in critical close states such as Arkansas, Tennessee, and of course Florida, without which Gore would have won the presidency. In fact if Bush had done only as well as Dole had among evangelicals in Florida, Gore would be in the White House today. But, more importantly, Bush did this well among evangelicals without alienating more moderate voters—and this was the key to his success.

How did Bush manage this feat? It was his "compassionate conservatism," but even more so it was his expert use of evangelical language, which conveyed to evangelicals that he was genuinely one of them, but without alienating him from more moderate voters. For example, Bush used the words "Jesus Christ" quite freely, whereas other candidates in this and earlier campaigns had kept to the more inclusive language of "God," "The Almighty," "The Creator," and so forth. Furthermore, Bush not only employed Christ's name but testified about the importance of Christ and His work in his life. Bush said that Jesus Christ was his favorite philosopher, that He changed his heart and cleaned up his life, and that He delivered him from alcohol abuse. Bush readily admitted that he is a "lowly sinner" and declared his belief that Jesus Christ "died for my sins and your sins." He testified that genuine faith is naturally evident in one's public actions:

> I was raised a Christian, recommitted myself to Christ. Got into the Bible. My life changed in many ways. . . . I was a more dedicated, more focused person. . . . It was a life-changing moment. I also recognize that a walk is a walk . . . a never-ending journey. . . . The more I got into the Bible, the more that admonition "Don't try to take a speck out of your neighbor's eye when you've got a log in your own" becomes more true, particularly for those of us in public life. . . . Many of the issues I talk about . . . are reinforced by my religion. [My recognition that we are all sinners] helps bring people together, and that's what is needed on some very practical issues that the country faces.

I'm going through one of the greatest challenges of all. And yet I'm
sustained by my faith. . . . I feel supported by the thousands of people
who [say they are praying for me], because I understand prayer.[38]

That Bush could employ this type of language in this campaign without fear of
alienating the less religiously committed is highly significant. In earlier years, this
could not have been done—remember the ridicule Carter received merely for
mentioning that he was "born again." But that Bush could have done so in 2000
provides additional evidence of the shift in America's religious culture. Religion
has become more pluralistic and diverse, and as a consequence less threatening and
divisive. Thus, as conservative Christianity loses its majority and dominant position
in American society, candidates like Bush can more safely and successfully employ
evangelical "Christ talk" without offending those of other faiths or those who are
less religiously observant, as it would have even four years ago.

Bush was successful in employing such language because he had already
established himself as a tolerant person of faith, a compassionate conservative open
to and even encouraging diversity. In his acceptance speech before the Republican
National Convention, for example, he testified about how his faith was
instrumental in making him a more tolerant person: "I believe in tolerance, not in
spite of my faith, but because of it," he said. "I believe in a God who calls us, not
to judge our neighbors, but to love them. I believe in grace, because I have seen it.
. . . In peace, because I have felt it. . . . In forgiveness, because I have needed it."[39]

Bush's initiative to expand federal funding for faith-based organizations
reinforced his image as a compassionate conservative. This "faith in action"
proposal includes assistance for programs providing child care, alcohol and drug
treatment, and prison programs, as well as an enforcement of the "charitable
choice" provision of the welfare reform law. In his campaign, Bush called for
church and state to "work together with respect for our differences and reverence
for our shared goals."[40] This initiative appeals to religious conservatives and
progressives alike—conservatives because it assists religious organizations,
progressives because it assists the poor. Thus this proposal by Bush is an example
of how the religious character of our contemporary lives has developed to such a
degree that faith in action can serve to unite diverse groups, rather than divide.

Conclusion

Despite the Democratic party's best efforts to win back the religiously committed
in the 2000 elections, come November 7 nearly two-thirds of voters who attend
religious services at least once a week (42 percent of all voters claim to attend this
frequently) voted for the Bush-Cheney ticket, and eight of ten voters identifying
with the Religious Right voted Republican. Sixty-three percent of all white
Protestants, making up 60 percent of all voters, voted for Bush, while 61 percent
of voters claiming no religion voted for the Gore-Lieberman ticket (only 9 percent

of voters claim no religious affiliation). While Gore and Lieberman were not successful in attracting the religiously committed and white Protestants to the Democratic camp in this election, this was due to their liberal policy positions and not because of any lack of religious piety.

Nonetheless, the Lieberman factor was significant for a number of reasons: it showed that a major party could successfully nominate a Jew for a national ticket, brought a renewed and different focus of religion into electoral politics, revitalized the Religious Left, prompted observers and the media to rethink the role of religion in American public life, and proved that public expressions of genuine orthodox faith by a political candidate (albeit not that of a conservative evangelical) could play well on the national scene. But, when it comes to making vote choices, religious conservatives are policy voters, unconvinced by expressions of religious faith alone.

More importantly, the 2000 presidential campaign was significant for American politics because it marked a major shift in the role and character of religion in American politics, a shift that parallels a transformation of the American religious landscape and experience. As Roof observed, "The boundaries of popular religious communities are being redrawn, encouraged by the quests of the large, post-World War II generations, and facilitated by the rise of an expanded spiritual marketplace."[41] These redrawn boundaries are accompanied by "a questing mood, a ferment, a search for a deeper spiritual life" that has transformed the character of American social life.[42] As a new millennium is dawning, Americans are more receptive to religious language from candidates than they were in the last half of the twentieth century, especially when the God talk appears to reflect a genuine faith and is cloaked in a tone of inclusivity sensitive to America's religious pluralism.

Thus religion is even more a part of American politics as we entered the new millennium than it was in the past generation, but the character of this intermixing of religion and politics has changed. A chastened Religious Right and a religiously engaged Progressive Left make for a different kind of spiritual politics than we have seen in recent decades. There is room in the public square for a diversity of faiths, and there is increased tolerance for the multiplicity of religious voices being heard today. This means that the rhetoric of the Religious Right is being challenged and softened by a dialogue with the Religious and the Secular Left, and both sides are joined, even bridged, by nontraditional spiritual and religious voices that resist conformity to established categories of belief and behavior. The character of religion in American public life will be enriched by the conversation. As one leader of the Evangelical Left recently wrote, this is all good, because the purpose of faith "is not simply to comfort the believers, but to transform the world," and this must be done "in ways that both respect religious liberty and enhance democracy." The reason for taking our faith into the public square, after all, is to "help bend the world toward justice."[43]

Notes

1. Wade Clark Roof, *Spiritual Marketplace: Baby Boomers and the Remaking of American Religion* (Princeton, N.J.: Princeton University Press, 1999), 4.

2. George Gallup, Jr., and Timothy Jones, *The Next American Spirituality: Finding God in the Twenty-First Century* (Colorado Springs, Colo.: Victor, 2000), 42.

3. Gustav Niebuhr, "Religion on the Hustings," *New York Times*, September 1, 2000, A1.

4. Michelle Bearden, "Running on Faith," *Tampa Tribune*, September 17, 2000, A6.

5. Franklin Foer, "Running on their Faith," *U. S. News Online*, December 6, 1999, <http://www.usnews.com/usnews/issue/120699/usnews/> (November 23, 2000).

6. Niebuhr, "Religion on the Hustings."

7. Niebuhr, "Religion on the Hustings."

8. Foer, "Running on their Faith."

9. Andrew Kohut, John C. Green, Scott Keeter, and Robert C. Toth, *The Diminishing Divide: Religion's Changing Role in American Politics* (Washington, D.C.: Brookings Institution, 2000), 123.

10. Paul Weyrich, "The Moral Minority," *Christianity Today*, September 6, 1999, 44.

11. Cal Thomas and Ed Dobson, *Blinded by Might* (Grand Rapids, Mich.: Zondervan, 1999).

12. Mark J. Rozell, ". . . Or Influential as Ever?" *Washington Post*, March 1, 2000, A17.

13. John C. Green, Mark J. Rozell, and Clyde Wilcox, *Prayers in the Precincts: The Christian Right in the 1998 Elections* (Washington, D.C.: Georgetown University Press, 2000).

14. Hanna Rosin, "A Maturing Christian Right: Diffuse Movement Turns More Mainstream, Less Loyal to GOP," *Washington Post*, April 7, 2000, A4.

15. Rosin, "A Maturing Christian Right," A4.

16. Rozell, ". . . Or Influential as Ever?" A17.

17. Kathleen A. Frankovic and Monika L. McDermott, "Public Opinion in the 2000 Election," in *The Election of 2000*, ed. Gerald M. Pomper (New York: Chatham House, 2001), 88.

18. William H. Swatos, Jr., and Kevin J. Christiano, "Secularization Theory: The Course of a Concept," *Sociology of Religion* 3 (1999): 211.

19. Gallup and Jones, *The Next American Spirituality*, 57.

20. Pew Research Center, "Religion and Politics: The Ambivalent Majority," September 2000, <http://people-press.org/reports/display.php3?PageID=175> (January 6, 2001).

21. Roof, *Spiritual Marketplace*, 81.

22. Robert Wuthnow, *After Heaven: Spirituality in America since the 1950s* (Berkeley: University of California Press, 1998), 2.

23. Wuthnow, *After Heaven*, 198.

24. Roof, *Spiritual Marketplace*, 84.

25. Swatos and Christiano, "Secularization Theory," 221.

26. R. Finke and Rodney Stark, *The Churching of America* (New Brunswick, N.J.: Rutgers University Press, 1992).

27. Kohut et al., *The Diminishing Divide*, 124.

28. Kohut et al., *The Diminishing Divide*, 6.

29. Bearden, "Running on Faith," A6.

30. Niebuhr, "Religion on the Hustings," A1.

31. Joseph Lieberman, <http://lieberman.senategov/speeches_schedule.cfm> (November 23, 2000).

32. Christopher Hanson, "God and Man on the Campaign Trail," *Columbia Journalism Review* 4 (November/December 2000): 40.

33. Melinda Henneberger, "Spiritual Seeker: Gore Has Explored a Range of Beliefs from Old Time to New Age," *New York Times*, October 22, 2000, A20.

34. Peter Steinfels, "Beliefs," *New York Times*, May 29, 1999, A11.

35. Steinfels, "Beliefs," A11.

36. Democratic debate, University of New Hampshire, January 5, 2000.

37. "Al Gore: Running on His Faith," *U. S. News Online*, December 6, 1999, <http://www.usnews.com/usnews/news/991206/goreint.htm> (March 13, 2003).

38. Steven Waldman, "Beliefnet Interviews Presidential Candidate George Bush," *Beliefnet*, October 2000, <http://beliefnet.com/story/47/story_4703_1.html&boardID=6303> (March 13, 2003).

39. George W. Bush, <http://www.c-span.org/campaign2000/gwbushspeeches.asp> (November 23, 2000).

40. Bush, <http://www.c-span.org/campaign2000/gwbushspeeches.asp> (November 23, 2000).

41. Roof, *Spiritual Marketplace*, 10.

42. Roof, *Spiritual Marketplace*, 254.

43. Jim Wallis, "Should Joe Lieberman Keep His Faith to Himself?" *Beliefnet*, September 6, 2000, <http://www.beliefnet.com/story/43story_4331_2.html> (March 13, 2003).

Chapter 6

Holy Books, Not Pocketbooks: Religious and Cultural Influences on the 2000 Presidential Election

Dale McConkey

The truisms of voting behavior have always focused on economic influences. "People vote with their pocketbooks," the time-honored saying goes. Bill Clinton certainly embraced this philosophy when he promised the American people that he would "focus on the economy like a laser beam." He reinforced this approach throughout his 1992 campaign with the mantra for his staff, "It's the Economy, Stupid." And Democratic presidential nominee Al Gore continued in this tradition in the 2000 campaign by pledging to "fight for the people, not the powerful," with the clear implication that "the powerful" were those with economic means to influence the political process.

But economic explanations did not immediately surface as pundits tried to make sense of the now-famous red and blue maps of America during the 2000 election. Geography more than economy apparently determined the fate of the electoral map, with Gore getting the coastal states and much of the northern Midwest, and George W. Bush sweeping the Deep South and Rocky Mountain regions. Even more striking is the county-level election map. Gore, the "blue" candidate, secured tiny patches of geographically small but densely populated urban cities on the East and West Coasts, while Bush's red regions spanned across the heartland in thinly populated rural regions.

While the regional divisions of the 2000 presidential election are clear, the causes behind the schism are not. Clearly the urban-rural distinctions are real, but several possible explanations for these divisions have been offered. This chapter utilizes several different types of data to investigate the 2000 election, and it concludes that cultural variables, most notably the relative presence or absence of conservative religion, significantly influenced the voting patterns of the 2000 election. It would appear that, rather than their pocketbook, people are more likely to vote with their holy book.

Literature

Structure or Culture?

David Brooks has provided perhaps the most straightforward account of the conflicting interpretations of the 2000 election.[1] The first interpretation, usually favored by the political left, argues that people vote according to their location in the social structure. Race, class, gender, and education all impact the way we vote, with those who are marginalized by society (minorities, the poor, women, and the less educated) more likely to vote Democratic. The fundamental division between red and blue America is thus along socioeconomic lines. Citing publications like *The American Prospect* and authors such as Stanley Greenberg, Ruy Teixeira, and Joel Rogers,[2] Brooks outlines how this position sees the Information Age unraveling any gains toward economic equality the labor movement achieved during the industrial era. A very real economic gap still exists between the haves and have-nots, and these two groups are increasingly being defined in terms of access to education. It is from these ranks that Clinton and Gore drew inspiration for their economy-oriented campaigns. Research indicates strong support for this position, as African Americans (90 percent), Hispanics (62 percent), women (54 percent), those earning less than $15,000 in family income per year (57 percent), and those lacking a high school diploma (59 percent) all decisively favored Gore.[3]

The second interpretation of red and blue America, the one usually preferred by the political right, argues that cultural issues are the quintessential influence on voting behavior. This position gained prominence with James Davison Hunter's *Culture Wars* (1991) and has recently been rearticulated in Gertrude Himmelfarb's *One Nation, Two Cultures* (1999).[4] It was given a caustic political face throughout the 1980s and 1990s with the Republican rhetoric for "traditional family values" and Pat Buchanan's austere "cultural war" speech during the 1996 Republican convention. Proponents of the cultural argument see red and blue America as a division of traditional community values of the heartland versus the progressive individualism of the cosmopolitan city. They point to the fact that rural communities were much more likely to vote for Bush (59 percent), while the big cities—filled with both the very rich and the very poor—went overwhelmingly for Gore (71 percent).[5] Although traditional and progressive values may be disproportionately dispersed geographically, the cultural explanation ultimately looks to religious ideology to explain the national divisiveness. Specifically, Hunter's fundamental insight is that evangelical Protestants, conservative Catholics, and orthodox Jews are now more likely to exhibit political preferences in line with each other than they are with the mainstream and progressive counterparts within their respective religious traditions.[6] A restructuring has occurred in American religion such that "Protestant," "Catholic," and "Jew" are less useful in understanding the parameters of faith.[7] Instead, terms like "conservative and orthodox" and "liberal and progressive" provide a better schema for understanding the religious landscape. The orthodox cherish timeless principles linked to the past, whereas progressives seek new and improved values found in a changing future.

Religion as a Key Cultural Category

It is not a coincidence that religion played a prominent role in the above discussion of culture, for religion is a fundamental way in which cultural values are expressed. Similarly, religion has been a visible factor in transmitting cultural and moral symbols in recent presidential elections. Surely this was true in the 2000 election. Perhaps the most profound religious event of the campaign was Al Gore's selection of Connecticut senator Joseph Lieberman as his vice-presidential running mate. Lieberman is a devout, theologically conservative Jew, the first to ever be on a major-party ticket for the presidency. Gore's historic selection of Lieberman was considered by most to be a bold move and was frequently compared to the breakthrough of the 1960 election of America's first Catholic president, John F. Kennedy. Many also interpreted the move as a way for Gore to muddy the cultural divide by selecting a religious conservative who is politically on the left. Similarly, it was a way to buttress the moral integrity of the Gore campaign, distancing itself from the scandal-prone Clinton presidency. Lieberman referred to his candidacy as a "miracle" and effortlessly made references to God and faith in his speeches.[8]

In addition to Lieberman's historic candidacy on behalf of the Democrats, Republican George W. Bush unabashedly referred to his evangelical Christian faith throughout his campaign. Perhaps the most famous incident occurred during a primary debate among Republican hopefuls when each was asked who their favorite political philosopher was. Bush replied, "Jesus Christ." When asked why he selected Jesus, Bush replied, "Because he touched my heart," and he acknowledged that such a transformation is difficult to explain to nonbelievers. Such visible embracement of conservative Christianity almost backfired at another point during the primary campaign when Bush agreed to give a speech at Bob Jones University. Bob Jones University is a fundamentalist college, far more conservative and exclusivist than mainstream evangelicalism. The university, for example, has had policies forbidding both the enrollment of Catholic students and the practice of interracial dating on its campus. Bush drew heavy criticism for his visit, and he subsequently made significant efforts to publicly distance himself from the university.[9]

Despite such visible displays of personal piety among the candidates, the religious identity of voters may have made little difference in the final 2000 election results. Despite Bush's visit to Bob Jones University, the gap in the 2000

Catholic vote was much smaller for him (two percentage points; 47 percent compared to Gore's 49 percent) than it was for Bob Dole in 1996 (16 percent gap) or for George H. W. Bush in 1992 (9 percent gap). And the country apparently gave a collective yawn over the fact that a Jewish candidate was running for office. Surveys reported that 92 percent of the country would vote for a Jew for president,[10] and surveys indicated that Lieberman's influence on his party's ticket was not substantially different from that of Cheney on his party's ticket. Ironically, it was the Anti-Defamation League who expressed the most concern about Lieberman's frequent references to the supernatural.[11] And in the end, all four candidates on the two major-party tickets seemed eager to keep divisive moral issues like abortion off the agenda throughout most of the campaign, opting instead to debate economic issues like social security and health insurance.

The above would agree with Wilson McWilliams that religion was an important part of the candidates' personal character, but they were each careful to distance their faith from their public policy.[12] (The one exception to this might be Bush's push for faith-based "charitable choice" in social services, an initiative that was not strongly contested and was even tepidly endorsed by Gore.) Even so, it is possible that the electorate still based its voting preference on religious and cultural grounds more so than the customary economic and structural reasons. We now explore whether this is, in fact, the case.

Methods

Four studies are used to determine which factors influenced voting patterns in the 2000 presidential election. The first study uses individual survey data. The second and third use aggregate regional data at the county and state levels, respectively. These three studies are similar in that eight common independent variables are regressed on the dependent variable of voting. The eight independent variables for each study are:

- religion
- marital status
- sex
- gender
- community size
- age
- income
- education

The fourth study builds upon the results of the third by including several cultural variables in addition to religion. Details of each study's methods are provided as follows.

Study One: Individual Survey Data

The first study is based on the 2000 National Election Study, conducted by the Center for Political Studies at the University of Michigan.[13] Of the 1,807 respondents, 1,165 voted in the 2000 election. Of these, only 491 are included in the study when listwise procedures were used. (Results were virtually identical when pairwise deletion was employed.) The survey variables included in this study are:

Dependent Variable:
Bush Vote. Asked only of those who voted in the 2000 presidential election, the variable inquires whether the respondent voted for George W. Bush. "Yes" responses are coded 1, and "No" responses are coded 0.

Independent Variables:
Biblical Literalism. Respondents are asked whether the Bible is: (0) a man-made book; (1) the nonliteral word of God; or (2) the literal word of God.

Married. Currently married respondents are coded 1; all others are coded 0.

Male. Men are coded 1; women are coded 0.

White. White/Caucasian respondents are coded 1; all others are coded 0.

City Size. Respondents are placed into the following categories: (0) rural area; (1) 2,500-9,999 residents; (2) 10,000-29,999 residents; (3) 30,000-49,999 residents; (4) 50,000-99,999 residents; (5) 100,000-149,000 residents; (6) 150,000-349,999 residents; (7) 350,000 residents and larger, unless located in a central metropolitan city; and (8) central metropolitan city.

Age. The age of each respondent is coded in years.

Household Income. Each respondent's family income is coded in 21 categories, ranging from "under $5,000" to "$200,000 and over." Most categories represent $10,000 intervals.

Education. Respondents are placed into one of four categories based on educational attainment: (0) no high school diploma; (1) high school diploma; (2) some college education; (3) bachelor's degree or higher.

Logistic regression is used to determine the net effects of the eight independent variables on the dichotomous dependent variable (that is, whether or not the respondent voted for Bush). Although not methodologically orthodox, ordinary least squares (OLS) regression is also employed for purposes of comparison with the next three studies.

Study Two: County-Level Aggregate Data

The second study uses county-level data to determine which factors impacted voting patterns in the 2000 presidential election. Of the 3,141 counties in the United States, 3,078 are included in the study. The variables used in the study are described below. Unless noted otherwise, data were obtained from the 1990 U.S. Census; county-level data from the 2000 census were not available at time of publication. One might wonder if this decade-old data accurately reflect the current status of U.S. counties. Correlations on these variables with their 1980 counterparts range between 0.728 and 0.994, all strong and highly significant. Based on this evidence, we can reasonably assume that the changes from 1990 to 2000 will be minimal and the older data will appropriately reflect current conditions.

Dependent Variable:
   Bush Vote. The percent of the vote going to George W. Bush is used to measure the voting patterns in each county. Data are based on certified election results obtained from <www.uselectionatlas.org>. All of the counties in Alaska were necessarily excluded from the study because that state uses districts rather than counties to report local election results.

Independent Variables:
   Conservative Religion. This variable measures the percentage of residents in each county that attend theologically conservative Christian denominations. Data are based on *Churches and Church Membership in the United States, 1990.*[14] This source provides a county-level tally of adherents in 133 Judeo-Christian denominations. Of these, sixty denominations were determined to be theologically conservative denominations (see table 6.1 for a list of these denominations and a description of the operational parameters for conservative theology). The number of adherents in each of these conservative denominations was summed together to determine the total number of theologically conservative adherents in each county. This number was divided by the county's population to determine the overall proportion of people practicing conservative religion in each county and ultimately converted into a percentage.

   Couples. This variable measures the percentage of all households with married couples.

   Male. This variable measures the percentage of the county population that is male.

Table 6.1 List of Conservative Denominations

American Baptist Church
Apostolic Christian (Nazarene)
Apostolic Christian Church of America
Apostolic Lutheran Church of America
Assemblies of God
Baptist General Conference
Baptist Missionary Assn. of America
Berean Fundamental Church
Black Baptist (Estimate)
Brethren Church (Ashland, Ohio)
Brethren in Christ Church
Central Baptist
Christian Church (Disciples of Christ)
Christian Church and Churches of Christ
Christian (Plymouth) Brethren
Church of God (Anderson, Ind.)
Church of God (Cleveland, Tenn.)
Church of God—Seventh Day (Denver, Colo.)
Church of God General Conference (Abrahamic Faith) (Oregon, Ill.)
Church of God in Christ (Mennonite)
Church of God of Prophecy
Church of God of the Mountain Assembly
Church of Jesus Christ of Latter-Day Saints
Church of the Brethren
Church of the Nazarene
Churches of Christ
Churches of God General Conference
Conservative Baptist Assn. of America
Conservative Congregational Christian Conference
Duck River/Kindred Baptist Assn.

Enterprise Baptist
Free Will Baptist, National Assn. of
General Six Principle Baptist
Hutterian Brethren
Independent Fundamental Churches of America
International Church of the Four-Square Gospel
International Pentecostal Church of Christ
Interstate Foreign Landmark Missouri Baptist
Jasper and Pleasant Valley Baptist
Lutheran Church—Missouri Synod
Mennonite Church
Mennonite Church—Eastern Penn.
Mennonite Church—General Conference
New Hope Baptist Association
North American Baptist Conference
Old Missouri Baptist Association
Old Regular Baptist
Open Bible Standard Churches
Pentecostal Church of God
Pentecostal Holiness Church
Presbyterian Church in America
Primitive Baptist Association
Regular Baptist
Seventh Day Adventist
Seventh Day Baptist General Conference
Southern Baptist Convention
Truevine Baptist Association
United Baptist
United Brethren in Christ
Wesleyan Church

To determine which denominations should be counted as theologically conservative, three doctrinal issues were used: (1) view of the Bible as the authoritative word of God; (2) insistence upon a strict standard of morality; and (3) an emphasis on adult baptism or conversion. Denominations that believe the Bible is the *literal* word of God were automatically coded as conservative. Denominations were also coded as theologically conservative if they believe that the Bible is the *inspired* word of God *and* at least one of the following: adherence to strict boundary markers for morality, or emphasis on adult baptism. Doctrinal positions of each denomination were determined using descriptions from Mead and Young.[15] (Thanks to Emily Wampler for her significant effort in the development of this variable.)

White. This variable measures the percentage of the county population that is white.

Rural. This variable measures the percentage of the county population that is rural.

Elderly. This variable measures the percentage of the county population that is at least sixty-five years old.

Income. This variable measures the 1989 average per capita income for each county.

High School Graduates. This variable measures the percentage of the county population twenty-five years old or older who have completed high school.

OLS regression is used to determine the net and joint effects of the eight independent variables on the dependent variable.

Study Three: State-Level Aggregate Data

The third study uses state-level data to determine which factors impacted voting patterns in the 2000 presidential election. Variables used in Study Three are described below.

Dependent Variable:
Bush Vote. The percent of the vote going to George W. Bush is used to measure the voting patterns in each state. Data are based on certified election results obtained from the Federal Election Commission (<www.fec.gov>).

Independent Variables:
Conservative Religion. This variable measures the percentage of residents in each state that attend theologically conservative Christian denominations. Data are based on Kosmin and Lachman's National Survey of Religious Identification which interviewed more than 113,000 people nationwide; the results of their research are reported in their book *One Nation under God.*[16] Of the thirty religious groupings used, eleven were identified as theologically conservative: Assemblies of God, Baptist, Born-Again/Evangelical, Church of Christ, Church of God, Holiness/Holy, Jehovah's Witness, Mormon (Church of Jesus Christ of Latter-Day Saints), Nazarene, Pentecostal, and Seventh-Day Adventist. Kosmin and Lachman provide the percentage of people claiming membership in each of these denominations within each state. These percentages are summed together to determine the total percentage of theologically conservative residents in each state. Alaska and Hawaii are exceptions to these procedures as they are excluded

from the National Survey of Religious Identification. For these two states, the county-level data previously described in Study Two are proportionally aggregated to calculate the overall percentage of theologically conservative residents in Alaska and Hawaii.

Couples. This variable measures the percentage of all households with married couples, based on the 1990 U.S. Census.

Male. This variable measures the percentage of the state population that is male, based on census data reported in 1999.

White. This variable measures the percentage of the state population that is white, based on the 2000 U.S. Census.

Rural. This variable measures the percentage of the state population that is rural, based on the 1990 U.S. Census.

Elderly. This variable measures the percentage of the state population that is at least sixty-five years old, based on census data reported in 1996.

Income. This variable measures the 1998 average per capita income for each state, as reported by *Statistical Abstracts* in 1999.[17]

High School Graduates. This variable measures the percentage of the state population twenty-five years old or older who have completed high school, as reported by *Statistical Abstracts* in 2000.[18]

OLS regression is used to determine the net and joint effects of these eight independent variables on the dependent variable.

Study Four: Additional State-Level Data: Cultural Variables

The fourth study builds upon Study Three. Nine cultural variables are correlated with the vote percentages for George W. Bush:

Pickups. This variable measures the number of pickup trucks per 1,000 population, as reported by the Federal Highway Administration in 1995.

Field & Stream. This variable measures the total circulation of *Field & Stream* magazine per 100,000 population, as reported by the Audit Bureau of Circulation Blue Book in 1996.

Hunting Licenses. This variable measures the number of hunting licenses purchased per 1,000 population, as reported by the U.S. Fish and Wildlife Service in 1990.

Reader's Digest. This variable measures the total circulation of *Reader's Digest* magazine per 1,000 population, as reported by the Audit Bureau of Circulation Blue Book in 1996.

Gourmet. This variable measures the total circulation of *Gourmet* magazine per 100,000 population, as reported by the Audit Bureau of Circulation Blue Book in 1990.

Psychiatrists. This variable measures the number of psychiatrists per 100,000 population in 1995, as reported by *Health Care State Rankings, 1997.*[19]

Plastic Surgeons. This variable measures the number of plastic surgeons per 100,000 population in 1995, as reported by *Health Care State Rankings, 1997.*

Wine. This variable measures the average number of gallons of wine consumed per person over age sixteen in 1995, as reported by *Health Care State Rankings, 1997.*

Abortions. This variable measures the number of abortions in 1996 per 1,000 women aged fifteen to forty-four years old, as reported by *Statistical Abstracts* in 2000.

In addition to calculating correlation coefficients to determine the relationship that each of these variables has with the 2000 presidential vote, each variable is also individually added to the regression analysis of Study Three. This procedure is used to determine the net, relative strength each variable has when structural and demographic variables are simultaneously considered.

Results

Study One: Individual Survey Data

Means and standard deviations are reported in table 6.2, while table 6.3 provides the essential regression results. Correlations are reported in table 6.4. Since the dependent variable is a dichotomous variable indicating whether or not the respondent voted for George W. Bush, logistic regression is the appropriate statistical test. The coefficients from this procedure are reported, along with "pseudo-standardized Betas" from a test of OLS regression. This latter test is not

Table 6.2 Means and Standard Deviations for Individual Data
(N = 491)

Variable	Mean	Standard Deviation
Biblical Literalism	1.155	0.676
Married	0.580	0.494
Male	0.466	0.499
White	0.827	0.379
City Size	2.768	2.588
Age	49.297	16.660
Household Income	7.342	3.809
Education	1.986	0.942
Bush Vote	0.430	0.496

Table 6.3 Regression Coefficients for Individual Data
(N = 491)

Variable	Beta (Logistic)	Pseudo-standardized Beta
Biblical Literalism	0.786**	0.220**
Married	0.405*	0.084
Male	0.504**	0.105*
White	2.026**	0.269**
City Size	-0.084*	-0.088*
Age	-0.006	-0.047
Household Income	0.082**	0.132**
Education	0.015	-0.002

Constant = -3.556
Pseudo-R^2 = 0.178**

$* = p < 0.05$
$** = p < 0.01$

Table 6.4 Correlation Coefficients for Individual Data (N = 491)

Variable	1	2	3	4	5	6	7	8	9
1. Bush Vote	-								
2. Biblical Literalism	0.136	-							
3. Married	0.188	-0.037	-						
4. Male	0.129	-0.087	0.133	-					
5. White	0.288	-0.174	0.145	0.050	-				
6. City Size	-0.201	-0.094	-0.134	0.016	-0.293	-			
7. Age	0.000	0.075	0.012	0.004	0.141	-0.047	-		
8. Household Income	0.180	-0.227	0.363	0.153	0.164	-0.042	-0.099	-	
9. Education	0.052	-0.298	0.154	0.118	0.119	0.086	-0.222	0.453	-

appropriate when dichotomous dependent variables are used, but it allows for approximate comparisons of relative net strength between the independent variables. A comparison of the results of the logistic test and the OLS test suggest that this approximation is not unwarranted.

Of the eight independent variables, six of them have a statistically significant impact on respondents' choice to vote for Bush or not. Only age and education level lack an influence on voting preference. Comparing the pseudo-standardized Betas, it appears that race is the strongest determinant, with whites more likely to vote for Bush than nonwhites (Beta = 0.269**). This is not surprising as there was much postelection media coverage on the paucity of the minority vote for Bush despite notable efforts to attract nonwhite support for the Republican standard-bearer throughout the campaign. Conservative religious belief, specifically a literalistic interpretation of the Bible, also had a strong positive impact on the 2000 vote for Bush (0.220**). Having a higher household income also increased the likelihood to vote for Bush (0.132**), as did being male (0.105*), being married (0.084*), and living in smaller communities (-0.088* for increased city size).

The OLS regression indicates that the combined effect of all eight independent variables explains about 18 percent of the total variance in the vote for Bush (pseudo-R^2 = 0.178**). Logistic regression indicates that the eight independent variables combine for 69.6 percent accuracy in predicting whether or not a respondent voted for Bush in the 2000 election.

Study Two: County-Level Aggregate Data

Means and standard deviations are reported in table 6.5. Essential regression results are reported in table 6.6, while table 6.7 provides the correlations.

All eight independent variables are statistically significant, each independently impacting the vote percentage for Bush. Comparing the standardized Betas, we see that the marital composition of counties had the strongest influence on the presidential vote: in general, the higher the overall percentage of households with married couples, the greater the vote for Bush (Beta = 0.422**). Not far behind, greater levels of conservative religion in a county typically increased the Bush vote (0.372**). Increased levels of education (0.286**) and white residents (0.151**) also positively impact the dependent variable. Per capita income level is only the fifth-strongest variable, and it is actually in the *inverse* direction of what one might expect: wealthier counties were actually *less* likely to support the Republican nominee (-0.128**). The other three variables have only a minimal impact on the presidential vote, with counties that are more male, elderly, and rural voting in greater percentages for Bush (0.095**, 0.088**, and 0.043*, respectively).

Overall, not quite half of the variance in the county-level presidential vote percentages is explained by the combined effect of the eight independent variables (R^2 = 0.453**).

Table 6.5 Means and Standard Deviations for County-Level Data
(N = 3,078)

Variable	Mean	Standard Deviation
Conservative Religion	29.538	21.127
Couples	61.466	5.862
Male	49.030	1.602
White	87.484	15.427
Rural	64.087	29.387
Elderly	14.944	4.331
Income	11,102.659	2,652.528
High School Graduates	69.541	10.346
Bush Vote	56.976	11.998

Table 6.6 Regression Coefficients for County-Level Data
(N = 3,078)

Variable	Beta	Standardized Beta
Conservative Religion	0.211	0.372**
Couples	0.864	0.422**
Male	0.709	0.095**
White	0.118	0.151**
Rural	0.017	0.043*
Elderly	0.244	0.088**
Income	-0.001	-0.128**
High School Graduates	0.332	0.286**

Constant = -68.837   * = $p < 0.05$
R^2 = 0.453**   ** = $p < 0.01$

Table 6.7 Correlation Coefficients for County-Level Data (N = 3,078)

Variable	1	2	3	4	5	6	7	8	9
1. Bush Vote	-								
2. Conservative Religion	0.204	-							
3. Couples	0.565	-0.009	-						
4. Male	0.198	-0.239	0.295	-					
5. White	0.382	-0.355	0.553	0.169	-				
6. Rural	0.258	0.140	0.334	0.137	0.133	-			
7. Elderly	0.135	0.038	0.019	-0.281	0.269	0.343	-		
8. Income	-0.106	-0.376	-0.028	0.052	0.182	-0.486	-0.258	-	
9. High School Graduate	0.088	-0.510	0.054	0.235	0.373	-0.360	-0.131	0.648	-

Study Three: State-Level Aggregate Data

Means and standard deviations are reported in table 6.8. Correlations are reported in table 6.9, while table 6.10 provides the essential regression results.

Unlike the county-level results, only three independent variables have a statistically significant influence on the 2000 presidential vote using state-level data: per capita income, percent conservative religion, and percent white. Also contrary to the county results, the average income of the state has the most significant impact. But the general pattern of prosperity and conservative vote remains the same as the counterintuitive results at the county level: wealthier states were *less* likely to support Bush (Beta = -0.406**). Higher percentages of conservative religious residents once again predict higher levels of support for Bush, and once again the strength of the relationship is relatively strong (0.362*). States with large percentages of white residents also have a greater likelihood to vote for Bush (0.231*). No other variables have a statistically significant influence at the state level.

More than 70 percent of the variance in the vote for Bush is explained by the combined effect of the eight causal variables ($R^2 = 0.715**$).

Table 6.8 Means and Standard Deviations for State-Level Data
(N = 50)

Variable	Mean	Standard Deviation
Conservative Religion	25.996	18.306
Couples	57.598	2.596
Male	48.980	0.869
White	79.474	12.962
Rural	31.826	14.667
Elderly	12.700	2.393
Income	25,131.860	3,916.288
High School Graduates	84.724	4.313
Bush Vote	50.445	8.715

Table 6.9 Correlation Coefficients for State-Level Data (N = 50)

Variable	1	2	3	4	5	6	7	8	9
1. Bush Vote	-								
2. Conservative Religion	0.512	-							
3. Couples	0.602	0.298	-						
4. Male	0.270	-0.273	0.159	-					
5. White	0.234	-0.176	0.338	-0.027	-				
6. Rural	0.391	0.249	0.424	-0.185	0.448	-			
7. Elderly	-0.318	-0.234	-0.034	-0.523	0.269	0.096	-		
8. Income	-0.675	-0.521	-0.475	0.012	-0.127	-0.577	0.058	-	
9. High School Graduate	0.020	-0.535	0.204	0.570	0.282	-0.149	-0.149	0.267	-

Table 6.10 Regression Coefficients for State-Level Data
(N = 50)

Variable	Beta	Standardized Beta
Conservative Religion	0.172	0.362*
Couples	0.647	0.193
Male	2.441	0.243
White	0.155	0.231*
Rural	-0.032	-0.054
Elderly	-0.458	-0.126
Income	-0.001	-0.406**
High School Graduates	0.104	0.051

Constant = -102.519   * = $p < 0.05$
R^2 = 0.715**   ** = $p < 0.01$

Study Four: Additional State-Level Data: Cultural Variables

Given the consistent predictive strength of conservative religion on the presidential vote, other cultural variables were correlated with state election returns. These results are reported in table 6.11, and they are striking. Cultural variables have a consistently strong association with the 2000 vote. Variables reflecting "heartland" culture correlate with increased Bush vote: pickup truck ownership (Beta = 0.699**), hunting license registration (0.537**), and circulation rates of *Field & Stream* and *Reader's Digest* magazines (0.610** and 0.505**, respectively) all exhibit patterns similar to that found with conservative religion (0.522**). Conversely, variables suggesting a cosmopolitan ethos such as rates of psychiatrists (-0.756**), plastic surgeons (-0.493**), wine consumption (-0.635**), abortions (-0.645**), and *Gourmet* magazine circulation (-0.747**) are all strongly and negatively correlated with the Bush vote.

Table 6.11 also provides the standardized Betas of all these variables when each is individually added to the eight-variable regression model used in Study Three. Nearly all of the cultural variables maintain their statistical association when added to the study. Moreover, the standardized Beta of each is almost always among the first or second strongest when compared to all the others (see table 6.11), indicating that the net effect of these cultural variables remains robust even when more traditional structural and demographic variables are considered. Moreover, the conservative religion indicator usually maintains its statistical influence on the Bush vote even when each additional cultural variable is included. And in all cases but one, conservative religion maintains either the strongest or second-strongest net effect among all the variables. *In six of the nine cases, religion and the other cultural variable are the strongest two variables in the study.* Usually, two or more variables measuring a similar phenomenon (cultural ethos in this case) would diminish the effects of one another due to multicolinearity, but here they remain strong. This provides powerful evidence that the cultural influences on political elections are of paramount importance.

Table 6.11 Influence of Other Cultural Variables for Survey Data
(N = 50)

Cultural Variable	Correlation	Standardized Beta[a]	Relative Rank of Variable[a]	Relative Rank of Conservative Religion[a]
Bush Vote	1.000			
Conservative Religion	0.522**			
Pickups	0.699**	0.366*	2	1
Field & Stream	0.610**	0.573**	1	2
Hunting Licenses	0.537**	0.332*	2	1
Reader's Digest	0.505**	0.617**	1	2
Gourmet	-0.747**	-0.578**	1	2
Psychiatrists	-0.756**	-0.350**	1	2
Plastic Surgeons	-0.493**	-0.313	3	1
Wine	-0.635**	-0.314*	2	3
Abortions	-0.645**	-0.232	4	1

[a] These values and ranks are determined by including each of these cultural variables individually with the other independent variables used in Study Three.

Discussion and Conclusion

Looking at the four studies together, several patterns emerge:

1. *Regardless of the level of analysis, religious conservatism consistently increased the vote for George W. Bush.* In each of the first three studies, religious conservatism is the second strongest factor in predicting conservative vote. Moreover, in each study it is a *different* variable—race (individual), percent couples (county), and per capita income (state)—that demonstrates more predictive power than religion. It thus seems that religious conservatism is the most consistent predictor of voting behavior in the 2000 election.

2. *When other cultural variables are considered at the state level, they have a strong impact on voting behavior, and religious conservatism maintains its influence.* At all levels of analysis, religion has a strong influence on voting behavior. The state data have many additional cultural variables to include. Remarkably, when considered in tandem, religion and other cultural variables usually both maintain a significant influence on the 2000 presidential vote. Structural and economic variables are much more likely to lose whatever influence they hold on the vote. This provides strong support for those who argue that red and blue America is divided along mostly cultural, rather than economic, lines. One could argue, however, that the current preeminence of cultural concerns is due to the relative prosperity and low unemployment that the United States has experienced throughout the past two election cycles. Articulated by proponents of the structural explanation, economic concerns will likely assume front stage if the Information Age ushers in increased inequality or widespread economic crisis. Time will tell.

3. *At the aggregate levels, income has a counterintuitive inverse effect on vote percentage for Bush.* Whereas the individual-level National Election Study survey displays a weak but anticipated positive relationship between income and conservative vote, the opposite is true for the county- and state-level data. This is especially true for the latter, as per capita income has a very strong inverse influence on the dependent variable: as a state's per capita income *increases*, the likelihood of increased vote percentage for Bush *decreases*. This finding flies in the face of common wisdom that the Republican party is primarily a party for the wealthy and the Democratic party primarily for the economically marginalized. While this common pattern modestly holds true at the individual level, the pattern reverses itself when aggregate units are considered.

4. *The relative impact of community size on the 2000 election may be overstated.* At first this, too, flies in the face of the common wisdom that we undeniably see with the maps of red and blue America. This is especially true when we see voting patterns broken down by community size: 59 percent of residents in rural areas or small towns voted for Bush, followed by 49 percent in the suburbs, 40 percent in midsize cities, and only 26 percent in large cities. But when several factors are simultaneously considered and the net effect of each variable is

determined, the influence of city size diminishes. Certainly this does not mean that the scope of one's community has no influence, but rather that the effect is indirect. The size of a community might ultimately call for a certain type of lifestyle, which in turn requires a certain type of values. These values ultimately influence voting behavior.

The evidence is striking: instead of voting with their pocketbooks, people vote with their holy books. Of course, some caution is in order. Much of the most acute findings in this study utilize state-level data, and states don't vote. One could easily commit the methodological sin of ecological fallacy, assuming individual behavior from aggregate results. Still, although individuals vote, states are the ones that provide electoral votes in presidential politics, and it is worth considering the importance of these results in light of a possible state-level cultural ethos that greatly influences national elections. Further research with additional cultural variables at the county and individual levels should prove illuminating.

Notes

1. David Brooks, "Are We Really One Country? A Report from 'Red' and 'Blue' America," *Atlantic Monthly* (December 2001): 53-65.

2. Stanley B. Greenberg, *Middle-Class Dreams: The Politics and Power of the New American Majority* (New York: Times Books, 1995); and Ruy A. Teixeira and Joel Rogers, *America's Forgotten Majority: Why the White Working Class Still Matters* (New York: Basic Books, 2000).

3. "CNN Exit Poll Results," <http://www.cnn.com/ELECTION/2000/epolls/US/-P000.html> (accessed November 25, 2001).

4. James Davison Hunter, *Culture Wars: The Struggle to Define America* (New York: Basic Books, 1991); and Gertrude Himmelfarb, *One Nation, Two Cultures* (New York: Alfred A. Knopf, 1999).

5. "CNN Exit Poll Results."

6. Hunter, *Culture Wars.*

7. Robert Wuthnow, *The Restructuring of American Religion* (Princeton, N.J.: Princeton University Press, 1988).

8. Ron Fournier, "Gore Picks Sen. Lieberman for VP," *Washington Post*, August 7, 2000, <http://www.washingtonpost.com/wp-srv/aponline/20000807/aponline121056_000.html>.

9. Wilson Carey McWilliams, "The Meaning of the Election," in *The Election of 2000*, ed. Gerald M. Pomper (New York: Chatham House, 2001), 177-201.

10. Frank Newport, "Senator Joseph Lieberman to Be Gore's Running Mate," *Gallup Organization*, August 7, 2000, <http://www.gallup.com/Poll/releases/pr000807b.asp >.

11. "Lieberman Qualifies Remarks on Religion; Reaction Continues," *Religion News Service*, August 31, 2000, <http:// www.religionnews.com/news4.html>.

12. McWilliams, "The Meaning of the Election," 177-201.

13. Nancy Burns, Donald R. Kinder, Steven J. Rosenstone, Virginia Sapiro, and the National Election Studies, *National Election Studies, 2000: Pre-/Post-Election Study* (Ann Arbor: University of Michigan, Center for Political Studies, 2001).

14. Martin B. Bradley, Norman M. Green, Jr., Dale E. Jones, Mac Lynn, and Lou McNeil, *Churches and Church Membership in the United States, 1990* (Atlanta: Glenmary Research Center, 1992).

15. Frank S. Mead, *Handbook of Denominations in the United States* (Nashville, Tenn.: Abingdon Press, 1995); and Alan Barclay Young, *Modernization and the Redefinition of Religion*, Ph.D. dissertation, University of Illinois at Urbana-Champaign, 1993.

16. Barry A. Kosmin and Seymour P. Lachman, *One Nation under God: Religion in Contemporary American Society* (New York: Harmony Books, 1993).

17. U.S. Bureau of the Census. *Statistical Abstract of the United States: The National Data Book, 1999.* (Washington, D.C.: U.S. Government Printing Office, 1999).

18. U.S. Bureau of the Census. *Statistical Abstract of the United States: The National Data Book, 2000.* (Washington, D.C.: U.S. Government Printing Office, 2000).

19. Kathleen O. Morgan and Scott E. Morgan, eds., *Health Care State Rankings, 1997* (Lawrence, Kans.: Morgan Quitno, 1997).

Chapter 7

Religious Civility, Civil Society, and Charitable Choice: Faith-Based Poverty Relief in the Post-Welfare Era

John P. Bartkowski and Helen A. Regis

In 1996, the federal government passed the most comprehensive welfare reform bill in recent memory—the Personal Responsibility and Work Opportunity Reconciliation Act.[1] One of the most noteworthy aspects of welfare reform law is its enactment of Charitable Choice, Section 104 of welfare reform legislation.[2] Charitable Choice mandates that state governments which opt to contract with independent-sector social service providers cannot legally exclude faith-based organizations from consideration simply because these organizations are religious in nature. This dramatic policy change is part of a broader commitment to political devolution. Political devolution, in short, is the philosophy that government deregulation empowers local communities to find grassroots solutions to social problems. From this vantage point, unencumbered locales are empowered communities. Despite the debates Charitable Choice has spawned,[3] presidential candidates from both major political parties promised to expand federal support for this provision during the Fall 2000 election campaign, and President George W. Bush has delivered on this promise since entering the White House.[4]

In what follows, we scrutinize the prospects of faith-based welfare reform by examining the dynamics of congregational antipoverty efforts undertaken by two prominent Mississippi churches—an African American Church of God in Christ (COGIC) congregation and a white Southern Baptist church. Situated in the same Mississippi township, both of these churches actively engage in poverty relief—though each does so with very different intentions and through highly distinctive means. Mississippi has the highest poverty rate in the nation and, at the same time, boasts one of the most highly churched populations in the United States.[5] Our intensive case-study analysis illuminates how the local milieu within which religious congregations are situated influences their views of the poor as well as their preferred strategies for poverty relief. Moreover, a comparative analysis of the two churches reveals how the meanings, motivations, and practices associated with faith-based poverty relief can vary greatly across congregational contexts.

Debating Civil Society, Citizenship, and Human Dignity: Libertarian, Communitarian, and Strong Democratic Paradigms

Our study of faith-based poverty relief is informed by ongoing disputes about the ideal structure of American civil society and competing visions of the citizen within this "parallel polis." Although proponents of civil society generally define civility as a respect for the inherent dignity of the human person, scholars often articulate divergent idealized visions of civil society and human dignity. The libertarian and communitarian models of civil society are among the leading contenders in ongoing debates over this issue.[6] A libertarian vision of civil society places a premium on personal freedoms in the "private" dimensions of social life. The private sphere is defined to include the realm of individual choice, as well as social relations in the market and the home. From the libertarian vantage point, the private sphere should remain untouched and untainted by government regulation. Given the government's public character, laws are viewed as inherently constraining and coercive.

By contrast, communitarians understand civil society as a "complex welter of ineluctably social relations that tie people together into families, clans, clubs, neighborhoods, communities, and hierarchies."[7] Communitarians typically emphasize the precontractual nature of social relations while highlighting the mutual obligations and responsibilities that eclipse individual choice. From this standpoint, community ties integrate individuals into the social fabric while providing moral guidance that is impossible to sustain in the libertarian pursuit of self-interest. Following from their divergent visions of civil society, libertarians and communitarians articulate distinctive metaphors of citizenship and human dignity. Whereas libertarians imagine the citizen as the *private rights-bearing consumer*, communitarians envision citizens as *publicly enmeshed clansmen* who are "tied to [their] community by birth, blood, and bathos."[8]

Within recent years, some scholars have argued that neither the libertarian nor the communitarian vision of civil society is adequate. Benjamin Barber argues for a "strong democratic" view of civil society that seeks to balance individual freedom with moral obligation. From this vantage point, "civil society's ideal citizen . . . is not as steeped in solidarity as the clansmen but is far more free; she is less radically autonomous than the consumer but better able to enjoy the comforts of neighborly associations."[9] Interestingly, churches are among the comforting, neighborly associations that Barber names in staking out this middle-range vision of civil society. Yet, of course, such claims raise questions about the appropriate place of religious congregations and faith-based organizations in American civil society. Are churches, as a rule, neighborly associations? What comforts do churches provide, and who are its beneficiaries? More broadly, how do congregations navigate around what Barber charges to be the extremes of an atomizing voluntarism (libertarianism) and a stifling collectivism (communitarianism)?

With these questions in mind, we now examine the distinctive social dynamics underlying poverty relief in two different Mississippi congregations. The first of the churches featured here is Temple Zion Church of God in Christ. A predominantly African American Christian denomination in the Holiness-Pentecostal tradition, COGIC is among the largest black denominational bodies in the United States and is the single largest black Pentecostal body in the world.[10] COGIC, which traces its origins to the early twentieth-century Holiness movement in Mississippi, currently boasts 5.5 million adherents.[11] It enjoys a strong presence among Southern blacks, with its headquarters located near the Mississippi-Tennessee border in Memphis.

We compare Temple Zion COGIC with the Main Street Southern Baptist Church. Main Street is a white, upper-middle-class church affiliated with the Southern Baptist Convention. Southern Baptists are the predominant denomination in the religious landscape of the South in general and Mississippi in particular. In east central Mississippi, confirmed Southern Baptist churchgoers alone account for as much as almost 50 percent of all church adherents.[12] With the Convention founded in 1845, Southern Baptists have a long history in the South and currently claim 15.7 million confirmed members nationwide.[13] Approximately one-quarter of all Southern Baptists reside in the four states of Mississippi, Alabama, Tennessee, and Kentucky.[14]

As the following accounts reveal, both Temple Zion COGIC and Main Street Southern Baptist are favorably disposed toward the forging of church-state partnerships in aid-provision to the local poor. Yet, despite this point of consensus, pastoral narratives of poverty relief in these two congregations are rooted in fundamentally different visions of civil society, citizenship, and human dignity.

Defending Big Government:
Tribulation and Transformation at Temple Zion COGIC

Temple Zion Church of God in Christ is a large, thriving, and politically engaged African American congregation located in an east central Mississippi town of approximately twenty thousand residents. As a congregation with four hundred members—and similar figures in Sunday service attendance—this church is competing effectively in its local religious economy. The membership of Temple Zion is quite young. Seventy percent of the membership is under thirty-five years old and virtually all are younger than fifty. Elder Cornelius Smith, Temple Zion's pastor of eighteen years, attributes his predominantly female membership—70 percent women—to the abundance of black males in the community "who have problems with authority due to their reaction to slavery and Jim Crowism." Despite its young and predominantly female membership, Temple Zion is a heterogeneous religious congregation in other significant ways. White-collar, skilled, and service-sector employees, as well as laborers, homemakers, and unemployed persons, are well represented at Temple Zion.

Temple Zion's physical facilities are impressive. The church has more than fifteen classrooms for Sunday school instruction, a cafeteria that can accommodate nearly three hundred persons, and a balcony that serves them well on Sunday mornings as they attempt to grow their membership to around five hundred. Temple Zion's annual budget of $300,000 is modest when compared with its slate of highly active relief programs: rental payment assistance, temporary shelter, clothing, various types of counseling, and financial assistance to those in need of medical services. Perhaps most notably, this church runs a food pantry that, according to Smith, serves more than five hundred families per month and utilizes a grocery voucher system for items not stored in their pantry. In all, Smith says that his church provides relief to nearly six hundred people in a typical month. Thus, in proportion to its financial and human resources, Temple Zion provides many different types of relief to a sizable number of people.

Debunking the Myths: Blackness, Welfare Recipiency, and the Question of Fraud

Elder Smith is forty-five years old, has a high school diploma, and is not seminary trained. His critical political sensibilities are clearly and unabashedly manifested throughout his discussion of state-sponsored welfare programs. "There is a myth in our country that welfare recipients are mostly black," Smith asserts. This erroneous belief, he contends, has found fertile soil in the minds of both whites and African Americans—even local black pastors: "I think that sometimes black preachers hear that [welfare services may be transferred to local churches], and we think 'My God, the whole welfare burden will be on our shoulders.' That is not true."

Smith also critiques what he views as other "welfare myths" as the opportunity arises. He has little patience for those who assume that the allegedly all-black recipients of public assistance commonly "abuse" the system through "welfare fraud." Like several other black pastors in the local area, Smith cites concrete instances in which welfare fraud—when understood in a broad, though very practical sense—has been perpetrated by privileged whites who extract benefits indirectly from welfare recipients. Among the most common examples cited are white landlords who artificially inflate rental prices in public housing for local blacks, and small-scale merchants who keep retail prices high in order to absorb the monies of welfare recipients in nearby neighborhoods. Smith, who has personally seen such abuse, adroitly redefines the notion of "welfare recipiency" when he says: "White people will be crying [about welfare reform]. It will be the mom and pop grocery stores who have been taking the food stamps and taking the welfare checks the first of every month [that will be adversely affected by welfare reform]. They will be going broke."

Interestingly, this critical appraisal of such welfare myths has not spawned jaundiced resignation or political apathy for Smith. To the contrary, Smith's vibrant religious convictions create for him an unyielding sense of confidence in his congregation's ability to minister effectively to many different disadvantaged populations. Material relief is provided at Temple Zion in many different forms—to the hungry at the church's food pantry, to the infirm who struggle with medical and prescription bills, to parents of limited means in need of dependable child care, and to those whose rental bills sometimes arrive before the tenants themselves are capable of paying them. Other types of sustenance—nonmaterial in character—are provided to the likes of struggling couples in need of marriage counseling, depressed persons with flagging self-esteem, or addicts requiring drug rehabilitation counseling.

If they are not already attending Temple Zion, clients of the congregation's food pantry and other relief programs are viewed unambiguously as future church members. In this sense, Temple Zion melds accountability standards—namely, the expectation of church membership—with compassionate relief. While some critics would characterize such expectations as aid provision with "strings attached," Smith does not. He proclaims unflinchingly, "We hope that somehow, if we show enough love, [aid recipients] will come back to our services and be a part of our church." He continues, "In our sessions, we offer Christ many times and there are those who don't really want Christ." The church's "solution" to those who reject such efforts at proselytization is pragmatic but uncompromising—ministers "give them counseling of a secular nature also. But we let them know that we believe [in Jesus Christ], and we teach that Jesus Christ is the answer to all of our problems."

Religious Civility and Kinship with the Poor

Smith adamantly states that the church's distinctive approach to relief provision moves public assistance recipients from welfare dependency into more economically productive endeavors. To discourage dependency on public assistance programs, Smith critically invokes the notion of the welfare "handout" from the libertarian ideology of *self-sufficiency*. However, he changes the meaning of terms such as "handout" and "dependency" by giving them a spiritual, otherworldly cast. By invoking the notion of *spiritual dependency*, Smith argues that all believers "depend" on the grace of God for their "welfare"—broadly understood:

> All I can tell you is two-thirds of our people when they came to us were on welfare. It is my Sunday morning sermon at some points [that is] on that [topic]. [I tell my congregants:] "If you are on welfare, get off as soon as you can because welfare is limiting your future. Welfare is hampering your success." That's how I teach it. I tell them this. "It is not God's will for you to be on welfare. And it insults God for Him to be our Father, [for] us to trust in Him, and we have to have a handout every day of our lives." So, therefore, I teach it is essential to us growing, to being proper witnesses, that we don't find ourselves on welfare. And I would dare to say [that] out of the numbers we called to you earlier [that is, two-thirds of those who came to the church on welfare], I would dare to say that less than 10 percent are on welfare.

Smith therefore critiques public assistance—rather than its recipients per se—because such programs are set up to undermine the believer's dependency on God. From this perspective, all believers—rather than just welfare recipients—must recognize their common state of dependency.

Through such sermons, Smith charismatically champions achieving "success" and fully exploring one's "future" through means other than welfare. Regardless of how terms such as "success" and "future" are interpreted by his diverse congregants, Smith claims to be achieving results by preaching against public assistance programs. In a similar fashion, he boasts a 95 percent success rate for marriage counseling with church members and estimates a one-in-two long-term success rate through the church's drug rehabilitation program.

If these dramatic success rates are taken at face value, how are we to make sense of them? Perhaps these outcomes result from the unique combination of compassion and judgment that characterize Temple Zion's relief efforts. At Temple Zion, the moral logics of compassion and judgment are seamlessly interwoven with another. Moreover, these twin moral imperatives are practiced as personalized convictions rather than merely preached as abstract principles. Smith claims kinship—literally and figuratively—with those on welfare: "My sister was a welfare recipient. Now she has a school of ministry." Redemption-from-public-assistance narratives such as these chart the move from tribulation (welfare dependency) to transformation (productive endeavors) and, ultimately, triumph (spiritual dependency complemented by proactive Christian service). Such stories mirror the retrospective accounts conveyed by ex-convicts or recovering alcoholics who have effectively wrestled with and scored victories over their own "demons."[15] Perhaps most important, recovery and redemption narratives at Temple Zion are personalized, autobiographical accounts of *my life* and *my family* in which the poor are understood not as "they" or "them" but as "us" and "ours." The sense of intimacy conveyed in these narratives provides fertile soil for cultivating social capital. Smith recounts how some churches lament that very poor persons "clutter

. . . their foyers and their lobbies." He is critical of such views, and also implicitly critiques outreach efforts that offer relief to the poor from afar: "To us, it is [the poorest people] who we want. We want to show love to the most dejected people who are nearest [by us] to help. And so we look for those kinds of folks."

It is in this spirit that Smith addresses the expectation of church attendance from recipients of congregational relief. According to him, success rates in their relief programs are significantly lower for nonmembers. The distinctively therapeutic interaction provided by *both* counseling *and* church attendance—the latter of which entails personal commitment and fosters a deep connection with the community of believers—is apparently the key to producing such positive results. Utilizing this "both/and" strategy of aid provision, Smith says that those who seek out the most holistic forms of counseling at Temple Zion "get their lives straight with the Lord and with each other." Continuing in this vein, he asserts: "You cannot expect to be irresponsible, cannot expect to be footloose and fancy free, not go anywhere near the church and expect the church to always help you. You have got to get into a church and support that church."

Thus, while Temple Zion stops short of formally *requiring* aid receivers to join *their church*, recipients are strongly encouraged to join *a church* or to reactivate their membership in the church they previously attended. In fact, Temple Zion aid workers will phone a church listed by a prospective recipient and inquire about his or her status at that church. In Smith's view, African American church membership in the South is not so much a question of rational choice or personal preference as it is a necessity for survival: "Because truly, in my opinion, the black church is the only hope black folk have. Always was."

Consequently, Smith is extremely positive about the potential for his church to expand their current slate of services with an infusion of government monies. Smith contends that, when compared with government welfare, church-based relief is far superior. Faith-based aid, he says, can "cut through the bureaucracy and get the money to the people in a much more efficient manner." In Smith's eyes, the efficiency of faith-based social service delivery is due, in part, to churches facing lower overhead costs "than they are paying downtown" in government offices. Under Charitable Choice, this reasoning goes, faith communities can use volunteer labor and existing congregational networks to register significant savings in wages, benefits, and operating expenses.

Denominationalism Trumps Blackness: Religious Incivility among African American Churches

Smith sees an important role for African American interfaith and parachurch organizations as Charitable Choice initiatives are expanded. However, he seems dismayed by the fact that parachurch groups have not developed strong social ties in his local township. Smith argues that white churches have been working cooperatively for some time now, and he believes that black churches must begin doing the same. Taking an optimistic future-oriented tone, Smith envisions black faith communities wielding significant power if they work collectively for social change. He charges that black churches in his county alone control nearly four million dollars. He laments the fact that these monies are currently spread over various financial institutions in the region.

Yet, if "the Black Church"—as he uses this singular term—were to pool their resources and invest such monies collectively, they could transform supra-congregational financial clout into political leverage:

> For that money, we [would] want that bank to give us a board position so that we can sit on that board and watch how that bank does business. How it makes its loans and is it fair and viable? Out of those concerns, we believe the Black Church can become [a social force] to get things done. Out of those concerns, we believe the Black Church could become a voting block that could control campaigns, that has the ability to do petitions, and to get things done as an effort to pull us together—both economically and socially—which is what has not been done in the past. The preacher in the past has made his money by amplifying differences. Your Baptist, our Pentecostal, your Methodist, our Presbyterian—through those differences, we have kept ourselves apart. And we are the only group that does it, because even though the white brothers may be Pentecostal or Baptist or Presbyterian, they have a council of churches. They get together and they make decisions in those church meetings that coincide with the church meetings down the road. And they get things done. That is what we haven't been doing.

In connecting the collective deployment of church-based resources to would-be institutional transformations outside of the congregational setting, Smith and pastors like him offer an extremely expansive conceptualization of faith-based aid. From this vantage point, churches should not simply be in the business of caring for down-and-out individuals on an intermittent or even semiregular basis. Rather, Smith argues that churches can and should function as critical institutions within civil society—critical in the sense that faith communities could represent the interests of the oppressed who may otherwise be invisible in the most powerful social institutions (e.g., banks, lending agencies). As the community's collective conscience, such churches could mobilize the oppressed through petition drives and marches to advance the causes of equity and justice.

Why, then, has "the Black Church" as envisioned by Smith not coalesced in his home community? His reply is short and pointed: "I think our prejudices and our Reformational racism is probably worse than the white people." It would seem that the collective interest of African Americans in local Southern communities has been undermined by denominational splintering that separates different factions of black Protestants, black Christians, and even black religious adherents in general (e.g., Christian versus Muslim) one from another. In this way, local black congregations have found the cultivation of broad-based, bridging capital most elusive. Because these faith communities remain divided by congregational and denominational boundaries, Smith recognizes that churches are not wholly insulated from producing pernicious social hierarchies of their own. Congregations that show great civility toward the poor can be most uncivil with one another.

Local Empowerment in Rural Mississippi: Redeeming Community or Resurrecting Jim Crow?

Divisions among churches, Smith warns, could influence Charitable Choice initiatives if not implemented with sensitivity to this issue. As noted above, Smith says that some of his fellow African American clergymen have bought into erroneous characterizations of welfare as a "black issue." Apart from the empirical inaccuracy of such conceptualizations, these notions could place the burden of responsibility for "fixing" welfare squarely—if not solely—on the shoulders of black social institutions, African American community leaders, and the alleged lack of initiative exhibited by "their" welfare recipients. Such reactions actually reinforce the idea that welfare—and, perhaps, welfare reform through Charitable Choice—is the problem of black America.

In addressing this prospect, Smith recounts how a white pastor from an affluent church nearby recently inquired about routing his church's aid through Temple Zion. While Smith was initially interested in the idea of serving more needy persons with monetary assistance from this nearby church, he found the other pastor's motivations for the proposed plan to be highly suspect upon hearing the details:

> A while back a large white church in Mississippi came to me. . . . [A pastor from that church inquired,] "Can we funnel our assistance programs through you?" I saw this as a great opportunity to get more money to more people. I said, "Certainly. What are you talking about putting through?" This was a large church. This church probably does $3 million a year or more, so [it is] a large white church. And so I said, "What are you talking about money-wise?" And the pastor said to me, "We will give you $4,000 a year." I was insulted. I stood up and walked out, and he said, "What is the problem?" I said, "I am insulted." . . . At this time our gross income was roughly $200,000 a year or a little better. I said, "We spend anywhere from $14,000 to $20,000 in helping people already. You mean to tell me you are going to offer me $4,000 a year to run all of your people through us? Your problem is you simply want to rid your lobby of a certain kind of people and put them in my lobby. You are not serious about the problem. So, when you want to spend some real money, we will talk." So I think the problem we are going to have is that if the government is going to do this, there has to be some real strict guidelines on how the money is appropriated at a

state level so that it won't get into the wrong hands and the wrong
churches [but] will get to where the people really need it.

Narratives such as these reveal the concerns that some pastors who are positively
disposed toward Charitable Choice harbor toward the actual implementation of
such initiatives. When offered a minuscule sum to perform a great deal more
antipoverty work, Smith realized that the pastor wishing to route that church's aid
programs through Temple Zion was less concerned with assisting the poor than
with maintaining a comfortable social distance between an increasingly visible
underclass and the affluent congregants of his white church.

Smith's last words on this subject clearly indicate his concern that pastoral and
congregational motivations to help the poor are an important consideration as
political devolution places the responsibility for welfare administration and work
placement on local communities. Local communities—for all of the merits of
grassroots empowerment—are not bereft of their own stratification mechanisms,
including denominational, racial, and class-based hierarchies:

> Whenever I hear people in Congress and the senators say things like,
> "We have to make government smaller and give power back to state
> governments" [pause]. To a Southern black person [pause]. Whenever
> I hear them say those kinds of terms, I know that means that [political
> power and resource control] is going to be put in the hands of the good
> old boys. It is going to be handled the way it was handled all the time.
> And the people who need [help] most won't get it. And so for that
> reason, I opt to say, "Let's keep the government [as it is]." I too would
> like to see a small government. But I would like to see a more fair
> system to where the government could be smaller because we have
> rectified the problem [of] each state being able to discriminate when
> they want to.

Thus, while expressing his generally positive affect toward Charitable Choice
partnerships, Smith advances a pointed critique of pro-welfare-reform discourse
and a stern warning about placing too much faith in the political devolution of
federal assistance programs.

Praising Local Empowerment at Main Street Southern Baptist

In many respects, Main Street Southern Baptist Church is a very different religious
congregation from Temple Zion. Whereas Temple Zion's Elder Smith is not
seminary trained, Main Street's pastor Robert Davidson obtained his doctorate of
ministry from New Orleans Baptist Seminary. Pastor Davidson, in his late fifties,
ministers to a large, affluent, upper-middle-class congregation. Main Street boasts
a membership of well over two thousand persons and operates debt-free with an
annual budget approaching $1.5 million. The complex of buildings that make up

this church houses a chapel capable of seating eight hundred Sunday service attendees, fifty classrooms, ten offices, expansive kitchen facilities, and one of the largest children's playgrounds among area churches. Main Street, situated at the geographical and social center of the small Southern town in which it resides, has been housed on its current site for more than 150 years. Davidson, an articulate minister who is well acquainted with Southern culture through his pastoral training and recent appointments, is proud that his church has "always been very strong and active locally" during his tenure there.

Religious Incivility toward the Poor? Faith-Based Benevolence and Highway Bums

Main Street, which offers church-door aid to about twenty persons in a typical month, administers a range of relief programs directly: payment of rental, utility, and medical bills; food assistance; temporary shelter; and counseling. These direct forms of congregational relief are complemented by Main Street's extensive support of several local interfaith efforts. As Davidson explains, Main Street's

> benevolence program . . . is well known in the city. Sometimes too well known because of the number of calls we get, and the people who refer people to us for help. We sometimes kid about it—that somewhere out on a bridge on the outside of town is our phone number with our names. So that people who are sort of the highway bums—and that's not a derogatory term, it just is a term—[we sometimes kid that] if they come to town . . . [they can easily find out] what our phone number is and who to call for a handout, for food, for money.

Davidson adds that his church gets referrals from "just about everyone" in town, including the police department and various aid agencies. In addition to the list of relief efforts described above, most of Main Street's Sunday School classes have adopted needy families. These adopt-a-family relief efforts often provide the children in less-privileged households with school clothes, winter coats, and other needed items over a sustained period of time.

Main Street Baptist is also involved in parachurch relief efforts. The church supports and coordinates some of their activities with Outreach and Uplift Relief (OUR) Ministries, an interfaith organization that provides select material goods (e.g., food, clothes) to needy residents. OUR Ministries commands more resources than many small churches in the area and serves as the "go-to" option for small-church pastors when faced with aid requests that would deplete their meager resources. Interestingly, Main Street's connection to OUR Ministries is the converse of that of many small churches. Davidson stresses that Main Street's own aid programs are more financially robust than virtually any nearby parachurch agencies. "They probably send more people to us than we do to them," he concludes, adding, "They probably have less to work with in that whole organization than our church."

In addition to these relief endeavors, Main Street has also offered assistance in opening a local emergency shelter for children. Main Street has allocated approximately $1,000 per month to underwrite that shelter, which is run by the local Salvation Army. Davidson refers to this cooperative partnership financed by Main Street as "great," adding: "I'm proud that we don't run [the children's shelter]. I told our Church family, I said, 'You've got to look at this and say, "A thousand dollars a month is cheap."'" Davidson considers all of their current relief efforts to be effective and explains tersely, "Our goal is ministry, not programs."

Welfare Culture and the Problem of Accountability

Yet, Davidson's tone takes a less than sanguine turn when he reflects on his church's experience with ex-Governor Fordice's Faith and Families of Mississippi program—the first faith-based welfare reform initiative of its kind in the United States.[16] Echoing the sentiments expressed by other pastors at white churches of privilege in our study, Davidson expresses frustration with the apparent failure of program applicants to appear for their designated appointments with the church. Davidson recounts the typical scenario: "The Faith and Families office will call us and they'll say, 'We've set up an appointment for you with Ms. So-and-so to come see you at a certain time related to your involvement [in Faith and Families].' And then the person doesn't show. . . . And [Faith and Families] will try to follow up and [the applicant] can't reschedule." Pastoral frustration with this state of affairs is amplified by the fact that Main Street was among the churches who were most supportive of this program in its initial stages.

As Davidson sees it, the underlying cause of this no-show outcome is the reluctance of welfare recipients to submit themselves to the church's scrutiny. From this vantage point, welfare recipients have a strong aversion to being held accountable for their lifestyle and actions. With choice words that underscore the social distance between Main Street and the undeserving poor, Davidson contends, "We've basically raised up a culture that says, 'We really do deserve the money and you don't deserve anything from us.'" Remembering the sixties as a period of cultural decadence rather than progressive social change, he asserts: "Since the 1960s, it has been a problem because we've developed a culture to allow people who really don't want any accountability required [of them]." He links this anti-accountability orientation to the problems associated with the Faith and Families program: "I think a lot of times, if a person realizes maybe if they are going to get involved in having a church and a mentorship, they are probably going to have to change some things in their lives. And they are going to have to face some responsibilities they don't want to face."

Memorializing Civility on the Southern Plantation

Davidson says that long-standing public assistance programs were initially predicated on an altruistic, "want to help" mentality. Yet, they blossomed into a "welfare system" fraught with corruption: "The welfare system basically operates in America today not for the poor person, but for the administrators." He asserts that such corruption is currently not incidental but intrinsic to federal government programs: "What is it they say? That something like twenty-something percent of all federal welfare money is gulped up in fraud. In dishonesty." In contrast to Smith at Temple Zion, Main Street's pastor reviles big government and strongly supports political devolution: "Most of those people [in the federal government] got those jobs through political appointments. They were put there to do just what they're doing—that's to lie, cheat, and steal. . . . I don't have a lot of appreciation for [federal government workers]."

As a counterpoint to federal government fraud, Davidson highlights the grassroots altruism that he says emerged in local Mississippi communities during the recent protracted power outage that resulted from a winter ice storm. This storm, which left thousands without electricity and in many cases heat for as much as one week, was met with "neighbors . . . show[ing] up with chain saws and drag[ging] limbs and help[ing] their neighbors. And they want to help. They want to cover that roof. They want to give food."

Consistent with his celebration of local altruism, Davidson is confident that his church could figure prominently in Charitable Choice initiatives if they were to be implemented in Mississippi. When asked what type of relief programs his church could sponsor with an infusion of block grant monies, he answers confidently, "Anything." However, his optimism toward Charitable Choice at Main Street does not translate into blanket support of such initiatives. Churches as a group, Davidson contends, are not above reproach where funds designed to underwrite relief provision are concerned. Now qualifying his optimism about Charitable Choice, Davidson mentions several instances in which financial partnerships between the state and local congregations have gone awry. In one instance, he says that a Memphis church "organized themselves to accept money—government money—to build public housing. And the pastor got sent to jail eventually because he spent most of the money on himself and his family, his brothers-in-law. . . . And eventually there were no houses built. The same thing happened on the Gulf Coast with a guy. . . . And so, sometimes the unscrupulous have a unique way of getting into those things."

In a striking point of departure from Temple Zion's Elder Smith, Pastor Davidson argues that attitudes about race and ethnicity would generally not affect the distribution of aid under Charitable Choice. When asked if race would affect the disbursement of funds to churches or, ultimately, to the needy, he responds point blank: "No, because any group involved in [providing] aid today, to anyone, has long since dealt with that one." So, whereas Smith points to the persistence of racism within both black and white local churches, Davidson claims that racism is an issue of the distant past—the quite distant past, it would seem.

According to Davidson, blacks were previously offered "help" by Southern plantation owners and farmers. Davidson's views of enduring white altruism toward "the black community" are most clearly evidenced when he is asked if he thinks race affects the way in which relief is currently provided by local congregations:

> No, I doubt that [race currently affects the distribution of church aid]. In fact, see, particularly in the South [pause]. And, you know, I'm a Southerner. [I] grew up in the South [and] have lived in a lot of other places, but [pause]. Southerners have always seen themselves as having to help, say, the black community. You know, the old plantation owner, he did it. The farmers did it. It's always been there. And so, race has—in my own lifetime—has never been a problem in relationships. Even when you had the active Ku Klux Klan and the marchers and everything, there's always been a desire to help. And I don't think that's ever been on a racial basis.

Using such language, Davidson suggests that even during tumultuous times—Klan activity and public marches supporting racial segregation and Jim Crow laws—white Southerners have "always seen themselves as having to help . . . the black community." One of the most striking features of this narrative is the way in which it portrays whites as the benevolent, compassionate agents of relief. Given this discursive memorializing of the past, white benevolence effectively trumps Klan activity and paints "old [Southern] plantation owners"—popularly viewed as a source of black oppression—in a positive light. This revisionist narrative, however, assumes a singular and homogeneously needy "black community," claims which would likely draw criticism from Temple Zion's Elder Smith. Recall that Smith pointedly criticizes racialized "welfare myths" which equate neediness and aid recipiency with membership in "the black community."

Civility toward the Deserving Poor: The Plight of Working Families

In the end, however, Davidson argues that the group about whom he is "most concerned" are not the recipients of welfare, but instead working poor families. The race of the hypothetical working poor family he describes is unmarked. However, the father in this nuclear family evinces an impressive work ethic, faces a heavy tax burden, and—through no fault of his own—cannot afford to provide the children he loves with the most basic forms of health care. Davidson explains:

> That's the man who's going out there and working every day—forty and fifty hours a week. And yet, after he pays his social security and gets his income tax taken out of this salary—his pay—he comes home and he

> doesn't have enough money to [look after] the basic needs of his family. And for whatever reason, the company he is working for does not provide insurance coverage or medical benefits. And he can't afford the hospitalization insurance for his family. So, his children can't go to the dentist. His children can't get their vaccinations and their check-ups. When they get a fever, they just do the best they can. That's the group now that I am most concerned about. And in our system we're destroying that family.

Although issues of "deservingness" are not addressed directly in this narrative of the struggling working poor family, one could argue that the committed breadwinner in such families makes a compelling foil against which the stereotypical "welfare mother"—bereft of a hard-working husband/provider, and perhaps prone to shiftlessness herself—can be counterposed. In fairness, Davidson does not draw such invidious comparisons. Yet, his overriding concern for this intact working poor family hints at a moral orientation that could affect the implementation of church-state partnerships in his congregation and others like it.

Compassion, Judgment, and Religious Civility: Pursuing Civil Society through Faith-Based Poverty Relief

In this era of Charitable Choice, how effectively can faith-based poverty ministry function in the "parallel polis" of American civil society? What are the prospects and pitfalls associated with inviting religious organizations to participate more centrally in social service provision to the poor? The portraits of poverty relief in two prominent Mississippi congregations presented here provide us with some intriguing—though admittedly programmatic—answers to such pressing questions.

Where poverty relief is concerned, congregations can act as comforting, neighborly organizations even as they impose various demands upon the recipients of their benevolence. Faith-based poverty relief, in many respects, adheres to the "strong democratic" vision of civil society by seeking to balance personal freedoms with moral obligations. Precisely how do congregations engaged in poverty relief navigate between rights and responsibilities? As illustrated here and in our other work on this topic,[17] congregations act upon their vision of the good society and the model citizen by melding together two otherwise competing moral logics—compassion and judgment.[18] As a moral imperative, compassion mandates empathy, mutuality, and forgiveness. Judgment, the moral counterpart of compassion, mandates accountability standards, ethical discernment, and (where needed) social hierarchies to adjudicate moral disputes. Religious organizations imagine and pursue their visions of civil society through poverty relief efforts that draw together compassion and accountability in congregationally distinctive ways.

At Temple Zion, compassionate giving is manifested in the kinship its congregants claim with the poor. Temple Zion assists over twenty times more persons per month via direct church-door relief than does Main Street—where religious leaders jest that they are too well-known among the local "highway bums." Temple Zion's Elder Smith argues that his relief providers consciously seek to aid the poorest of the poor within the local community. On the face of it, then, Temple Zion seems to evince a more compassionate orientation toward the poor. Yet, compassionate benevolence at Temple Zion is only part of the "moral" in this story. Such compassion is deftly interwoven with accountability standards at this COGIC congregation. The church's pastor and aid providers strive to convert recipients of church relief to become members of their congregation by continually "offering Christ" to nonbelievers. Temple Zion's aid providers want beneficiaries of their benevolence to belong to a church and will even call the home congregation named by prospective aid recipients to determine if these individuals are committed church members or "footloose" solicitors. Such accountability standards are imposed with the hope that aid recipients will recognize their dependency on God and avoid welfare dependency, which Smith chides from the pulpit as an "insult" to the Almighty.

Compassion, of course, is not absent from Main Street's benevolence programs. Here, too, the moral logics of compassion and accountability are woven together—albeit differently—within this congregation. Main Street offers financial support to many local benevolence agencies. Agencies underwritten by Main Street's financial support serve as a liaison—even a buffer—between this upper-middle-class congregation and the less privileged poor. Compassion in this context is manifested not through direct kinship, but rather via congregational philanthropy to middleman charitable organizations. Moreover, Main Street's Pastor Davidson exudes compassion for the hard-working, two-parent family whose father's income, after taxes, leaves him unable to meet his children's basic needs. Yet, this same compassion is not manifested toward those families unwilling to submit their lives to the scrutiny of the church—which Davidson chides as an aversion to "accountability."

The decidedly different mixes of compassion and accountability within these two congregations produce divergent definitions of civility and disparate appraisals of political devolution. As an African American raised in the South, Temple Zion's Smith worries that political devolution under welfare reform will effectively prevent the federal government from supervising local "good old boy" networks which historically functioned to reproduce class- and race-based hierarchies in rural Southern townships. The federal enforcement of civil rights legislation in states such as Mississippi may generate antipathy against "government interference" among some local residents, including white conservatives, whose enthusiasm for a new federalism may be rooted in a desire to preserve racial privilege rather than in more genuine philosophical commitments to grassroots democracy or local empowerment. Terms such as "local empowerment" raise concerns for this Southern black pastor who fears a return to Jim Crow politics in which local power structures trump federal civil rights legislation and erode gains made through federal mandates of equal opportunity and Affirmative Action.

By contrast, Main Street's Pastor Davidson is a champion of the new federalism and political devolution. He believes that racial issues in the South are largely resolved. In his view, Southern whites have always looked after local African Americans—even during the plantation era. Much of his support for welfare reform and Charitable Choice is linked to his support for grassroots empowerment, which he has seen manifested most recently during harsh winter power outages in his local community.

In the end, our study reveals that pastoral visions of civil society vary dramatically across congregational contexts.[19] To be sure, the pastors featured in this study are not thoroughgoing libertarians, nor are they wholehearted communitarians. By melding the logics of compassion and judgment, congregational poverty relief gravitates between these moral poles. In many respects, the pastoral discourse of poverty relief featured here aligns closely with a strong democratic vision of civil society in which freedom and flexibility are placed in ongoing tension with moral obligation and accountability.[20] Although Temple Zion and Main Street share a joint commitment to a strong democratic vision of civil society, these two congregations utilize very different poverty relief strategies and mix the moral antinomies of compassion and judgment in culturally distinctive ways. Thus, as religious organizations become more central to social service provision in twenty-first-century America, there is much to be gained by observing—carefully yet critically—the complex moral orientations adopted by religious leaders and the congregations they serve. Civility demands nothing less.

Notes

1. Mary Jo Bane and David T. Ellwood, *Welfare Realities: From Rhetoric to Reform* (Cambridge, Mass.: Harvard University Press, 1996); and Gwendolyn Mink, *Welfare's End* (Ithaca, N.Y.: Cornell University Press, 1998).

2. *A Guide to Charitable Choice: The Rules of Section 104 of the 1996 Federal Welfare Law Governing State Cooperation with Faith-Based Social-Service Providers* (Washington, D.C.: Center for Public Justice; Annandale, Va.: Christian Legal Society, Center for Law and Religious Freedom, 1997); Mary Jo Bane, Brent Coffin, and Ronald Thiemann, eds., *Who Will Provide? The Changing Role of Religion in American Social Welfare* (Boulder, Co.: Westview Press, 2000); John P. Bartkowski and Helen A. Regis, "Religious Organizations, Anti-Poverty Relief, and Charitable Choice: A Feasibility Study of Faith-Based Welfare Reform in Mississippi" (Arlington, Va.: Pricewaterhouse Coopers Endowment for the Business of Government, 1999); John P. Bartkowski and Helen A. Regis, *Charitable Choices: Religion, Race, and Poverty in the Post-Welfare Era* (New York: New York University Press, 2002); Mark Chaves, "Religious Congregations and Welfare Reform: Who Will Take Advantage of 'Charitable Choice'?" *American Sociological Review* 64 (1999): 836-46; and Ram A. Cnaan, *The Newer Deal: Social Work and Religion in Partnership* (New York: Columbia University Press, 1999).

3. See, for example, John D. DiIulio, Jr., "In America's Cities: The Lord's Work, the Church, and the 'Civil Society' Sector," *Brookings Review* 15 (1997): 27-31; Laurie Goodstein, "Religious Groups See Larger Role in Welfare," *New York Times*, December 14,

1997; Cathy Lynn Grossman, "Lawyers Not Swayed by 'Charitable Choice,'" *USA Today*, December 8, 1995; and Joe Klein, "Can Faith-Based Groups Save Us?" *Responsive Community* 8 (1998): 25-39. See Bartkowski and Regis, *Charitable Choices* for reviews.

4. Bartkowski and Regis, *Charitable Choices*.

5. Bartkowski and Regis, *Charitable Choices*.

6. Benjamin Barber, "Clansmen, Consumers, and Citizens: Three Takes on Civil Society," in *Civil Society, Democracy, and Civic Renewal*, ed. Robert K. Fullenwider (Lanham, Md.: Rowman & Littlefield, 1999), 9-29.

7. Barber, "Clansmen, Consumers, and Citizens," 14.

8. Barber, "Clansmen, Consumers, and Citizens," 15.

9. Barber, "Clansmen, Consumers, and Citizens," 23.

10. Hans A. Baer and Merrill Singer, *African American Religion in the Twentieth Century: Varieties of Protest and Accommodation* (Knoxville: University of Tennessee Press, 1992), 155.

11. Eileen W. Lindner, ed., *Yearbook of American and Canadian Churches, 2000: Religious Pluralism in the New Millennium*, 68th ed. (Nashville, Tenn.: Abingdon, 2000).

12. Martin B. Bradley, Norman M. Green, Jr., Dale E. Jones, Mac Lynn, Lou McNeil, *Churches and Church Membership in the United States, 1990* (Atlanta: Glenmary Research Center, 1992).

13. Lindner, *Yearbook of American and Canadian Churches*.

14. Bradley et al., *Churches and Church Membership*.

15. Cf. Norman K. Denzin, *The Alcoholic Self* (Newbury Park, Calif.: Sage, 1987); and *The Alcoholic Society: Addiction and Recovery of the Self* (Piscataway, N.J.: Transaction, 1993).

16. Bartkowski and Regis, "Religious Organizations"; and Bartkowski and Regis, *Charitable Choices*.

17. Bartkowski and Regis, *Charitable Choices*.

18. Cf. John P. Bartkowski, *Remaking the Godly Marriage: Gender Negotiation in Evangelical Families* (New Brunswick, N.J.: Rutgers University Press, 2001); John P. Bartkowski, Christopher G. Ellison, and W. Bradford Wilcox, "Charting the Paradoxes of Evangelical Family Life: Gender and Parenting in Conservative Protestant Households," *Family Ministry* 14 (2000): 9-21; and Penny Edgell Becker, "What Is Right? What Is Caring? Moral Logics in Local Religious Life," in *Contemporary American Religion: An Ethnographic Reader*, eds. Penny Edgell Becker and Nancy L. Eiesland (Walnut Creek, Calif.: AltaMira Press, 1997), 121-45.

19. See also Bartkowski and Regis, *Charitable Choices*.

20. Barber, "Clansmen, Consumers, and Citizens."

Chapter 8

Speech, Not Religion: The Dilemma of Religious Conservatives in the Public Square

Steven P. Brown

Of the various interest groups that have been organized within the last quarter-century, few have shared the meteoric political ascension of the New Christian Right. Coming to political prominence only in the mid-1970s, the efforts of Christian conservatives on such controversial issues as abortion, school prayer, and "family values" have propelled this movement to the forefront of contemporary American politics. Through their outspoken but organized activism, the broad mosaic of individuals and organizations that comprise the New Christian Right has sought to influence electoral campaigns from the local school board to the White House.[1]

While maintaining an emphasis on electoral races, supporters of the New Christian Right have increasingly looked to other avenues of political influence, including the judiciary. Several New Christian Right organizations have come into existence with the intention of using the courts as the next battleground of conservative Christian activism. For these groups, the law represents an opportunity to establish their vision for America without screening candidates, canvassing for votes, or lobbying Capitol Hill. With a cadre of well-trained lawyers, the experience of liberal public interest organizations before them, and a unique emphasis on the Free Speech Clause in religious liberty cases, New Christian Right public interest law firms are leaving their imprint upon the American legal landscape.

New Christian Right Legal Organizations and Strategies

The New Christian Right's recent embrace of the judiciary is consistent with the already well-documented relationship between interest groups and the courts.[2] Given the broad spectrum of issues pursued by New Christian Right organizations within the electoral arena, it is not surprising to learn that the movement's judicial branch efforts reflect a similarly diverse field of interests encompassing such issues as parental rights, abortion clinic protesting, opposition to the gay rights agenda, and traditional family values. The greatest proportion of New Christian Right activity in the courts, however, is devoted to questions of religious liberty.

Of the organizations that pursue the New Christian Right agenda in the judicial branch, the most active in religious liberty litigation are the Alliance Defense Fund, the American Center for Law and Justice, the Christian Legal Society's Center for Law and Religious Freedom, Liberty Counsel, and the Rutherford Institute. As table 8.1 illustrates, these groups differ considerably in terms of size, financial and personnel resources, and willingness to cooperate with other New Christian Right legal organizations. While at the most basic level these groups are one in purpose, enlisted together in the battle to protect religious liberty against the forces of secular humanism, there is, nevertheless, considerable competition for funding, cases, and public recognition.[3]

In the courtroom, New Christian Right public interest law firms have generally patterned their litigation strategies after those utilized by the American Civil Liberties Union and other organizations that have looked to the courts to bring about social change.[4] These strategies include the submission of third-party *amicus curiae* briefs as well as more-direct participation as counsel or financier of sponsored cases.[5] Of equally strategic importance is the role that some public interest law firms play as "legal overseers" in providing outside funding and legal expertise to the lawyers and organizations actually named in the briefs. In most cases, the amount of external financial or technical assistance (as well as the degree to which the legal overseer influences the course of the litigation) is virtually unknown except to the parties directly involved.[6]

Interest groups from across the political spectrum that maintain a presence in the courts have adopted these litigation tools as part of a larger campaign to create a legal environment favorable to their interests. The New Christian Right is no exception. However, in addition to the aforementioned techniques, New Christian Right attorneys have perfected a litigation strategy of their own—one which forges a unique jurisprudential link between the Free Speech Clause and religion.

More than any other constitutional principle, the Free Speech Clause of the First Amendment has come to characterize the religious liberty efforts of New Christian Right public interest law firms. Admittedly, the notion that, in certain matters of faith, the Free Exercise and Establishment clauses of the Constitution would take a back seat to the Free Speech Clause seems an especially odd strategy for religious conservatives to embrace. Yet, it is just this approach which, after years of frustrating losses in the courts, has provided the New Christian Right with a

Table 8.1 New Christian Right Legal Organizations

Firm, Year Founded, and Key Personnel	1997 Budget	Staff Attorneys	Characteristics of Group
Alliance Defense Fund Scottsdale, AZ (1994) President: Alan Sears	$3 million	No staff attorneys since it does not actually litigate cases	ADF provides funding for the legal defense of religious liberty and other is-sues. It also helps coordinate the liti-gation efforts of other New Christian Right firms.
American Center for Law and Justice Virginia Beach, VA (1990) CEO and Chief Counsel: Jay Sekulow	$12 million	30 staff attorneys and 500 affiliated volunteer lawyers	Founded by Pat Robertson, the ACLJ benefits from exten-sive media exposure, a huge budget, and Sekulow, a frequent advocate before the Supreme Court.
Center for Law and Religious Freedom Annandale, VA (1975) Director: Carl H. Esbeck	$1.3 million	3 staff attorneys and 4,500 members of CLS	Affiliated with the Christian Legal Society, the Center is known for its ability to work with its ideo-logical opponents as well as litigate.
Liberty Counsel Orlando, FL (1990) President: Matthew Staver	$1 million	7 staff attorneys	Typical of many small firms engaged in public interest law, Liberty Counsel maintains a strong regional presence but is also increasing its efforts nationally.
Rutherford Institute Charlottesville, VA (1982) President: John Whitehead	$4 million	15 staff attorneys and 2,300 affiliated volunteer lawyers	Rutherford pursues claims of religious liberty infringement worldwide. It stead-fastly refuses allian-ces with other New Christian Right legal groups.

number of significant legal victories in both the Supreme Court and lower federal courts. Couching religious liberty interests in free-speech language is obviously not always possible. But where New Christian Right lawyers have been able to argue religion claims within the context of the Free Speech Clause, they have done so with repeated success.

The Free Speech-Religion Nexus in the Supreme Court

From at least one perspective, the emergence of this approach to religious liberty litigation should have come as no surprise. Writing for the majority in *Capitol Square Review and Advisory Board v. Pinette* in 1995, Justice Antonin Scalia proclaimed:

> Our precedent establishes that private religious speech, far from being a First Amendment orphan, is as fully protected under the Free Speech Clause as secular private expression. Indeed, in Anglo-American history, at least, government suppression of speech has so commonly been directed precisely at religious speech that a free-speech clause without religion would be *Hamlet* without the prince.[7]

Although Justice Scalia asserts an almost banal judicial recognition of religious expression as speech protected by the First Amendment, that legal perspective is of relatively recent origin.

One of the most significant religion cases of the early 1980s, *Widmar v. Vincent* (1981), saw a near-unanimous Supreme Court formally extend Free Speech Clause protection to religious expression. In its 8-1 decision, the Supreme Court ruled that public universities could not deny the use of their facilities to student religious clubs if such facilities were made available to other student organizations of a secular nature. Brought by the Christian Legal Society, this case focused on the University of Missouri at Kansas City's refusal to allow an evangelical Christian student group to meet in buildings owned by the university.[8] Justice Powell's opinion for the majority in *Widmar* set forth the court's hierarchy of rights where religion, speech, and the state intersect:

> On one hand, respondents' [members of the Christian student group] First Amendment rights are entitled to special constitutional solicitude. Our cases have required the most exacting scrutiny in cases in which a State undertakes to regulate speech on the basis of its content. . . . On the other hand, the state interest asserted here—in achieving greater separation of church and State than is already ensured under the Establishment Clause of the Federal Constitution—is limited by the Free Exercise Clause and in this case by the Free Speech Clause as well. In this constitutional context, we are unable to recognize the State's

interest as sufficiently "compelling" to justify content-based discrimination against respondents' religious speech.[9]

The reordering of rights in the court's opinion is critical because, while acknowledging the university's Establishment Clause fears in this case, it held that such concerns were essentially "trumped" by the students' free speech right to use university facilities to express themselves religiously. In doing so, the court deftly, and significantly, placed religious expression clearly under the guardianship of the Free Speech Clause. A position it reiterated in several subsequent cases in which New Christian Right public interest law firms figured prominently, including *Westside Community Schools v. Mergens* (1990), *Lamb's Chapel v. Center Moriches Union Free School District* (1993), and *Rosenberger v. Rector and Visitors of the University of Virginia* (1995).[10]

Yet, aside from this legal bond that joins the Free Speech Clause and issues of religious liberty, there are other important spiritual and strategic reasons that guide New Christian Right public interest law firms in their appeal to free speech. Among those that litigate the New Christian Right agenda, for example, there is a shared sense that religion in general has been marginalized by secular forces.[11] They lament the political and legal culture in America that, in Harvard professor Stephen Carter's words, "presses the religiously faithful to be other than themselves, to act publicly, and sometimes privately as well, as though their faith does not matter to them."[12] Thus, in turning to the judiciary to make the public square available to religious speech, New Christian Right lawyers are attempting to do more than simply "level the playing field" between religious and secular speech. The larger goal is to ensure that religious expression is allowed to compete with other types of speech in the marketplace of ideas and, in successfully doing so, reestablish the larger societal relevance of religion that New Christian Right supporters believe existed in an earlier era.[13]

This is not to say, as many critics of the New Christian Right contend, that the ultimate public policy aim of these groups is to obliterate the wall between church and state en route to christianizing America.[14] The groups in this study have also litigated religious liberty cases and performed other legal services for non-Christians. As a general rule, New Christian Right public interest law firms adhere to the principle that the loss of religious expression by any one group necessarily contracts the religious rights of all. Yet, the majority of cases these firms pursue are, in fact, brought by Christians who claim that their religious expression has been chilled, if not censored altogether, because it was deemed inappropriate.

This has led New Christian Right public interest law firms to make an ironic free speech link between the religious expression of the 1990s and the sexually explicit materials of the 1960s.[15] They again take their cue from Justice Scalia who dissented from the Supreme Court's decision in *Lee v. Weisman* in 1992. Denouncing the court's majority opinion which found school-sponsored invocations at public school graduation ceremonies unconstitutional, Scalia declared, "Church and state would not be such a difficult subject if religion were, as the Court apparently thinks it to be, some purely personal avocation that can be indulged entirely in secret, like pornography, in the privacy of one's room."[16]

In his later opinion for the majority in *Capitol Square Review and Advisory Board v. Pinette* (1995), Scalia again addresses the prospect of driving religious expression "underground." Referring to the dissenting opinions of Justices Stevens, Souter, and O'Connor, Scalia wrote, "[Their view] exiles private religious speech to a realm of less-protected expression heretofore inhabited only by sexually explicit displays and commercial speech. . . . It will be a sad day when this Court casts piety in with pornography, and finds the First Amendment more hospitable to private expletives than to private prayers."[17]

While the "religion as porn" analogy plays well to sympathizers as a caustic indictment against the court's treatment of religion, it also serves as a model legal strategy guiding New Christian Right efforts in the courts. Just as free speech advocates during the 1960s and 1970s maintained that the First Amendment was broad enough to protect sexually explicit materials, New Christian Right attorneys must also argue for an expansive reading of the Free Speech Clause in order to find relief for religious liberty claims. In doing so, however, these lawyers recognize that swelling the Free Speech Clause to accommodate religion extends the protection of that clause to other viewpoints as well.

In that sense, the Free Speech Clause as promoted by New Christian Right lawyers becomes a strange mixture of legal pragmatism and faith. On the one hand, the free speech approach to religious liberty has been upheld by the Supreme Court as a valid legal precedent. On the other, the judicial recognition of this strategy necessarily protects the views of non-Christian groups, other organizations nonreligious in nature, and some that are decidedly in opposition to the principles for which New Christian Right lawyers are fighting.

Yet, the success of appealing to the Free Speech Clause is undeniable. During the last two decades, New Christian Right public interest law firms participated as counsel or amici in some thirty religious liberty cases decided by the Supreme Court. The outcomes of these cases reflect the strategic value of arguing religion as speech. As tables 8.2 and 8.3 illustrate, in the religion cases in which they participated, the parties that New Christian Right law firms served as counsel, supported with amicus briefs, or helped to finance were successful just sixteen times (or 53 percent). Nearly three-fourths of these were grounded in the Free Exercise and Establishment clauses of the First Amendment, with largely mixed results for the New Christian Right. The fact that these clauses yielded little consistent success even with the changing composition of the federal bench under the Reagan and George H. W. Bush administrations was a source of considerable frustration for New Christian Right attorneys. As Mathew Staver of Liberty Counsel described it, "We were beating our heads against the wall by arguing most of these cases as 'establishment clause' and 'free exercise.'"[18] In the late 1980s, however, New Christian Right lawyers came to embrace a broad interpretation of the Free Speech Clause in their religious liberty efforts and saw their legal fortunes change.

Table 8.2 Supreme Court Decisions Involving New Christian Right Public Interest Law Firms

Supreme Court Terms and New Christian Right (NCR) Firms	Religion Cases Decided	Type of NCR Participation		
	Number	Amicus	Counsel	Financier
1980-89 Terms				
Number of Supreme Court cases	37			
Christian Legal Society	17 (45%)	14	3	
Rutherford Institute	16 (43%)	15	1	
Other (Sekulow with ACLJ)	1 (2%)		1	
Total Cases with NCR Participation	**21 (57%)**	**20**	**5**	
1990-98 Terms				
Number of Supreme Court cases	9			
Christian Legal Society	9 (100%)	9		
Rutherford Institute	5 (55%)	5		
Liberty Counsel	3 (33%)	3		
ACLJ	7 (77%)	5	2	
Alliance Defense Fund	3 (33%)			3
Total Cases with NCR Participation	**9 (100%)**	**9**	**2**	**3**

Table 8.3 Supreme Court's Decision and Position Supported by New Christian Right (NCR)

Supreme Court Terms	Establishment Clause Arguments of NCR	Free Exercise Arguments of NCR	Free Speech/Equal Access Arguments of NCR	Other	Totals
1980–89 Terms					
Recognized by Court	3	5	2	0	10
Rejected by Court	2	6	0	3	11
Total Cases	5	11	2	3	21
1990–98 Terms					
Recognized by Court	3	1	2	0	6
Rejected by Court	3	0	0	0	3
Total Cases	6	1	2	0	9

Free Speech, Religion, and the Lower Federal Courts

The most consistently successful line of argumentation for the New Christian Right in Supreme Court religion cases has been the free speech approach. Legal disputes which formerly raised questions of religious exercise are transformed through this process into questions of speech—which happens to be religious. When religious liberty claims are cloaked in the Free Speech Clause, they are undefeated at the Supreme Court level (see table 8.3). Those cases that primarily relied upon the Constitution's religion clauses offered no similarly consistent pattern of success for the New Christian Right.

Thus, compared with the mixed results of Establishment Clause and Free Exercise Clause arguments in other Supreme Court cases, the strength of the free speech strategy to the New Christian Right appears obvious. Yet, despite its undefeated record before the Supreme Court, the religion-as-free-speech argument is not without its weaknesses. While the free speech approach to religious liberty remains a viable legal strategy, lower federal court religion cases in which the New Christian Right has been involved reveal the ultimate limitations of this strategy.

Because the Supreme Court takes such few cases each term, organizations that are serious about creating legal change must be prepared to participate in other judicial venues. Accordingly, New Christian Right law firms have actively pursued religious liberty claims in both the U.S. Courts of Appeals and U.S. District Courts. These lower federal courts rule with a remarkable degree of finality. While recourse to the Supreme Court is always possible, most decisions rendered by the lower federal courts are not appealed, are denied review by the Supreme Court, or are upheld by the justices.[19]

The free speech strategy utilized by the New Christian Right with success in the Supreme Court has also been the catalyst for the majority of New Christian Right victories in the lower federal courts. However, it is in the lower courts that the limitations of the free speech approach to religious liberty become apparent, as does the conclusion that the Free Speech Clause can never be an effective long-term ally of the New Christian Right.

Since 1980, the New Christian Right has participated in sixty-nine religion cases in the lower federal courts, forty of which saw religion-as-free-speech arguments. Of these, the party supported by New Christian Right law firms in their role as counsel, amicus, or financier prevailed twenty-six times (65 percent). While the free speech strategy has been successful in the lower federal courts (albeit to a lesser degree than in the Supreme Court), the inherent boundaries to this argument also become evident. Constitutional scholar Mark Tushnet once claimed that with the free speech emphasis in the Supreme Court's 1981 *Widmar v. Vincent* decision, "religion entered the Court's analysis by the back door."[20] He might have phrased it "the school's back door." Of the forty lower federal court religion cases categorized as free speech cases, 80 percent (thirty-two) take place in schools from the elementary level through the university. Although there have been many changes in the way the courts view religious expression since *Widmar*, the educational setting central to that case still predominates in its legal progeny.

In the lower courts, access to school facilities, recognition of religious school clubs, and school policies on the distribution of religious literature are the most consistently litigated issues of New Christian Right public interest law firms. Outside of the classroom, the Free Speech Clause has been invoked in just a handful of disparate cases ranging from license plate lettering to noise and loitering ordinances that restrict speech. The limitations of the free speech strategy thus become increasingly apparent in the lower federal courts. New Christian Right lawyers have succeeded in building upon *Widmar's* foundation and have used that case to free some religious expression from its traditional Establishment Clause or Free Exercise Clause bonds. Yet, as demonstrated by their efforts in the lower federal judiciary, New Christian Right attorneys are themselves constrained in how far they can stretch the free speech rationale. Their general inability to successfully transplant the free speech argument into other areas neutralizes the overall effect of this strategy. In other words, it is unlikely that the free speech-based religious liberty victories in the *schools* will precipitate the widespread changes in *society* sought by the New Christian Right.

There are other concerns as well. Not every religion case can or should be argued using the Free Speech Clause. Inapplicable because of the legal facts in some cases, critics have suggested that it may also be inappropriate from both a constitutional and spiritual standpoint. In his solo dissenting opinion in *Widmar v. Vincent*, Justice Byron White questioned the constitutional relevancy of the religion clauses under the free speech model:

> A large part of respondent's argument, accepted by the court below and accepted by the majority, is founded on the proposition that because religious worship uses speech, it is protected by the Free Speech Clause of the First Amendment. Not only is it protected, they argue, but religious worship qua speech is not different from any other variety of protected speech as a matter of constitutional principle. I believe that this proposition is plainly wrong. Were it right, the Religion Clauses would be emptied of any independent meaning in circumstances in which religious practice took the form of speech.[21]

Finally, there is considerable irony to the religion-as-speech argument. Religious conservatives have long voiced their opposition to the perceived subordination of the religion clauses to other constitutional rights enunciated by the federal courts.[22] Yet, the free speech arguments made by New Christian Right lawyers in religious liberty cases do essentially the same thing. They rely upon an expanded interpretation of the Free Speech Clause to provide what, as they claim, the enervated Free Exercise and Establishment Clauses cannot. The irony of this practice is twofold: On the one hand, it reinforces the perception that the religion clauses contain little more than second-rate rights—the very attitude that some New Christian Right supporters hold responsible for judicial rulings against religion.[23]

On the other, this preferred free-speech litigating strategy of New Christian Right public interest law firms is inherently inconsistent with their professed desire to return to an earlier constitutional era when the Free Exercise and Establishment clauses meant something.[24]

New Christian Right lawyers maintain that the judicial application of the Free Speech Clause elevates this aspect of religious liberty to a protected level enjoyed by other types of speech. Others dispute these claims, contending that, in appealing to the secular to protect the sacred, religious expression is degraded from a position of singular importance to just another form of speech. As one critic of the religion-as-free-speech argument has written: "If religion is understood as just a benign point of view that some people happen to have, then by implication religion is harmless, a meaningless difference. It becomes simply a brand name, or a political party, or a Hallmark card sentiment. . . . Religion is important enough to be treated differently."[25]

Conclusion

The importance of the Free Speech Clause strategy to New Christian Right public interest law firms cannot be overstated. It has brought new life to their litigation efforts, rewarded them with major victories in the federal judiciary, and brought about a genuine transformation in how religion and speech are perceived in the courts. In that sense, New Christian Right lawyers seem to agree with the above declaration that religion is "important enough to be treated differently." So much so, in fact, that they have turned from traditional methods of political activism to the courts, adopted the litigating strategies of their ideological rivals, and sought religious liberty's refuge not in the religion clauses but the Free Speech Clause—the long-term consequences of which remain to be seen.

Notes

1. Steve Bruce, "The Inevitable Failure of the New Christian Right," in *The Rapture of Politics*, ed. Steve Bruce, Peter Kivisto, and William H. Swatos, Jr. (New Brunswick, N.J.: Transaction, 1995), 7-20; James L. Guth, John C. Green, Lyman A. Kellstedt, and Corwin E. Smidt, "Onward Christian Soldiers: Religious Activist Groups in American Politics," in *Interest Group Politics*, ed. Allan J. Ciglar and Burdett A. Loomis (Washington, D.C.: Congressional Quarterly Press, 1996), 55-76; and Mark J. Rozell and Clyde Wilcox, eds., *God at the Grassroots, 1996: The Christian Right in the 1996 Elections* (Lanham, Md.: Rowman & Littlefield, 1997).

2. Lee Epstein, *Conservatives in Court* (Knoxville: University of Tennessee Press, 1985); Richard Kluger, *Simple Justice: The History of* Brown v. Board of Education *and Black America's Struggle for Equality* (New York: Alfred A. Knopf, 1976); Karen O'Connor, *Women's Organizations, Use of the Courts* (Lexington, Mass.: Lexington Books, 1980); Frank J. Sorauf, *The Wall of Separation: Constitutional Politics of Church and State*

(Princeton, N.J.: Princeton University Press, 1976); Mark V. Tushnet, *The NAACP's Legal Struggle against Segregated Education, 1925-1950* (Chapel Hill: University of North Carolina Press, 1987); and Clement E. Vose, *Caucasians Only* (Berkeley: University of California Press, 1959).

3. Mark Curriden, "Defenders of the Faith," *ABA Journal* (December 1994): 86-89; and John W. Moore, "The Lord's Litigators," *National Journal* 2 (July 1994): 1560.

4. Keith Fournier, *A House United? Evangelicals and Catholics Together* (Colorado Springs, Colo.: NavPress, 1994).

5. Gregory A. Caldeira and John R. Wright, "Organized Interests and Agenda Setting in the Supreme Court," *American Political Science Review* 82 (1988): 1109-27; Lee Epstein, "Interest Group Litigation during the Rehnquist Era," *Journal of Law and Politics* 9 (Summer 1993): 639-717; Donald R. Songer and Reginald S. Sheehan, "Interest Group Success in the Courts: Amicus Participation in the Supreme Court," *Political Research Quarterly* 46 (1993): 339-54; and Stephen L. Wasby, *Race Relations Litigation in an Age of Complexity* (Charlottesville: University Press of Virginia, 1995).

6. Lee Epstein, "Courts and Interest Groups," in *The American Courts: A Critical Assessment*, ed. John B. Gates and Charles A. Johnson (Washington, D.C.: Congressional Quarterly Press, 1991), 339.

7. 515 U.S. 753, 760 (1995); citations omitted.

8. 454 U.S. 263 (1981).

9. 454 U.S. 263, 277.

10. By an 8-1 margin, the Supreme Court in *Mergens*, 496 U.S. 226 (1990), extended the rationale of *Widmar* to religious expression in high schools. In *Lamb's Chapel*, 508 U.S. 384 (1993), a unanimous court held that the Free Speech Clause protected the right of a religious organization to use school facilities (provided such facilities were made available to other secular groups). The 5-4 vote in *Rosenberger*, 515 U.S. 819 (1995), was not a reflection of the constitutional difficulty of protecting religious expression with the Free Speech Clause as much as supporting that speech with taxpayer money.

11. Fournier, *A House United?* and John W. Whitehead, *Religious Apartheid: The Separation of Religion from American Public Life* (Chicago: Moody Press, 1994).

12. Stephen L. Carter, *The Culture of Disbelief* (New York: Basic Books, 1993), 3.

13. Pat Robertson, "Religion in the Classroom," *William and Mary Bill of Rights Journal* 4 (Winter 1995): 595-606.

14. Sara Diamond, "Watch on the Right," *Humanist* 53 (May/June 1994): 35-37.

15. David Melton, "The Free Exorcise of Religion," speech delivered to Students for Individual Liberty and the Liberty Coalition, University of Virginia, January 29, 1997.

16. 505 U.S. 577, 645 (Scalia, J., dissenting).

17. 515 U.S. 753, 767 (1995).

18. Curriden, "Defenders of the Faith," 88.

19. Henry J. Abraham, *The Judicial Process*, 7th ed. (New York: Oxford University Press, 1997), 157; and Donald R. Songer, "The Circuit Courts of Appeals," in *The American Courts*, 35-59.

20. Mark V. Tushnet, "Constitution of Religion," *Review of Politics* 50 (Fall 1988): 652.

21. 454 U.S. 263, 284 (White, J., dissenting).

22. David Barton, *Original Intent: The Courts, the Constitution, and Religion* (Aledo, Texas: Wallbuilder Press, 1996); Mark A. Beliles and Stephen K. McDowell, *America's Providential History* (Charlottesville, Va.: Providence Foundation, 1994); and John W. Whitehead, *The Stealing of America* (Westchester, Ill.: Crossway Books, 1982).

23. Barton, *Original Intent*.

24. Robertson, "Religion in the Classroom."
25. Winnifred Fallers Sullivan, "The Difference Religion Makes: Reflections on Rosenberger," *Christian Century* 13 (March 1996): 292-95.

Chapter 9

Faith, Tolerance, and Civil Society

Beverly Gaddy

[After the religious wars in seventeenth-century Europe,] tolerance was necessary to civil peace, and religion was the chief threat to tolerance. In this account, tolerance is a secular achievement won at great cost in a battle against religion. . . . But a number of funny things have happened on the way to the end of the twentieth century. For one, secular tolerance has become profoundly intolerant. For another, there is widespread agreement today, also among secular liberals, that secular liberalism cannot provide a convincing philosophical defense of tolerance that was once the great achievement of secular liberalism. The truth about tolerance is that tolerance requires truth. But . . . modernity has ineluctably corroded intellectual confidence in the possibility of truth.

—Richard John Neuhaus

Two assumptions must obtain to make the marriage of truth and tolerance work. First, it must be assumed that truth exists and that it is worth preserving and passing on to future generations. And second, tolerance needs to be understood not as an end but as a means, a crucial ingredient in the preservation and cultivation of truth. Under such assumptions tolerance is not something we celebrate but something we acknowledge as a necessity in a fallen world. What we celebrate, instead, is the truth. It is truth we honor, it is truth we cherish, and it is truth on which we stake our lives. . . . [But] modernity has managed to reverse the equation entirely, elevating tolerance to a virtue and relativizing truth in total, affirming the latter only when it promotes the goal of tolerance.

—S. D. Gaede

A basic tenet of democracy is that all citizens are entitled to certain basic civil liberties, including a right to a voice in the public square. But if this liberty is to be guaranteed to all, citizens must be willing to respect the right of all others to also express their ideas in public, even in their own communities and regardless of how unpalatable their ideas may appear. This, in essence, is the classic liberal defense of political tolerance. Etymologically, "tolerance" refers to "enduring, or putting up with, items of various kinds."[1] The implication is that the "putting up with" is of something that is disapproved; hence tolerance is "the degree to which we accept things of which we disapprove."[2] Political tolerance can be defined, then, as the willingness of individuals to put up with the public expression of ideas they oppose.[3] The classical liberal defense for enduring the expression of ideas one abhors is that open discourse, free expression, and rational debate of ideas are necessary for a society to progress toward the "truth."

But what if a category of people is unwilling to tolerate the public expression of ideas they find especially offensive or perceive as harmful to their values and community? What if they are unwilling to extend civil liberties to members of certain groups because of their ideas or behaviors? Then other citizens might understandably be less willing to extend the same civil liberties to these intolerant citizens.[4] This is a dilemma people of faith face in the public square—particularly doctrinally conservative Christians. Widely perceived as bigoted, dogmatic, hate-filled, quick to judge, and intolerant, many believe religious conservatives are less deserving of the protection of their civil liberties than are others.[5]

Moreover, this portrayal of religious conservatives as intolerant bigots has empirical support. Nearly a half-century of research has confirmed that religious belief is indeed associated with intolerance—with, as far as I have been able to find, no evidence to the contrary. In fact few, even among the religiously committed themselves, have challenged this linkage between religion and intolerance, perhaps because many view tolerance as resting upon assumptions opposed to orthodox belief.[6] The classical, liberal argument for tolerance—that in a community where diverse views are freely expressed and debated, "truth" will ultimately prevail—may hold less value for believers who hold to the depravity of man and the imperfection of man's ideas and believe that truth has already been revealed by God through scripture and the Incarnation. The ideal of tolerance, some argue, assumes the acceptance of relativism and individualism—a position the orthodox view as incompatible with religious commitment.[7]

Is this portrayal of the religiously orthodox and committed believers as intolerant accurate? Actually there has been little comprehensive empirical examination of the relationship of religion to tolerance, and almost none using content-controlled tolerance measures (an approach developed by Sullivan, Piereson, and Marcus in 1982). Improved measurement approaches for both religion and political tolerance developed over the past several years permit the researcher to measure these constructs more accurately than they were measured in the earlier studies that found that believers are intolerant.[8]

There has also not been, in my estimation, satisfactory theory developed as to *why* the religiously committed should be more intolerant than other citizens. Some of the doctrinal explanations offered for why religious belief predisposes citizens to be intolerant have not been empirically demonstrated. *Is* a belief in Biblical inerrancy truly associated with dogmatism? *Is* anti-intellectualism more predominant among religiously committed evangelicals than it is among the less committed or seculars?[9] Furthermore, how could religious belief promote intolerance when many Christian believers today—even those within evangelical denominations—remain largely ignorant of orthodox beliefs and the Bible?[10]

Even for that minority who are knowledgeable of scripture and doctrine, there is not a dominant or consistent message regarding political tolerance within the evangelical community as there is regarding other political issues. Rather, there are mixed messages and orientations within evangelicalism, some of which may encourage tolerance and others that may lead to intolerance.[11] Religious beliefs appear to affect political attitudes mainly when there are clear messages regarding how the religiously committed should think regarding the issues.[12]

And as for the religiously committed, we can no longer assume, even for those who attend evangelical churches, that their beliefs are orthodox. American religiosity today is often thought of as "spirituality" rather than "religion"—an attitude of constant "seeking" rather than acceptance of historic doctrines and creeds of the faith, or a chaotic mixture of assorted bits and pieces of religions and belief systems to suit individual tastes, even self-defined beliefs—a far cry from the orthodoxy G. K. Chesterton so eloquently defended.[13]

For these and other reasons, we should be skeptical about the claims that the religiously committed have a greater tendency toward intolerance than do nonbelievers. The purpose of the analyses presented here is to examine the relationship between religion and political tolerance using improved measurements of political tolerance and religion. Three linkages (or the absence of linkages) will be demonstrated: (1) between political tolerance and certain social, political, and psychological predispositions, (2) between these predispositions and religion, and (3) between religion and tolerance. My expectation is not only that religion will not be associated with intolerance, but that the predispositions that are sources of political tolerance are not related to religious belief or to orthodoxy. The hypotheses are:

I: *Religion is related to political tolerance.* Religion is measured by religious tradition (evangelical affiliation to measure orthodoxy) and commitment.

II :   Religion is related to political tolerance partly because *religiously committed and orthodox believers differ from the religiously less-committed and seculars in their social, political, and psychological characteristics.* The focus will be on those predispositions that earlier political tolerance studies have found relevant to tolerance. These include social or demographic characteristics (age, rural residence, social class, education, sex, income, and Southern residence), political characteristics (ideology, level of political engagement, and support for democratic principles), and psychological characteristics (threat perceptions, dogmatism, self-esteem, and traditionalism).

III: *Those characteristics that are related to religion are also related to political tolerance.*

Data for the analyses come from two surveys of the same respondents, taken a couple of months apart in 1987 and merged into one data set. The religion and demographic variables are from the 1987 General Social Survey (GSS). The source for the tolerance variables is the "Freedom and Tolerance in the United States" study (F&T), conducted by James Gibson. This re-survey of 1,267 of the respondents who had participated in the GSS study two months earlier is a rich source of variables measuring political tolerance, measured with both least-liked and Stouffer-type measures, and other related attitudes.

Linking Religious Belief to Intolerance

Of the many studies of political tolerance that have been published, few actually include religious variables, but those that do have generally demonstrated an association between religion and intolerance. The first major work on political tolerance in the United States—Stouffer's *Communism, Conformity, and Civil Liberties*—was also the first to demonstrate this link empirically.[14] Stouffer, whose tolerance measures have served as the model for the GSS tolerance indicators for the past quarter-century, examined attitudes of tolerance for three groups unpopular in the 1950s: communists, socialists, and atheists. He not only found that church attendance was linked with greater intolerance toward each of these groups but also concluded that church attendance is associated with greater intolerance overall.[15]

Among those who have repeated Stouffer's study over the past few decades, the work by Nunn, Crockett, and Williams is particularly significant.[16] Replicating Stouffer's survey to see if tolerance levels had changed in the intervening two decades, Nunn and colleagues found that Americans had indeed become more tolerant by 1973. However, the religiously committed within every faith tradition were still less tolerant than the less-committed and seculars, both in the mass and in the elite samples.[17] They also found that the more frequently believers attended church, the less tolerant they were.

A major development in the study of political tolerance came in 1982 with the development of the content-controlled or "least-liked" measurement approach by Sullivan, Piereson, and Marcus. They claimed that the Stouffer-type measures were biased against people who were not leftist in their ideology. To control for this, they had respondents self-identify their disliked groups. They then asked the respondents if members of the groups they identified should be permitted to engage in various public activities (serve as president, teach in public schools, make a speech, hold a public rally) or whether the government should be allowed to outlaw the group or tap their phones. Using this measurement approach, they found that Americans in the 1980s were just as intolerant as were Americans in the 1950s, except that their targets of intolerance had become more diverse and dispersed: liberals tended to be less tolerant of groups on the far right, conservatives less tolerant of groups on the far left—a "pluralistic intolerance." Even so, they still found a linkage between intolerance and religion, although only for Baptists;[18] they found no difference in tolerance levels with identifiers of other Protestant denominations, Catholics, or Jews.

While much of the other major empirical work on political tolerance has ignored religion, there have been a few articles that have focused specifically on the relationship between religion and tolerance. The problem is that these have generally relied upon GSS for their data; thus the biases inherent in the Stouffer-type measures have tainted their conclusions.

Smidt and Penning, for example, using GSS data (from 1974, 1977, and 1980) focused on differing tolerance levels among religiously committed conservatives and liberals, and nonreligious conservatives and liberals.[19] While they found that nonreligious liberals were consistently most tolerant, tolerance levels for the other groups varied depending on the groups asked by GSS that year.[20] They observed a growing gap between the religious and secular in their tolerance levels, due primarily to the growing level of tolerance of the nonreligious. They also noted that religious commitment was more strongly associated with intolerance when the issue was perceived as having a moral aspect, such as abortion. With less of a tie to moral values, the relationship between religion and tolerance was weaker.[21]

Beatty and Walter, also employing GSS data (the 1976, 1977, and 1980 surveys) to examine the relationship of denominational affiliation and church attendance on tolerance, found fundamentalist and Pentecostal denominations to be the least tolerant, and liberal denominations most tolerant. They also noted that intolerance increased as church attendance increased.[22]

Wilcox and Jelen, likewise relying on GSS, searched for doctrinal explanations for the greater intolerance of evangelicals.[23] The primary culprit, they argued, is Biblical inerrancy: those who believe that truth has been revealed in scripture may be less willing to tolerate open and free discussions of ideas they view as inconsistent with God's revealed Word. They also suggested that fundamentalists and Pentecostals may be less tolerant than other evangelicals due to their anti-intellectualism and separatist tendencies (particularly fundamentalists).[24] In short, they concluded that evangelicals, and especially fundamentalists and Pentecostals, are intolerant because their doctrines encourage dogmatism and narrow-mindedness. They did not, however, actually demonstrate a greater tendency toward dogmatism and anti-intellectualism among these religious groups.

The one study I found that employed content-controlled tolerance measures was a survey of religious activists only, so it was unable to compare the religiously committed with other citizens. Green, Guth, Kellstedt, and Smidt found that intolerance could be explained by certain doctrinal beliefs held by fundamentalists: Biblical literalism, social separation, premillennialism (and other doctrines associated with this eschatological view), and pessimism about the world.[25] Fundamentalists are also more likely to feel threatened by the dominant political culture, which could also serve to increase intolerance.[26] However other religious measures commonly associated with tolerance—religious tradition, orthodoxy, religious salience, and religious involvement—were not related to tolerance once controls were added. The authors suggested that nonfundamentalist believers might be more tolerant than fundamentalists because they have a reduced sense of threat, fewer concerns about traditional morality, higher levels of education, and greater engagement in politics.[27]

Thus, what little empirical research there is that focuses on religion and tolerance has concluded that religious commitment, or commitment to specific orthodox or fundamentalist denominations or doctrines, does lead to greater intolerance. My investigation of this topic was prompted largely because the explanations for this linkage were not consistent with recent literature on the sources of intolerance, because the measurement approaches employed by these studies have since been improved upon, and also because of the changing nature of the religiously committed and religious beliefs.

Attitude Accessibility and Tolerance Judgments

Religious belief can be a potent force for political attitudes and behaviors. It is a significant influence on political participation, partisan identification, vote choice, and attitudes on social and moral issues, among other things.[28]

Since Americans are among the most religious people in the world,[29] the relationship between religious belief and political behavior is particularly significant in the United States. Nevertheless, there are other political attitudes— opinions on foreign policy and domestic spending, for example—that are not significantly affected by religious belief.[30] Linkages between religion and political variables have been found only when there is an explicit application of religious belief to secular issues, as in certain moral or social issues.[31] Also, for many political attitudes and behaviors that show a linkage to religion, the influence of religion on the dependent variable is indirect—through partisanship, for example. There are instances when religion has more of a direct influence, however.

Political tolerance may be among those political attitudes that are not strongly or directly influenced by religious belief. There are several reasons to consider this. One is that scripture does not speak directly on the subject of political tolerance as it does on other issues for which there is a direct relationship between religion and attitude, as, for example, the sanctity of life. Religious leaders—even considering only those within the evangelical tradition—also offer inconsistent messages regarding tolerance. This is because political tolerance is not an essential element of faith, but a democratic ideal. Therefore orthodox believers may differ in their views as to how Christians should respond in situations that may call for tolerance. Given the absence of a consistent message in scripture and from religious leaders, believers are likely to learn tolerance in much the same manner as other American citizens—through the learning, acceptance, and internalization of liberal democratic norms. This is all the more true when we consider that citizens, even those heavily involved in their churches, receive much of their *civic* socialization from families, schools, the media, and other nonreligious sources.[32]

If religion does not influence political tolerance, what does? Earlier research (beginning with Stouffer) suggested that tolerance could be explained primarily by demographic and social characteristics: education, age, residence, ideology, and religious commitment. However, tolerance studies using the content-controlled measures pioneered by Sullivan, Pierson, and Marcus have found that psychological and political attitudes may be more important than social and demographic characteristics in predicting levels of political tolerance.[33] Theories of political information-processing and attitude accessibility could help to explain why political and psychological predispositions are more important than the more stable social and demographic characteristics in explaining how people make political tolerance judgments, and why religious beliefs may not be a significant influence on tolerance.

Political psychologists have demonstrated that individuals exposed to the same information will remember it differently, and those exposed to the same situation will respond differently. This is because individuals vary in their *antecedent considerations*: predispositions, beliefs, attitudes, and information relating to an object—in this case, a tolerance judgment.[34] But when individuals are faced with making a decision (a tolerance judgment), they do not search through their whole store of relevant knowledge, beliefs, attitudes, and impressions. Instead, being "cognitive misers," they rely upon only a few of the most immediately accessible, relevant, and salient ones.[35]

Certain antecedent considerations—*predispositions*—are more centrally located and prior to others and therefore shape other attitudes and information and affect how they are attended to.[36] Marcus and colleagues demonstrated that, in the case of political tolerance, these predispositions include some demographic traits, but mostly psychological characteristics and the internalization of political norms. Religious beliefs, like worldviews, are also predispositions because they are "general and enduring" and because they "hold a more central position than attitudes in individuals' belief systems."[37] Since religious beliefs, like other worldviews, structure or organize other attitudes and information by accommodating only those constructs that are consistent with it, information or attitudes inconsistent with them are rejected, ignored, altered, or adjusted to fit. Thus religion *can* have a significant influence on other antecedent considerations.

In their conceptual framework, Fishbein and Ajzen distinguished between four separate but connected elements within an individual's attitude structure: beliefs, attitudes, intentions, and behaviors. *Beliefs*—an individual's "understanding of himself and his environment"—are foundational predispositions, the "fundamental building blocks" of individuals' belief systems.[38] Religious beliefs, as centrally located beliefs, can be especially influential in "serving as the informational base that ultimately determines . . . attitudes, intentions, and behaviors.[39]

Some beliefs are more salient or prominent than others within an individual's belief hierarchy in regard to a particular object. Also, some beliefs are rather stable, while others vary over time and according to the specifics of a particular situation. Beliefs that are strongly held are likely to be more stable, more influential, and more accessible. Other beliefs may be less strongly held and less stable, altering over time as individuals respond to experiences or are exposed to other beliefs. Religious beliefs may be of either type: for some individuals they may be strongly held and stable, for others less strong and less stable. Like any beliefs, they may even be lost, rejected, or forgotten.[40]

Attitudes are guided by a limited set of salient and accessible beliefs individuals hold about a particular object.[41] Accessibility of attitudes is likewise dependent upon a number of factors: the importance of the attitude to the individual, motivation (goals, needs, values, and affective state), recency of activation, salience, and relation to other accessible constructs.[42] Furthermore, since individuals are generally capable of attending to only five to nine items of information at any one time, only the most readily accessible attitudes will be elicited at the time the tolerance judgment is made.[43] When it comes to accessibility of attitudes for tolerance judgments, Marcus et al. demonstrated that "standing decisions" on such issues as support for democratic values and civil liberties and the general predisposition to tolerate a disliked group are normally more accessible than other beliefs or predispositions.[44] Contemporary information and judgments are also predispositions influential to tolerance judgments.[45] Information can be even more influential than other antecedent considerations (such as religious beliefs) not only because they may be more recent but also because they help provide context.[46]

Thus predispositions relevant to an object influence attitudes and other less-stable antecedent considerations; similarly, attitudes and other antecedent considerations influence *intentions* (the "subjective probability that [an individual] will perform some behavior") and intentions influence *behaviors*.[47] However, not all predispositions that are related to the object are involved—only those few that are most related, salient, and accessible. Therefore, religious beliefs will influence a tolerance decision only if the belief is important to the individual; is interpreted in a way that makes it particularly important to the tolerance judgment; is strongly held, stable, and salient to the object; has been recently and frequently activated; is linked to other constructs related to the decision within the individual's memory; and is more so than other predispositions (including threat perceptions, democratic norms, attitudes toward the disliked group, contextual information) within the individual's conceptual framework.

A goal of religious education is to have believers internalize the teachings of their faith so that these teachings inform their everyday lives. Paul admonished Christians to "not be conformed to this world, but be transformed by the renewing of your mind" (Romans 12:2). However, as religious leaders and scholars have lamented in recent years, most self-identified believers today do not show evidence of "renewed" (Christian) minds and have not demonstrated that they know how to apply their faith consistently to everyday life situations.[48] Rather, especially in situations that are not specifically related to religion or morality, they are likely to think and behave much as nonbelievers. They have separated their world into two spheres, sacred and secular (a dichotomy not found in scripture).[49] Or, they separate "private" faith from "public" attitudes.[50] In situations they judge to be within the secular sphere, they may be less guided by their religious beliefs, making them indistinguishable from other citizens with similar social and demographic characteristics. They may relegate their "Christian" thinking only to those situations that, in their view, fall within the moral, private, or sacred sphere. It may well be that political tolerance judgments, like many other political decisions, normally fall within this "secular" sphere. Therefore, "secular" attitudes (civic education, liberal democratic norms) may be more accessible to the tolerance judgment than religious beliefs.

Thus if a survey question is phrased in a way that activates the respondent's religious beliefs, as when respondents are asked how they would respond to certain activities of homosexuals or atheists, then religious beliefs may become more salient to the response. But when respondents, in the context of a survey on political and social attitudes, are asked to choose their own most disliked group and they do not attend specifically to their religious beliefs when selecting a group, their tolerance judgments may be less dependent upon their religious beliefs. For example, the majority of Americans have strong moral objections to the Ku Klux Klan. While there are obviously religious grounds for such objections, the objections are more likely rooted in civic concerns regarding liberty, equality, nonviolence, justice, and fairness. Their objections to this group may be consistent with their religious beliefs but are not necessarily founded in their religious beliefs. Thus when respondents are asked how they would respond to hypothetical situations concerning the KKK, these strong moral objections, civic concerns, attitudes specific to the Klan (that they are racist, promote violence, intimidate and instill fear in others, fail to play by the rules, etc.), and current or contextual information may be more accessible and salient to their response than specifically religious beliefs.

In sum, religious beliefs can be influential in political attitudes and behaviors, particularly when those beliefs are strongly held. Yet many believers today, even those with strong commitment, have not developed a distinctly Christian worldview to equip them to bring their faith to bear across the myriad issues they encounter in everyday life. Rather, their religious beliefs may be salient in only limited cases: (1) when faced with an issue that is easy for religion to speak to because it is strongly related to religious concerns (as in some moral or social issues), (2) when the issue has been made religiously salient (as in some elections), (3) when religious beliefs are closely related to other constructs that are accessible to the object (as perhaps with tolerance judgments toward atheists), or (4) when the respondent lacks other more accessible beliefs or attitudes upon which to rely for guidance.

Additionally, even among those for whom religious beliefs are strongly held, these beliefs are not likely to be strongly salient to political tolerance judgments, at least not in the aggregate, because there is no consensus among the orthodox regarding how believers should respond in situations calling for tolerance. Some may have an orientation toward tolerating diverse ideas in the public sphere, and others may be less willing to tolerate opposed views. As Wald explains, "Religion may sometimes sustain democratic values and sometimes undermine them. The source of the paradox is simply that religious values are ambiguous with regard to politics. They contain messages that can lead persons of common faith in different directions.[51]

Measuring Political Tolerance

At the beginning of this chapter, political tolerance was defined as the willingness of individuals to "put up with" or endure the public expression of ideas they dislike, disapprove of, or oppose. The words "disapprove" and "oppose" are the key to measuring political tolerance. If there is no opposition and disapproval, there is no tolerance. Individuals cannot be said to tolerate ideas or groups they do not oppose, since they do not "put up with" something with which they agree. Indifference is not tolerance, since indifference means there is no opposition. Tolerance is active, not passive; it is a "principled commitment," a commitment to tolerate *in spite of* opposition to or dislike of a group.[52]

Therefore, how can we say that those without religious commitment are tolerant of atheists, unless they have objections to religious nonbelief? Similarly, it makes no sense to claim that individuals who have no moral objection to homosexual lifestyles are tolerant of homosexuals, or that those who oppose abortion are tolerant of pro-life groups. On the other hand, religiously committed individuals may be tolerant if they are willing to put up with public lectures by atheists in their community, those with moral objections to homosexual behavior demonstrate tolerance if they are willing to put up with public advocacy of homosexuality, and abortion supporters who are willing to permit a pro-life demonstration in their community are likewise tolerant.

It is rather obvious, then, that in order to measure political tolerance we must first ascertain which groups respondents oppose or dislike, and then determine if they are willing to permit members of these groups their civil liberties. And the most straightforward way to ascertain which groups respondents dislike is to ask them. This is the "content-controlled" or "least-liked" measurement approach developed by Sullivan, Piereson, and Marcus. By contrast, the approach developed by Stouffer and adopted by GSS attempts to measure tolerance by asking respondents about their willingness to "tolerate" a few specific, though traditionally widely disliked, groups. The 1987 GSS asked respondents about five groups: atheists ("somebody who is against all churches and religion"), racists ("a person who believes that Blacks are genetically inferior"), Communists, militarists ("a person who advocates doing away with elections and letting the military run the country"), and homosexuals. Respondents were asked about their willingness to allow a member of each of these groups to engage in three activities: (1) making a public speech, (2) teaching in a college or university, and (3) having a book written by a member of the group in the public library. Responses were provided in a three-point Likert scale.

In the F&T survey, respondents were presented with a list of thirteen groups and asked their feelings toward each. They were then asked to identify any other groups they disliked, and to what degree they disliked them. These self-identified groups were added to the list. Next, they were asked to select *four* most-disliked groups from all those on the list.[53] Respondents were then asked about their willingness to allow certain activities of their four target groups.[54] The activities included (1) running for public office, (2) teaching in public schools, (3) making a speech, and (4) holding a public rally. They were also asked if (5) the group should be outlawed and (6) the government should be allowed to tap their phones.[55] Responses were selected from five-point Likert-type response sets.[56] They were summed and scaled so that a "1" indicates highest tolerance and a "0" least tolerance.[57]

The resulting tolerance scales are highly reliable, with a coefficient alpha for the least-liked group of .83, and those for the GSS scales ranging from .73 (racists) to .80 (homosexuals). Tolerance scores for the GSS measurement approach (an average of .57) are higher than when respondents choose their own disliked group (average tolerance score of .40). Respondents also vary in which activities they are least willing to tolerate from their disliked groups: the majority felt that government wiretapping should not be permitted even for members of their disliked group (.60), yet these group members should not be permitted to teach in public schools (.29). Scores for the other activities varied from .32 (running for public office) to .48 (making a public speech), with an average of .40. These results are summarized in table 9.1.

Measuring Religious Belief and Commitment

Religion is measured using the approach developed by Kellstedt, Green, Guth, and Smidt, with a few adaptations necessitated by GSS item availability (Kellstedt et al. developed their approach with American National Election Studies [ANES] data).[58] The GSS survey includes measures of religious preference, denominational affiliation, church attendance, religious intensity, and private prayer. These items can be combined to provide measures of religious tradition (used here to tap orthodoxy since doctrinal measures are not available) and religious commitment—the two religious variables employed in this analysis.

Following Kellstedt et al., respondents not meeting minimal requirements regarding affiliation and commitment are categorized as secular, even though they

Table 9.1 Tolerance Scores by Measurement Approach and Activity

Measurement Approach	Mean Tolerance Score
Least-Liked Group	.40
Second Least-Liked Group	.42
GSS items (overall mean)	.57
Atheists	.62
Communists	.57
Homosexuals	.62
Militarists	.53
Racists	.57
Tolerance by Activity (Least-Liked Approach)	**Mean Tolerance Score**
Run for public office	.32
Outlaw group	.40
Make a speech	.48
Allow government to tap phones	.60
Teach in public schools	.29
Hold a public rally	.38
Average for all six items	.40

All scores are scaled from 0 to 1, with 1 = greatest tolerance.

may express a religious preference. Seculars include those with (1) no religious preference, (2) a preference, but not religious commitment, or (3) a stated religious affiliation, but with such low commitment they are only "nominally" religious. Seculars are classified into two groups: *seculars* either have no religious preference or have no religious commitment (10 percent of the population is in this group); the *nominally identified* have a religious preference, but very low commitment (20 percent of respondents). While Kellstedt et al. combined these two groups, since they found that nominal identifiers behave politically more like seculars than they do the religiously committed, here the group sizes are sufficiently large to permit separate categories.

The measurement approach developed by Kellstedt et al. requires that respondents first be assigned to a religious tradition based on their preference and (for Protestants) denominational affiliation.[59] Religious commitment is operationalized by measures of four separate dimensions of religiosity: denominational affiliation (affiliation or belonging), religious intensity (salience),[60] church attendance (involvement), and frequency of prayer (devotionalism).[61] Minimal commitment means the respondent reports an affiliation, reports some religious intensity, attends services more than a couple of times a year, and reports praying more than once a week. This is truly *minimal* commitment, thus it is easy to see why respondents failing to meet more than one of these criteria should be classified as secular, while those meeting no more than two are "nominally committed." If they met three criteria, they are "moderately" committed. Only those meeting all four criteria are considered highly committed, and if they also have a high level of commitment on all dimensions (i.e., report a specific affiliation, a strong religious intensity, attend church at least weekly, and pray at least daily), they are coded with the highest commitment score. A reliability analysis of the items yielded an alpha of .68.

Table 9.2 displays the frequency of respondents within each religious category, by religious commitment and tradition. The largest religious categories are evangelical (20 percent) and Catholic (19 percent), with over half of these measuring strong commitment. But since some of the nonevangelical groups are too small to permit analysis, for the remaining analyses they are combined into one "religious, but nonorthodox" grouping, while the evangelical identifiers are the "orthodox."[62] The nominally identified and secular are generally maintained as separate categories.

Choice of Disliked Groups

Which groups did the respondents select as their most disliked, and did this vary by religious group? As table 9.3 shows, most respondents selected the same few groups as their most disliked regardless of their religious beliefs or level of religious commitment. The same six groups were selected as least liked by 95 percent of all respondents: the KKK, American Nazis, Communists, atheists, militarists, and homosexuals; in fact these six groups also make up 85 percent of *all* mentions in the top four least liked groups.[63] The KKK is by far *the* most disliked of all the groups—82 percent of all respondents selected it as one of their four least liked, and 42 percent as their *most* disliked. Other groups mentioned by a majority of respondents as one of their four disliked include Communists, atheists, American Nazis, and militarists. But no group other than the KKK is mentioned by more than 20 percent of all respondents as *most* disliked.

Table 9.2 Religious Tradition by Level of Commitment

Religious Tradition	None/Very Low	Low	Moderate	High	Total
Evangelical			136 (46.1)	159 (53.9)	295 (20.2)
Mainline			133 (54.5)	111 (45.5)	244 (16.7)
Black Protestant			48 (36.9)	82 (63.1)	130 (8.9)
Conservative			11 (29.7)	26 (70.3)	37 (2.5)
Liberal Nontraditionalists				3 (100)	3 (0.2)
Catholic			125 (45.1)	152 (54.9)	277 (19.0)
Jew			5 (55.6)	4 (44.4)	9 (0.6)
Other Non-Christian			13 (56.5)	10 (43.5)	23 (1.6)
Nominally Identified		296 (100)			296 (20.3)
Secular	144 (100)				144 (9.9)
Total	144 (9.9)	296 (20.3)	471 (32.3)	547 (37.5)	1,458 (100)

Notes: The figures in parentheses in the None/Very Low through High columns represent the percentage of the religious tradition members who have the indicated level of commitment. The figures in parentheses in the Total column are the percentage of the 1,458 respondents who were categorized into each religious tradition. For most of this chapter, the Evangelical group is identified as Orthodox. All other religiously committed traditions (Mainline, Black Protestant, Conservative Nontraditionalists, Liberal Nontraditionalists, Catholic, Jew, and Other Non-Christian) are combined into a Religious Non-Orthodox category. The Nominally Identified and Secular are both treated as secular, that is, nonreligious.

Table 9.3 Percentage of Respondents Selecting Group as First through Fourth Most Disliked

Group	First Disliked	Second Disliked	Third Disliked	Fourth Disliked	Mentioned as One of Four Most Disliked
Ku Klux Klan	42.0	19.0	13.7	7.6	82.3
American Nazis	8.1	26.8	19.7	15.2	69.7
Communists	19.3	16.2	16.7	12.2	64.2
Atheists	10.0	12.8	15.3	16.8	54.9
Militarists	9.2	8.1	13.2	18.5	48.9
Homosexuals	5.7	6.4	5.8	9.2	27.1
Abortion Supporters	2.6	5.0	5.4	2.5	15.5
Religious Fundamentalists	0.9	2.1	3.1	4.8	10.8
Anti-Abortionists	0.6	1.4	2.6	3.8	8.4
Feminists	0.1	0.5	0.5	1.1	2.1
Society for New America	0.2	0.2	0.9	0.7	2.1
Conservatives	0.0	0.3	0.3	1.3	1.9
Liberals	0.2	0.0	0.8	0.9	1.8

Do the religiously committed and orthodox believers differ from other respondents in which groups they selected as most disliked? While the Religious Right is often portrayed as "hate-filled," particularly toward homosexuals, the data in table 9.4 show that average religious commitment scores are *not* higher for respondents selecting homosexuals as least liked. In fact, the religiously committed—both orthodox and nonorthodox believers—are *less* likely than the nonreligious to single out homosexuals as most disliked than either of the two secular groups. The only outlier group is "religious fundamentalists" (a religious commitment score of .46, but with only eleven respondents).

The data presented in table 9.4 also demonstrate only slight differences in choice of least-liked group by religious category, but two differences that run counter to conventional wisdom stand out: seculars are *more* likely than the religiously committed groups to select homosexuals as their most disliked group, and evangelicals are *more* likely than the other groups to select the KKK as their most disliked (and white evangelicals are even more likely to select the KKK than are Black Protestants).

Do the religiously orthodox differ from the others in their *degree* of like/dislike toward their least-liked group? The results are not shown here, since there is remarkable similarity across the groups, but three differences are worth noting: seculars tend to dislike liberals more than either of the two religiously committed groups (p < .01), they tend to dislike homosexuals more than the religiously committed (p < .10), and they dislike Communists more (p < .05). These results demonstrate that, contrary to popular belief, the religiously orthodox are *not* more hate-filled than the nonreligious; in fact, where there are significant differences in dislike toward groups, seculars tend to "hate" *more* than the religiously committed and the orthodox.

Do believers and seculars vary in their willingness to tolerate their least-liked group? The data presented in table 9.5, displaying mean tolerance scores by religious group and target group, suggest they do not, despite the reputation for intolerance of the religiously committed. There are differences in average tolerance score by target group, but not as much as we might expect. Gibson had hinted that since respondents who select "trivial" groups as their most disliked may not be as intolerant of these groups, tolerance scores would likely vary by group selected.[64] We might expect, for example, that respondents selecting a group with a reputation for not "playing by the rules" as their least liked, or a group perceived to be particularly threatening, may be less willing to permit group members their civil liberties than respondents selecting a less threatening group. But the data do not bear this out. Tolerance scores are lower for the KKK, Communists, and homosexuals and higher for atheists, militarists, and fundamentalists—but not by much.

Table 9.4 Level of Religious Commitment, Orthodoxy, and Tolerance by Choice of Least Liked Group

Group Selected as Least Liked	Mean Religious Commitment	Orthodox	Religious, Not Orthodox	Nominally Committed	Secular	Tolerance Score	N
Ku Klux Klan	.64	124 (48.1)	261 (42.9)	98 (40.6)	45 (36.6)	.36	531
Communists	.61	42 (15.9)	127 (20.8)	52 (22.1)	22 (17.9)	.35	244
Atheists	.64	27 (10.5)	63 (10.4)	25 (10.2)	11 (8.9)	.49	127
Militarists	.61	26 (10.1)	56 (9.2)	20 (8.2)	14 (11.4)	.55	116
American Nazis	.57	18 (7.0)	49 (8.0)	21 (8.6)	15 (12.2)	.44	103
Homosexuals	.59	15 (6.2)	29 (4.8)	17 (7.0)	10 (8.1)	.37	72
Abortion Supporters	.66	5 (1.9)	19 (3.1)	4 (1.6)	4 (3.3)	.40	33
Religious Fundamentalists	.46	1 (.01)	4 (.06)	4 (.01)	2 (.01)	.66	11
Total	.62	262 (100)	608 (100)	246 (100)	123 (100)	.40	1,237

Note: Religious Commitment and Tolerance are scaled from 0 to 1, with 1 = highest.

Table 9.5 Tolerance of Least Liked Group by Religious Category

Group Selected as Least Liked	Orthodox	Religious, Not Orthodox	Nominally Committed	Secular	Mean Tolerance
Ku Klux Klan	.35	.36	.36	.31	.36
Communists	.32	.34	.36	.36	.35
Atheists	.42	.55	.47	.40	.49
Militarists	.51	.55	.55	.60	.55
American Nazis	.41	.45	.45	.41	.44
Homosexuals	.37	.40	.31	.38	.37
Abortion Supporters	.45	.35	.45	.49	.40
Religious Fundamentalists	.33	.73	.65	.69	.66
Total	.38	.41	.40	.39	.40

Tolerance: 1 = Most tolerant, 0 = Least tolerant

Characteristics of Believers and Sources of Political Tolerance

To test my hypotheses—that religion is related to political tolerance (H-I), that this is partly because religiously committed and orthodox believers differ from other citizens in their social, political, and psychological characteristics (H-II), and that those characteristics related to religion are also related to political tolerance (H-III) —I examine the differences between respondents in each of the religious categories and also employ multiple-regression analyses (with religious commitment, orthodoxy, and tolerance scores as the dependent variables). As my results will show, religion is not related to tolerance. This is partly because the religiously committed and orthodox vary from the nonorthodox and nonbelievers only in their social and demographic characteristics, and not in the political and psychological characteristics that are actually the sources of political tolerance.

The earlier literature, using the GSS (Stouffer) measurement approach, suggested that tolerance could be explained primarily by social or demographic characteristics (e.g., education, income, social class, age, sex, Southern residence, and size of community of residence) and some of the political characteristics (particularly ideology) that are not significant using the least-liked measures. It is in this difference that the crux of my argument lies: almost without exception, *for those characteristics that the GSS measurement approach found were associated with tolerance, the religiously committed and orthodox do differ from other groupings; but in those characteristics that the content-controlled approach found to be significant predictors of tolerance* (the psychological and certain political predispositions), *orthodox and highly committed believers do not differ from other citizens*. It is my contention that the GSS measures found religion to be linked with intolerance largely because religion is also linked with social and demographic characteristics this older measurement approach found predicted intolerance, and also because they employed poor measures of religion which inadequately captured religious belief and commitment. Thus *the long-held assumption that religion is associated with intolerance is largely an artifact of outmoded measurements of both tolerance and of religion*, while employing the more accurate measurements of these two concepts described in the Sullivan et al. and Kellstedt et al. publications will enable us to correct our misconceptions of the relationship of religion to tolerance.

As mentioned above, demographic traits were found to be strong predictors of tolerance in the work utilizing the GSS measures. The results in the last column of table 9.6 (the GSS tolerance measure is the dependent variable) show that among the strongest predictors of tolerance are education, age, religious commitment, and Southern residence, with the education coefficient being the most significant. Two political characteristics—ideology and political engagement (interest and involvement) also have significant coefficients.

Table 9.6 OLS: Explaining Political Tolerance, Religious Commitment, and Orthodoxy

	Religious Orthodoxy	Religious Commitment	Tolerance, Least Liked	Tolerance, GSS Measures
Constant	.148	.527***	.467***	.545***
Age	-.014	.0946***	-.019	-.267***
Education	-.206**	-.153***	.066	.569***
Income	.000	-.034	-.048**	.080**
Social Class	.035	.034	-.015	.023
Southern Residence	.163***	.023	.001	-.066***
Urban/Rural	.095**	.009	-.065***	-.068
Female	.000	.084***	.000	-.036
Vote	.000	.064	-.012	.045**
Political Interest	-.045	-.066**	-.032	-.097***
Political Knowledge	.025	.033	.005	.020

t value: * p < .10, ** p < .05, *** p < .01. All variable values range from 0 to 1. Direction of variables: Age: 1 = oldest; Education: 1 = highest; Income: 1 = highest; Social Class: 1 = highest; Southern Residence: 1 = higher; Urban/Rural: 1 = more rural; Female; Vote: 1 = yes; Political Interest: 1 = least; Political Knowledge: 1 = highest.

Table 9.6—continued

	Religious Orthodoxy	Religious Commitment	Tolerance, Least Liked	Tolerance, GSS Measures
Ideology	.281***	.143***	-.002	-.107***
Democratic Principles	-.115	.062	.377***	-.027
Dogmatism	-.097	-.046	.395***	-.024
Perceived Threat	-.094	.011	-.126***	-.076
Self-esteem	.023	.055	-.015	-.029
Traditionalism	.062	.017	.139***	-.025
Religious Commitment			.015	-.222***
Orthodox Believer			-.014	-.009
Religious, Not Orthodox			.012	.039
Adjusted R^2	.326***	.093***	.252***	.312
F	36.762***	8.651***	22.179***	29.482***
N	1,211	1,217	1,217	1,211

t value: * p < .10, ** p < .05, *** p < .01. All variable values range from 0 to 1. Direction of variables: Ideology: 1 = most conservative; Democratic Principles: 1 = most supportive; Dogmatism: 1 = least dogmatic; Perceived Threat: 1 = higher threat, Self-esteem: 1 = higher esteem; Traditionalism: 1 = least traditionalistic; Religious Commitment: 1 = highest commitment.

As we note from table 9.7, these same social and demographic characteristics are also generally found to be associated with religiosity. Higher education, Southern and rural residences, and conservative ideology are associated with religious orthodoxy, while being older, less educated, female, politically conservative, and having low political interest are characteristic of higher religious commitment. Furthermore, the data presented in table 9.7 demonstrate that the religious do vary significantly from the nonreligious in their social and demographic characteristics (education, income, social class, age, sex, and residence) and in those political traits that are also significant to tolerance when the GSS measurements are employed (ideology and political engagement),[65] but they do not differ from one another on those political and psychological traits that are significant predictors of tolerance when the content-controlled measurement approach is used (support for democratic norms, perceptions of threat, dogmatism, self-esteem, and traditionalism).

However, the variables which have significant coefficients in the "tolerance, least liked" column of table 9.6, reporting the regression results with the least-liked tolerance score as the dependent variable, are almost a mirror image of those with the GSS measure: of the demographic variables, only income and rural residence have significant coefficients (but the income coefficient is in the opposite direction). Of the political characteristics, only support for democratic norms—one of the political variables *not* significant with the GSS approach—remains a predictor of tolerance (in fact it is second in strength only to dogmatism).[66] The other variables with significant coefficients are psychological traits, none of which had significant coefficients with the GSS measure: dogmatism (with the largest coefficient), perception of threat,[67] self-esteem, and traditionalism.[68]

Looking again at table 9.6, we note that with one exception, none of the variables with significant coefficients when tolerance is measured with the least-liked approach have significant coefficients for the religious variables. The only exception is rural residence (a predictor of religious orthodoxy), but the coefficient is in the opposite direction (rural residents are *more* tolerant than urban). Yet we note that, with the exceptions of income and political involvement, every variable that is a significant predictor of tolerance measured with the GSS approach also has a significant coefficient with at least one of the religious variables: age, education, Southern residence, political interest, and ideology.

The reason for these differences is that the content-controlled tolerance measures were developed to more accurately reflect the actual definition of tolerance (to put up with groups which one strongly opposes), and thus controls for the social and cultural biases inherent in the GSS measurement approach. The assumption is that tolerance itself does not vary by social characteristic, but only who it is that must be tolerated. Marcus et al. suggest that willingness to tolerate is largely explained by having made standing judgments to support the principles of democracy and also by psychological characteristics (e.g., threat perceptions, dogmatism, and self-esteem). Thus, religion should be associated with tolerance only if believers are

Table 9.7 A Comparison by Religious Category in Social, Political, and Psychological Characteristics

	Orthodox			Religious, Non Orthodox			Secular			Mean
		Commitment			Commitment				Non-	
	All	High	Moderate	All	High	Moderate	All	Low Commit.	religious	
Age	.41	.44	.37	.40	.42	.38	.32	.33	.30	.38***
Education	.60	.61	.58	.61	.61	.62	.64	.63	.67	.62***
Income	.61	.63	.58	.57	.56	.60	.65	.65	.64	.60***
Social Class	.51	.54	.48	.48	.49	.47	.50	.50	.52	.49**
Southern Res.	.43	.37	.49	.29	.31	.25	.24	.25	.20	.30***
Urban/Rural	.51	.53	.48	.34	.33	.35	.36	.39	.31	.37***
Female	.59	.64	.52	.64	.69	.58	.42	.39	.48	.57***
Vote	.64	.73	.52	.69	.73	.64	.55	.57	.50	.64***
Political Interest	.40	.35	.46	.40	.41	.39	.44	.45	.43	.41**
Political Knowledge	.52	.54	.49	.47	.48	.45	.44	.47	.39	.47***
Ideology	.56	.60	.52	.49	.50	.48	.48	.50	.43	.50***
Democratic Principles	.60	.59	.61	.60	.61	.60	.60	.61	.59	.60
Dogmatism	.47	.46	.48	.50	.49	.50	.49	.48	.51	.49
Perceived Threat	.70	.70	.70	.72	.72	.71	.71	.70	.71	.71
Self-esteem	.59	.59	.59	.60	.60	.60	.59	.58	.60	.59
Traditionalism	.24	.24	.23	.23	.22	.23	.23	.22	.24	.23
N	299	163	136	1,019	586	433	501	334	167	1,819

Numbers represent mean scores. *** p < .01, ** p < .05, * p < .10. All variables are measured so that 0 = lowest, 1 = highest. Age: 1 = oldest; Education: 1 = highest; Income: 1 = highest; Social Class: 1 = highest; Southern Residence: 1 = Yes; Urban/Rural: 1 = more rural; Female: 1 = female; Vote: 1 = yes; Political Interest: 1 = least; Political Knowledge: 1 = least; Ideology: 1 = most conservative; Democratic Principles: 1 = most supportive; Dogmatism: 1 = least dogmatic; Perceived Threat: 1 = higher threat; Self-esteem: 1 = higher esteem; Traditionalism: 1 = least traditionalistic.

distinct in the psychological and political predispositions relevant to tolerance, if the beliefs are closely linked to the antecedent characteristics within their conceptual framework that are sources of intolerance, or if the beliefs themselves are accessible, salient, and activated at the time of making the tolerance judgment. But as demonstrated in table 9.7, believers do not differ from nonbelievers in those characteristics that influence political tolerance, although they do in the social and demographic traits found to be sources of tolerance when using the Stouffer measurement approach (education, income, social class, age, sex, and residence). The same conclusion can be made regarding political and psychological characteristics. The religiously committed and orthodox tend to be more conservative in their ideology, and ideology has been shown to be an important predictor of political tolerance, but only when the Stouffer-type measurements are employed. Yet this relationship disappears when the content-controlled measures are used.[69]

In sum, religious belief and religious commitment are unrelated to political tolerance. Although there are significant demographic differences by religious category, only two demographic variables (income and urban residence) significantly influence political tolerance. With the exception of support for democratic principles, political variables are not associated with political tolerance. The religious categories do not differ from one another on support for democratic principles, but they do on ideology and political engagement. The religiously committed and orthodox believers do not differ from other citizens on the psychological predispositions that are significantly related to political tolerance. When tolerance is measured by the least-liked method, it can be largely explained by dogmatism, support for democratic principles, perception of threat, traditionalism, and (to a lesser extent) urban residence and income. Religion does not contribute to tolerance attitudes and, for the most part, is not associated with characteristics that do contribute to tolerance attitudes, at least when tolerance is defined so as to require opposition or dislike.

All this is not to claim that believers are tolerant—only that they are no more *in*tolerant than are other citizens. On average, U.S. citizens are intolerant—or at least more so than would be ideal in a democracy (scoring an average of .40 on a 0-1 scale, with 0 being least tolerant). But this intolerance characterizes believers and seculars alike, and the tendency is for believers (and nonbelievers) *not* to be influenced by their religious beliefs when making tolerance judgments, but rather by their psychological predispositions and their support for the principles of democracy.

Religious Orientation, Tolerance, and Truth

Since these findings run counter to the empirical evidence presented by other scholars, some scholars may remain unconvinced by what has been presented here. There are a number of additional arguments that could be made in support of these findings, but space will permit only one. It is related to the precision by which religion was measured in this analysis, which permitted the distinction between the religiously committed and the nominally committed (a secular group). In most tolerance analyses, the religious groups are tainted by the presence of a large number of individuals who claim a religious attachment but are actually secular in their outlook. In fact, many of these may have an "extrinsic" religious orientation, while those in the strongly committed group may be more likely to be intrinsically religious. This difference between these two orientations has been found to have large significance for prejudice and could have implications for *why* one is prepared to tolerate diversity.

It should be abundantly clear to even the casual observer that not all people are "religious" in the same way—some believers have internalized the teachings of their faith (and their behavior testifies to that fact), while others are merely outwardly religious. Distinguishing between "genuine" and "false" belief is nothing new—Jesus did so,[70] as have many others more recently: for example, Kierkegaard's musings on "official Christianity" versus "true Christianity," and William James' distinction between "personal" religion (a genuine, firsthand conversion or religious experience) and religion as an "institutional, corporate, or tribal product."[71] In much of the early work on religion and prejudice, done by psychologists Gordon Allport (*The Nature of Prejudice*) and T. W. Adorno, Else Frenkel-Brunswick, Daniel J. Levinson, and R. Nevitt Sanford (*The Authoritarian Personality*), this distinction has tremendous relevance.

In his work on prejudice in the 1950s and 1960s, Allport had observed a positive relationship between church attendance and ethnic prejudice. Yet these attitudes were contrary to what was being taught in the churches during the 1960s: that is, concerns for social equity, civil rights, and so forth.[72] Examining the data more closely, Allport noted a curvilinear relationship between attendance and prejudice. Those who did not attend church at all scored low on prejudice, but so did those who attended church quite often. But those attending church infrequently (once or twice a month) scored *highest* in prejudice. Allport concluded that both prejudice and church attendance were motivated by a third factor: religious orientation. He found that many of the infrequent attendees are actually extrinsically religiously oriented. These individuals can be expected to be more prejudiced than the other groups because

> a person with an extrinsic religious orientation is using his religious views to provide security, comfort, status, or social support for himself—religion is not a value in its own right, it serves other needs, and it is a purely utilitarian formation. Now prejudice too is a "useful" formation: it too provides security, comfort, status, and social support. A life that is dependent on the supports of extrinsic religion is likely to be dependent on the supports of prejudice.[73]

Thus, Allport observed, "the extrinsically motivated person *uses* his religion, whereas the intrinsically motivated *lives* his religion."[74] Extrinsic religion is "self-serving, conferring safety, status, comfort and talismanic favors upon the believer. . . . People who are religious in this sense make use of God. . . . [They are] dependent and basically infantile."[75] Such individuals may be motivated to become involved in church by the need for "security and solace, sociability and distraction, status and self justification," rather than out of a heartfelt desire to worship God or to learn of His teachings. For such persons, doctrine or creed "is lightly held or else selectively shaped to fit more primary needs. In theological terms the extrinsic type turns to God, but without turning away from self."[76]

As Wald notes, the extrinsically religious find in religion confirmation for their way of life and their social order, but there is nothing about their religion that changes their attitudes or challenges them to conform to its teachings internally. He continues: "What is missing from such conventional or nominal religiosity is deeply rooted acceptance of the nobler values associated with major religious traditions—love, charity, compassion, and forgiveness. Some adherents do not hear these messages either because they do not attend often enough or, more likely, because 'while hearing they do not hear, nor do they understand' (Matthew 13:13)."[77]

On the other hand, those with intrinsic religious sentiments do not view religion as "an instrumental device. It is not a mere mode of conformity, nor a crutch, nor a tranquilizer, nor a bid for status. All needs are subordinated to an overarching religious commitment. In internalizing the total creed of his religion the individual necessarily internalizes its values of humility, compassion, and love of neighbor. In such a life . . . there is no place for rejection, contempt, or condescension toward one's fellow man."[78] The individual with such an orientation "regards faith as a supreme value in its own right."[79] For such persons, religion is a central, master motive in life. Contrary to the view of the religiously committed as rigid and closed-minded, persons with a mature faith or intrinsic orientation share a critical, open-ended approach to existential questions. They "take seriously the commandment of brotherhood, and strive to transcend all self-centered needs. Dogma is tempered with humility, and in keeping with the Biblical injunction the possessor withholds judgment until the day of the harvest. A religious sentiment of this sort floods the whole life with motivation and meaning."[80] Those with genuine belief tend to be more trusting, compassionate, and humble: "Having embraced a creed the individual endeavors to internalize it and follow it fully. It is in this sense that he *lives* his religion."[81]

This corresponds with what Adorno and colleagues found in their research on the authoritarian personality which began in 1944.[82] Seeking to discover the types of personalities attracted to Nazism, they measured two major personality dimensions: authoritarianism (defined by a high regard for and tendency to acquiesce to authority, adherence to conventional values, rigidity in thinking, and the need for clear structure) and ethnocentrism (defined by in-group loyalty and distrust and dislike of out-groups). They sought to determine "whether religion represents to the subject a further effort toward belonging to a privileged group and the explicit acceptance of a set of conventionalized mores and rules of behavior prevalent within a majority group, or whether religion represents a system of more internalized, genuine experiences and values."[83] What they found is that it is not religious belief that is linked to authoritarianism and ethnocentrism, but rather "conventionalized" or "neutralized" religion—an "emasculation" of the more "profound" claims of religion, where all that is left is "the doctrinal shell" arranged in "a rigid and haphazard way."[84]

Adorno et al. also found that neutralized religion correlated negatively with a second way of being religious: "personally experienced belief." A personally experienced belief, or "genuine" religiousness, leads believers to "take religion seriously in a more internalized sense."[85] Thus the genuinely religious are not as likely to be prejudiced as are the religious conformists because the genuinely religious attend church not out of convention, but because they have embraced and internalized its teachings. They speculated that such individuals are the least prejudiced because "the more 'human' and concrete a person's relation to religion, the more human his approach to those who 'do not belong' is likely to be."[86]

Allport also identified a third religious orientation: the "indiscriminately pro-religious" (IPR).[87] He observed that the IPR tend to be the *most* prejudiced of any group (although they are actually a subgroup of the extrinsically religious), because of their "undifferentiated thinking," a type of thinking Rokeach also found present in the dogmatic mind.[88] Allport and Ross observed that these individuals "take a superficial or 'hit and run' approach" in their responses to the religious statements on the survey, indicating their agreement with any pro-religious sentiment, even if the statements were inconsistent. This is significant because, in the same way, "prejudice itself is a matter of stereotyped overgeneralization, a failure to distinguish members of a minority group as individual."[89]

Both sets of scholars found that seculars, like the intrinsically religious, also tend to be less prejudiced. But we should keep in mind that seculars are a diverse group, and not all are irreligious for the same reason. According to Adorno et al., seculars' reasons for rejecting religious belief may have implications for their attitudes toward other groups:

> It may turn out to be an important criterion of susceptibility whether a person is opposed to religion as an ally of repression and reaction, in which case we should expect him to be relatively unprejudiced, or whether he adopts an attitude of cynical utilitarianism and rejects everything that is not "realistic" and tangible, in which case we should expect him to be prejudiced. There also exists a fascist type of irreligious person who has become completely cynical after having been disillusioned with regard to religion. . . . The true candidates of neo-paganism of the fascist extreme are recruited from the ranks of these people.[90]

In sum, these scholars found a curvilinear relationship between religion and prejudice, with seculars being less prejudiced than all church attendees combined, but with the intrinsically religious as the least prejudiced. Conversely, the extrinsically religious are the most prejudiced, and among this group the "indiscriminately pro-religious"—those individuals with a favorable but casual attitude toward religion—are the most prejudiced of all. Other researchers have replicated these findings.[91]

Granted, prejudice and political intolerance are not the same. One can be prejudiced against a group and still be tolerant of them, or vice versa. But this research on prejudice has significance for the present study because it provides additional theoretical and empirical support for why the religiously committed may be more tolerant than earlier work on religion and tolerance suggested, and why seculars (a group that includes many extrinsically religious) may be much less so.

It may be that this work on religious orientation may have more implications for *reasons* for tolerance—and what constitutes "true" tolerance—than it does for *levels* of tolerance. The explanations provided by these scholars for why the extrinsically religious are more prejudiced takes us back to the "truth and tolerance" theme alluded to earlier—the argument made by Neuhaus, Gaede, Markham, and others that genuine political tolerance requires a commitment to truth. If "the truth about tolerance is that tolerance requires truth,"[92] who is more prepared to tolerate than those who most value truth? Since the classical liberal defense of political tolerance is to permit maximum freedom of expression and rational debate on diverse ideas, in the hopes that communities may progress toward the "truth," might we conclude that those who most desire truth—those who most believe that truth exists and is valuable for all—might possess the firmest foundation from which to tolerate diverse ideas and opinions? Might it be true that, as one scholar explains it, individuals who have "given up the quest for truth and therefore moral debate and rational dialogue," have less ground from which to tolerate ideas they disagree with?[93] Relativists and postmodernists may value tolerance as an end in itself, but that is a weaker foundation for tolerance than to value tolerance as a means to a higher end: truth.

In the passage by Adorno et al. quoted below, the extrinsically religious are identified as among those individuals who have "given up the quest for truth":

> It is the disposition [of the extrinsically religious] to view religion as a means instead of an end. Religion is accepted, not because of its objective truth, but on account of its value in realizing goals that might also be achieved by other means. This attitude falls in line with the general tendency toward subordination and renunciation of one's own judgment so characteristic of the mentality of those who follow fascist movements. Acceptance of an ideology is not based upon understanding of or belief in its content but rather upon what immediate use can be made of it, or upon arbitrary decisions. Here lies one of the roots of the stubborn, conscious, and manipulative irrationalism of the Nazis, as it was summed up by Hitler's saying: "*Man kann nur fur eine Idee sterben, die man nicht versteht.*" (One can die only for an idea which one does not understand.) This is by its intrinsic logic tantamount to contempt for truth *per se*. One selects a "*Weltanschauung*" after the

pattern of choosing a particularly well-advertised commodity, rather than for its real quality. This attitude, applied to religion, must necessarily produce ambivalence, for religion claims to express *absolute* truth. If it is accepted for some other reason alone, this claim is implicitly denied and thereby religion itself rejected, even while being accepted. Thus, rigid confirmation of religious values on account of their "usefulness" works against them by necessity.[94]

Thus those who profess a belief in God, or an affiliation with a religious tradition, but have little real religious commitment or do not provide evidence of having internalized the teachings of their faith, are committed not to the truth their religious faith teaches but to their own needs (security, social status, etc.). The truth of their religion is no longer the supreme value, the end; their religion has become a means to a more self-centered goal. The extrinsically religious are prejudiced because they treat religion the same as they treat any other ideology: as a commodity to be used, not as truth, valuable in itself.

Such persons may not be capable of "true" tolerance because they do not *believe*—not in religion, truth, or the possibility for good from people they dislike—so they cannot be wholly committed to any of these things. Their "commitment" is but a superficial assent, not a heartfelt embracement. They may be outwardly religious, but only because their religiosity gives them what they need, not because they are drawn to its truth claims. Without a reflective commitment to truth, they have little foundation for tolerance.

Conclusion

Although there are important distinctions among religious believers and the non-religious, these distinctions are not relevant to the making of political tolerance judgments. Religious beliefs are not salient to these judgments in part because the predispositions that are important to tolerance judgments are not related to religion. Americans learn support for the fundamental principles of democracy regardless of their religious beliefs—from their families, schools, the media, civic organizations, popular culture, and so on. Religious beliefs are not highly relevant to the learning and internalization of democratic values, and they are generally not among the most accessible attitudes to making political tolerance judgments, even for those with strong commitment.

The evidence does not support the characterization of orthodox or religiously committed believers as intolerant bigots. This myth of intolerance is an artifact of poor measurement of religion and the Stouffer-type tolerance measures, which are biased against certain demographic and cultural groups, most significantly conservatives, Southerners, the less educated, and older adults. These variables are also linked to religiosity, but they do not help to predict intolerance when tolerance is measured by least-liked measures. Religion does not affect political tolerance because religious beliefs are not the most salient and accessible attitudes when respondents are asked to make political tolerance judgments. Rather, the sources of tolerance for the religiously committed are much the same as they are for other people: psychological predispositions and the internalization of liberal democratic norms.

Thus, the widespread notion of modern Americans that religious expression has no place in the public square, in part because orthodox belief is linked to political intolerance—and by implication to a disrespect for democratic principles—is not supported by this analysis. While there are indeed other (likewise unfounded) arguments for why religion does not belong in the public square, they shall have to be refuted elsewhere. But as for the democratic principle that citizens must be willing to tolerate diversity, people of faith are just as qualified to fully participate in civil society as anyone else.

Notes

1. Preston King, *Toleration* (London: Allen and Unwin, 1976), 12.

2. Bernard Crick, "Toleration and Tolerance in Theory and Practice," *Government and Opposition* 6 (1971): 144.

3. John L. Sullivan, James Piereson, and George E. Marcus, *Political Tolerance and American Democracy* (Chicago: University of Chicago Press, 1982), 2.

4. The widespread belief that religion is linked to intolerance is only one excuse for excluding religious voices in the public square. Another justification for such exclusion in the United States is the private-public and secular-sacred splits that came out of the Reformation and Enlightenment and that prominently influenced our political philosophy. This resulted in a strong belief (one that is even stronger today) that religion is inherently divisive and destructive of civil society, and thus religious expression must be kept private and out of the secular realm. Of course such a position is ludicrous—religious belief is not only not harmful to civil society but, at least some would argue, is essential for a healthy moral body politic. But this is a whole other issue and will not be addressed more fully here.

5. While such a characteristic is not accurate, as I will demonstrate in this chapter, it is nonetheless pervasive. For evidence of this, see especially two articles by Louis Bolce and Gerald De Maio in *Public Opinion Quarterly* 63, nos. 1 and 4 (Winter and Spring 1999): "The Anti-Christian Fundamentalist Factor in Contemporary Politics" and "Religious Outlook, Culture War Politics, and Antipathy toward Christian Fundamentalists." Bolce and De Maio used American National Election Studies data from 1988 to 1996 to demonstrate the widespread and intense dislike toward conservative Christians (fundamentalists). This antipathy is particularly pervasive among the highly educated and seculars—the very groups most tolerance literature portrays as most tolerant.

6. The convention among scholars of U.S. religion and political behavior is to speak of "evangelicals" or "fundamentalists," rather than "orthodox." While employing the term *orthodox* is not without problems, I prefer to use it rather than the more conventional *evangelical* primarily because orthodoxy has rich implications for the "truth" subtheme of this paper—an essential linkage when speaking of religion and tolerance.

"Orthodox" derives etymologically from the Greek words *orthos*, meaning "straight," and *doxa*, "opinion." Thus, it literally means "straight opinion" or "right belief." As used here, the word *orthodoxy* means to conform to the traditional doctrines of one's faith. As G. K. Chesterton reminds us, Christian orthodoxy means adherence to the Apostle's Creed and the conduct of those who hold to this creed (*Orthodoxy* [San Francisco: Ignatius, 1908], 17). The literal translation of *orthos doxa* assumes some authoritative criterion to establish what is the "right belief." In the United States, this authoritative criterion for Christianity is the Bible. Since it is the view toward the Bible that primarily separates evangelical from old-line Protestants (evangelicals viewing the Bible as the inerrant Word of God, while old-line denominations are moving away from this orthodox position), the word *orthodox* is used here to refer to evangelicals.

Although the word *orthodoxy* is employed in this chapter to refer to evangelicals, not all those within evangelical denominations hold to or live by the orthodox doctrines of the Christian faith, while some outside the tradition do. Thus "orthodox" does not accurately describe all evangelicals, but it does tend to be a more accurate description of evangelicals than of those in other religious traditions.

7. In his recently published book, *Politics, Religion, and the Public Good* (San Francisco: Jossey-Bass, 2000), Martin Marty made the following observation about this: "Relativism strikes fundamentalists as the key feature of modernity, the main assault on the grasp of truth. Interestingly, relativism is a problem not because every system of thought, every contention, every moral decision is perceived as equally false. Just the opposite: they can all be presented positively by advocates, sold by the tolerant, until the victim of modernity decides that all truths are equally satisfying: "You have yours, I have mine. I must tolerate you." And in the process, say not only fundamentalists, all seriousness in moral, intellectual, and spiritual searches get sapped" (35).

Also see Clyde Wilcox and Ted Jelen, "Evangelicals and Political Tolerance," *American Politics Quarterly* 18 (1990): 25-46, about relativism as an explanation for the intolerance of fundamentalists.

8. John L. Sullivan, James Piereson, and George E. Marcus, *Political Tolerance and American Democracy* (Chicago: University of Chicago Press, 1993).

9. I am not the only one who doubts the empirical evidence. In his most recent edition of *Religion and Politics in the United States*, Kenneth Wald commented about the empirical evidence linking religious belief to intolerance: "These results paint a disturbing portrait of the capacity for democratic thinking and action among deeply religious people and lead to concern about the implications of their increasing involvement in political life. Dogmatism, closed-mindedness, and intolerance are not traits that promote civility or the free exchange of ideas. If such traits are pronounced among religious activists and their opponents, there is a solid basis for concern about the increasing politicization of religious issues. In my view, however, the evidence supporting a link between religiosity and the propensity to intolerance is not strong enough to warrant alarm. Kenneth Wald, *Religion and Politics in the United States*, 3d ed. (Washington, D.C.: Congressional Quarterly Press, 1997): 327.

10. It is not difficult to find documentation and discussion of the doctrinal ignorance of the religiously committed in the United States, which is just as pervasive (though arguably more dangerous) than the civic ignorance of American citizens. See, for example, David F. Wells, *No Place for Truth; or, Whatever Happened to Evangelical Theology?* (Grand Rapids, Mich.: Eerdmans, 1993); David F. Wells, *God in the Wasteland: The Reality of Truth in a World of Fading Dreams* (Grand Rapids, Mich.: Eerdmans, 1994); and George Gallup, Jr., and D. Michael Lindsey, *Surveying the Religious Landscape: Trends in U.S. Beliefs* (Harrisburg, Pa.: Morehouse, 1999), 49.

11. Various orientations of believers toward tolerance have also been identified and discussed in Rienhold Niebuhr, *The Children of Light and the Children of Darkness* (London: Nisbet and Co., 1945), and Ian S. Markham, *Plurality and Christian Ethics* (Cambridge: Cambridge University Press, 1994). (Niebuhr's work actually concerned approaches to the problem of religious and cultural diversity.) The first type, an exclusive orientation, Niebuhr identified as an approach seeking to overcome diversity and restore traditional culture. This type of orientation is evident in some of the fundamentalist and evangelical literature, such as that of the Christian Reconstructionist movement. Niebuhr identified the secular approach as a second orientation, one that attempts to achieve cultural unity through denial of traditional religion. However, as Markham recognized, this second orientation is quite evident within evangelicalism—it is an "inclusive" approach. Two examples of the inclusive orientation might be Glenn Tinder, *Tolerance and Community* (Columbia: University of Missouri Press, 1995), and Clarke Cochran, *Religion in Public and Private Life* (London: Routledge, 1990). The third approach—the "orthodox, but committed to tolerance" orientation—seeks to maintain both religious vitality and diversity. This orientation is committed to absolute and orthodox truth as revealed in scripture, and yet encourages promotion of truth through tolerance (consistent with classical liberalism). This is the position of several orthodox scholars who have written on tolerance, among them Niebuhr in *The Children of Light*; Markham in *Plurality and Christian Ethics*; Richard John Neuhaus in a number of his writings, including *The Naked Public Square* (Grand Rapids, Mich.: Eerdmans, 1984); and S. D. Gaede in *When Tolerance Is No Virtue*.

12. Kenneth D. Wald, *Religion and Politics in the United States*; see also Ted Jelen, "Research in Religion and Mass Political Behavior in the United States: Looking Both Ways after Two Decades of Scholarship," *American Politics Quarterly* 26 (1998).

13. See, for example, Robert Wuthnow, *Spirituality in America since the 1950s* (Berkeley: University of California Press, 1999); Wade Clark Roof, *Spiritual Marketplace* (Princeton, N.J.: Princeton University Press, 1999); Ingolf U. Dalferth, "I Determine What God Is! Theology in the Age of 'Cafeteria Religion,'" *Theology Today* 57 (2000): 5-23. See also Wells, *No Place for Truth* and *God in the Wasteland*.

14. Samuel A. Stouffer, *Communism, Conformity, and Civil Liberties*, 2d ed. (New York: Doubleday, 1966).

15. Stouffer, *Communism, Conformity, and Civil Liberties*, 142.

16. Clyde Z. Nunn, Harry J. Crockett, Jr., and J. Allen Williams, Jr., *Tolerance for Nonconformity* (San Francisco: Jossey-Bass, 1978).

17. Nunn, Crockett, and Williams, *Tolerance for Nonconformity*, 140.

18. Sullivan, Piereson, and Marcus measured religious affiliation by major tradition and mainline denomination: Protestant, Catholic, Jewish, other religion, and nonreligious; and within Protestantism: Presbyterian, Methodist, Baptist, Episcopalian, and Lutheran. Religious affiliation was not combined with any sort of religiosity measure. Since Baptists were the only Protestant group for which there was a significant difference in tolerance scores, they used it as their religious explanatory variable. Presumably, they were using it to tap fundamentalism.

19. Corwin Smidt and James Penning, "Religious Commitment, Political Conservatism, and Political and Social Tolerance in the United States: A Longitudinal Analysis," *Sociological Analysis* 43 (1982): 231-46.

20. Religious liberals increased in their tolerance of atheists and declined in their tolerance of Communists from 1974 to 1980. They were more tolerant of homosexuals in 1977 than they were in 1974 or 1980. Religious conservatives were less tolerant toward all three groups in 1977 than they were in either 1974 or 1980. Nonreligious conservatives were the least

tolerant of all four groups in 1974, but religious conservatives had the lower tolerance levels in 1977 and 1980.

21. Smidt and Penning, "Religious Commitment," 244.

22. Kathleen Murphy Beatty and Oliver Walter, "Religious Preference and Practices: Reevaluating Their Impact on Political Tolerance," *Public Opinion Quarterly* 48 (1984): 318-29.

23. Ted Jelen and Clyde Wilcox, "Denominational Preference and the Dimensions of Political Tolerance," *Sociological Analysis* 51 (1990): 69-80.

24. Jelen and Wilcox, "Denominational Preference," 28.

25. John C. Green, James L. Guth, Lyman A. Kellstedt, and Corwin Smidt, "Uncivil Challenges: Support for Civil Liberties among Religious Activists," *Journal of Political Science* 22 (1994): 29.

26. Green et al., "Uncivil Challenges," 29.

27. Green et al., "Uncivil Challenges," 43.

28. This has been demonstrated repeatedly in studies of the political behavior of the religiously committed. For example, see Wald, *Religion and Politics in the United States*; David Leege and Lyman A. Kellstedt, "Religious Worldviews and Political Philosophies: Capturing Theory in the Grand Manner through Empirical Data," in *Rediscovering the Religious Factor in American Politics*, ed. David Leege and Lyman Kellstedt (Armonk, N.Y.: Sharpe, 1993), 216-34; Ted Jelen, ed., *Religion and Political Behavior in the United States* (New York: Praeger, 1989); and Ted Jelen, "Research in Religion and Mass Political Behavior in the United States: Looking Both Ways after Two Decades of Scholarship," *American Politics Quarterly* 26 (1998): 110-34.

29. George Gallup, Jr., and Jim Castelli, *The People's Religion: American Faith in the Nineties* (New York: MacMillan, 1989), 3.

30. Jelen, "Research in Religion and Mass Political Behavior," 120.

31. James L. Guth, Ted G. Jelen, Lyman A. Kellstedt, Corwin E. Smidt, and Kenneth D. Wald, "The Politics of Religion in America: Issues for Investigation," *American Politics Quarterly* 16 (1988): 360.

32. See, for example, David Leege, "Religiosity Measures in the National Election Studies: A Guide to the Use, Part II," *Votes and Opinions* 3 (1995): 28, and Jelen, "Research in Religion and Mass Political Behavior," 125.

33. See also George E. Marcus, John L. Sullivan, Elizabeth Theiss-Morse, and Sandra L. Wood, *With Malice toward Some* (Cambridge: Cambridge University Press, 1995); and John L. Sullivan, Michal Shamir, Patrick Walsh, and Nigel S. Roberts, *Political Tolerance in Context: Support for Unpopular Minorities in Israel, New Zealand, and the United States* (Boulder, Colo.: Westview Press, 1985).

34. Marcus et al., *With Malice toward Some*, 25. See also Martin Fishbein and Icek Ajzen, *Belief Attitude, Intention, and Behavior: An Introduction to Theory and Research* (Reading, Mass.: Addison-Wesley, 1975).

35. Marcus et al., *With Malice toward Some*. See also John R. Zaller, *The Nature and Origins of Mass Opinion* (New York: Cambridge, 1992); Susan T. Fiske and Donald R. Kinder, "Involvement, Expertise, and Schema Use: Evidence from Political Cognition," in *Personality, Cognition, and Social Interaction*, ed. Nancy Cantor and John F. Kihlstrom (Hillsdale, N.J.: Lawrence Erlbaum, 1981); and Jon A. Krosnick, "Attitude Importance and Attitude Accessibility," *Personality and Social Psychology Bulletin* 15 (1989): 297-308.

36. Fishbein and Ajzen, *Belief Attitude, Intention, and Behavior*; Marcus et al., *With Malice toward Some*; and Zaller, *The Nature and Origins of Mass Opinion*.

37. Zaller, *The Nature and Origins of Mass Opinion*, 23.

38. Fishbein and Ajzen, *Belief Attitude, Intention, and Behavior*, 14, 131.

39. Fishbein and Ajzen, *Belief Attitude, Intention, and Behavior*, 14.

40. Fishbein and Ajzen, *Belief Attitude, Intention, and Behavior*, 217.

41. Fishbein and Ajzen, *Belief Attitude, Intention, and Behavior*, 14, 218.

42. Krosnick, "Attitude Importance and Attitude Accessibility," 304. See also Tory E. Higgins and Gillian King, "Accessibility of Social Constructs: Information Processing Consequences of Individual and Contextual Variability," in *Personality, Cognition, and Social Interaction*, eds. Nancy Cantor and John F. Kihlstrom (Hillsdale, N.J.: Lawrence Erlbaum, 1981), 71, 75, 77.

43. Fishbein and Ajzen, *Belief Attitude, Intention, and Behavior*, 218. See also Fiske and Kinder, "Involvement, Expertise, and Schema Use"; and Zaller, *The Nature and Origins of Mass Opinion*.

44. Marcus et al., *With Malice toward Some*, 212.

45. Marcus et al., *With Malice toward Some*, 33.

46. Higgins and King, "Accessibility of Social Constructs," 70.

47. Fishbein and Ajzen, *Belief Attitude, Intention, and Behavior*, 288.

48. For example, Mark A. Noll, *The Scandal of the Evangelical Mind* (Grand Rapids, Mich.: Eerdmans, 1994); Harry Blamires, *The Christian Mind* (New York: Seabury, 1963); Wells, *No Place for Truth*; and Wells, *God in the Wasteland*.

49. See especially Eric Voegelin's account of the development of this split between the secular and the sacred in "The Emergence of Secularized History: Bousset and Voltaire," in *From Enlightenment to Revolution* (Durham, N.C.: Duke University Press, 1975).

50. For evidence of this, see Alan Wolfe, *One Nation, After All: What Middle-Class Americans Really Think about God, Country, Family, Racism, Welfare, Immigration, Homosexuality, Work, the Right, the Left, and Each Other* (New York: Viking, 1998).

51. Wald, *Religion and Politics in the United States*, 342.

52. Paul M. Sniderman, Philip E. Tetlock, James M. Glaser, Donald P. Green, and M. Hout, "Principled Tolerance and the American Mass Public," *British Journal of Political Science* 19 (1989): 25-45; Susan Mendus and David Edwards, *On Toleration* (Oxford: Clarendon Press, 1987), 2.

53. The groups that were asked about included conservatives, the U.S. Communist party, religious fundamentalists, the Ku Klux Klan, "people who are against all churches and religion," American Nazis, "those who would prohibit abortions," liberals, the Society for a New America (a fictitious group), "those who would allow abortions," feminists, "those who advocate doing away with elections and letting the military run the country," and homosexuals. There were a number of other group names volunteered by respondents as groups they strongly disliked. These included such groups as Lyndon La Rouche supporters (18 respondents), the John Birch Society (11), the NAACP (10), Republicans (7), Socialists (6), Democrats (6), the Moral Majority (5), the ACLU (4), Asians (4), Christian radio/TV talk show hosts (3), gay rights organizations (3), Black Panthers (3), and about thirty other groups with one or two respondents (including everything from liars, terrorists, "troublemakers," and the Mafia, to the National Rifle Association, Jesse Jackson, Ronald Reagan, the Mormon Church, TV evangelists, "Catholic ministers who advocate homosexuality," "groups supported by Jane Fonda and Tom Hayden," and "people who bring in illegal aliens").

54. In the F&T survey, the respondents were asked to name their first four most disliked groups, and they were asked about six activities for their first two most disliked groups. Those respondents who listed the KKK as their first or second most disliked group were asked about their third most disliked; all others (38 percent) were asked about the KKK. If

they had not yet been asked about Communists (49 percent of the sample), they were asked about Communists for the final question. Those respondents who had already been asked about Communists for one of their first two most disliked groups were asked about their third most disliked group, or if they had already been asked about their third most disliked (because they had identified the KKK as one of two most disliked), they were asked about their fourth most disliked (12 percent of the sample were asked about their fourth most disliked, and 38 percent their third most disliked).

55. For the third and fourth most disliked groups (or, for some respondents, the KKK and Communists), respondents were asked about only four activities: banning the group or barring it from public office, public speaking, or public rallies. Since only 12 percent of the respondents were actually asked about their third and fourth most disliked, while the 88 percent were asked about the KKK and/or Communists in place of their third or fourth most disliked, and because Gibson asked about only four activities for the third and fourth groups rather than the six asked of the first two groups, I do not include the third and fourth most disliked in my analyses.

56. Following Gibson's practice, I treated the "don't knows" the same as the "uncertains," by scoring them a "3" (between "agree" and "disagree") on the five-point Likert response sets (James L. Gibson, "Alternative Measures of Political Tolerance," *American Journal of Political Science* 36 [1992]: 563).

57. All my variables are scaled from 0 to 1, in order to make the coefficients more easily comparable.

58. Lyman A. Kellstedt, John C. Green, James L. Guth, and Corwin E. Smidt, "Grasping the Essentials: The Social Embodiment of Religion and Political Behavior," in *Religion and the Culture Wars: Dispatches from the Front*, ed. John C. Green, James L. Guth, Corwin E. Smidt, and Lyman A. Kellstedt (Lanham, Md.: Rowman & Littlefield, 1996), 174-92.

59. Black Protestants are identified either by affiliation with a majority black denomination or by race. Kellstedt et al. in "Grasping the Essentials" found in their analysis that black Protestants in historically white evangelical denominations in the South really should be included in the Black Protestant tradition along with those in the historically black denominations.

60. For religious salience, Kellstedt et al. used the National Election Studies item that asks respondents the importance of religion in their lives. GSS does not have this item, so I substituted the GSS item most analogous to it, a religious intensity measure. It asks the respondent: "Would you call yourself a strong (religious preference) or a not very strong (religious preference)?"

61. The commitment measure developed by Kellstedt et al. also included a belief measure: belief that God exists. This item is not included in my analysis because it is not included in GSS. Since GSS does not include a similar belief item that could be substituted for the NES item, and since about 95 percent of all Americans say they believe in God anyway, I dropped this dimension from my religious commitment measure.

62. The reasons for this are explained in note 8.

63. The fact that only six groups are selected by 95 percent of all respondents as their most disliked appears to refute Sullivan et al.'s theory of pluralistic intolerance. Note, however, that three of these six groups—the KKK, Nazis, and militarists—are considered extreme right groups, not the leftist nonconformist groups Stouffer was concerned about. In fact these three extreme right groups alone were identified as the most disliked by almost 60 percent of all respondents. Since groups on both the extreme left and the extreme right are evenly represented in these six groups, there is some support for Sullivan et al.'s contention that target groups are more dispersed across the ideological spectrum than earlier scholars had

maintained. However, the KKK is selected as disliked by the vast majority of the public, so it is not true that one group is not at risk for receiving the brunt of the harm, contrary to what Sullivan et al. had maintained.

64. Gibson, "Freedom and Tolerance in the United States," 575.

65. Political engagement is a multidimensional concept. Norman Nie, Jane Junn, and Kenneth Stehlik-Barry (*Education and Democratic Citizenship in America* [Chicago: University of Chicago Press, 1996], 21) identify several attributes of engagement, including knowledge of leaders, knowledge of political facts, political interest or attentiveness, and political participation and voting. Political engagement is measured here by vote turnout (in the 1984 presidential elections), political interest (self-reported), and political knowledge (correctly identifying governor, Congress member, and school superintendent). The three elements are not scaled, but maintained as separate variables, to be consistent with earlier research.

Table 9.5 demonstrates significant variation in all three elements of political engagement by religiosity, but the picture is mixed: commitment is positively associated with voting and political knowledge, but (for evangelicals) is negatively associated with interest. Seculars have higher interest, but lower knowledge. And though there are strong theoretical reasons to suspect that citizens who are more politically engaged would be more tolerant (e.g., Herbert McClosky, "Consensus and Ideology in American Politics," *American Political Science Review* 58 [1964]: 361-382; Herbert McClosky and Alida Brill, *Dimensions of Tolerance* [New York: Sage Publications, 1983]; Herbert McClosky and John Zaller, *The American Ethos: Public Attitudes toward Capitalism and Democracy* [Cambridge: Harvard University Press, 1984]; Marcus et al., *With Malice toward Some*), and scholars have frequently found that political elites or the more politically involved and well educated are more tolerant than other citizens (Samuel Stouffer, *Communism, Conformity, and Civil Liberties* [New York: Doubleday, 1955]; McClosky and Brill, *Dimensions of Tolerance*; Nunn, Crockett, and Williams, *Tolerance for Nonconformity*; Robert Jackman, "Political Elites, Mass Publics, and Support for Democratic Principles," *Journal of Politics* 34 [1972]: 753-773; Nie, Junn, and Stehlik-Barry, *Education and Democratic Citizenship in America*), none of the elements of political engagement (knowledge, interest, and voting) have significant coefficients in the regression analysis in table 9.4.

66. Since political tolerance is a primary liberal democratic value, we expect that support for democratic norms would be associated with greater tolerance. Marcus et al. suggest that this is because commitment to democratic principles is a type of "standing decision" to tolerate a disliked group (*With Malice toward Some*, 77). They found *strength* of commitment to democratic values an important predictor of tolerance: those respondents who had strong prior commitments to democratic principles were less swayed by contemporary information than were those whose support for democratic norms was less firm (214). My results confirm that support for democratic principles is crucial—in fact, it is the second most potent explanatory variable (dogmatism is the strongest). Note, however, that there are no significant differences across religious groups in support for democratic norms in table 9.5.

67. Threat can actually be a political or a psychological predisposition, depending on whether it is external or internal. There has been some research on how threat influences tolerance judgments (especially in Marcus et al., *With Malice toward Some*, 1995), but not on whether the religiously committed are more likely than the nonreligious to perceive threat from their least-liked group.

68. Traditionalism was not included in the Sullivan et al. and Marcus et al. studies. I include it, although it may be more accurately thought of as a value orientation rather than

a psychological predisposition, because it may have particular relevance for the tolerance of believers. Traditionalism scale reliability coefficient alpha is .62.

69. See also Sullivan et al., *Political Tolerance in Context*, 183.

70. An example is the following, spoken by Jesus to the Pharisees: "Woe to you, scribes and Pharisees, hypocrites! For you pay tithe of mint and anise and cummin, and have neglected the weightier matters of the law: justice and mercy and faith. . . . Woe to you, scribes and Pharisees, hypocrites! For you are like whitewashed tombs which indeed appear beautiful outwardly, but inside are full of dead men's bones and all uncleanness. Even so you outwardly appear righteous to men, but inside you are full of hypocrisy and lawlessness. . . . Serpents, brood of vipers! How can you escape the condemnation of hell?" (Matthew 23: 23, 27-28, 33).

71. William James, *The Varieties of Religious Experience* (New York: Simon & Schuster, 1997), 261.

72. Gordon Allport and J. M. Ross, "Personal Religious Orientation and Prejudice," *Journal of Personality and Social Psychology* 5 (1967): 432-43.

73. Allport and Ross, "Personal Religious Orientation and Prejudice," 441.

74. Allport and Ross, "Personal Religious Orientation and Prejudice," 434.

75. Gordon Allport, *The Individual and His Religion* (New York: Macmillan, 1960), 33.

76. Allport and Ross, "Personal Religious Orientation and Prejudice," 434.

77. Wald, *Religion and Politics in the United States*, 328-29.

78. Allport and Ross, "Personal Religious Orientation and Prejudice," 441.

79. Gordon Allport, "Religious Context of Prejudice," *Journal for the Scientific Study of Religion* 5 (1966): 455.

80. Allport, "Religious Context of Prejudice," 455.

81. Allport, "Religious Context of Prejudice," 434.

82. T. W. Adorno, Else Frenkel-Brunswick, Daniel J. Levinson, and R. Nevitt Sanford, *The Authoritarian Personality* (New York: Harper and Brothers, 1950).

83. Adorno et al., *The Authoritarian Personality*, 240.

84. Adorno et al., *The Authoritarian Personality*, 212.

85. Adorno et al., *The Authoritarian Personality*, 731.

86. Adorno et al., *The Authoritarian Personality*, 731.

87. Allport and Ross, "Personal Religious Orientation and Prejudice," 441.

88. Allport and Ross, "Personal Religious Orientation and Prejudice," 441.

89. Allport and Ross, "Personal Religious Orientation and Prejudice," 442.

90. Adorno et al., *The Authoritarian Personality*, 732.

91. For example, see L. A. Kirkpatrick, "A Psychometric Analysis of the Allport-Ross and Feagin Measures of Intrinsic-Extrinsic Religious Orientation," in *Research in the Social and Scientific Study of Religion,* vol. 1, ed. M. L. Lynn and D. O. Moberg (Greenwich, Conn.: JAI, 1989): 1-31. See also L. A. Kirkpatrick and R. W. Hood, "Intrinsic-Extrinsic Religious Orientation: The Boon or Bane of Contemporary Psychology of Religion?" *Journal for the Scientific Study of Religion* 29 (1990): 442-62.

92. Neuhaus, *The Naked Public Square*, 75.

93. Markham, *Plurality and Christian Ethics*, 16.

94. Adorno et al., *The Authoritarian Personality*, 733.

Chapter 10

Aliens and Citizens:
Competing Models of Political Involvement
in Contemporary Christian Social Ethics

David Oki Ahearn

A perceived tension between the kingdoms of this world and the eschatological Kingdom of God is an enduring feature of the Christian tradition. All manner of positions on this issue can be found in Christian history, ranging from the demonization of the Roman Imperial state in the Apocalypse of John at one end of the spectrum to the caesaropapism of medieval Orthodoxy at the other. The mainstream of the Christian tradition has tended to seek out a middle position between these extremes, however, seeking a relative peace between the human and divine orders without losing sight of the limited, penultimate nature of the former.

In American history, too, the debate concerning the proper relationship between the church and the political order has tended to gravitate toward two centrist positions. The first, *pluralistic separationism,* traces its origins to the Anabaptists and other separatists groups in America's colonial past.[1] Churches that fall within this category tend to define the role of the church in the world through the matrix of interlocking dualisms: love versus justice, face-to-face relations versus complex institutions, and transcendent and ultimate versus immanent and penultimate. Many churches that exemplify this type are pacifist. They thus reject the ultimate goodness of the state, which necessarily achieves its purposes through coercion. The political order, to use the memorable phrase of the Schleitheim Confession, reflects God's will for the world "outside the perfection of Christ." Perennial outsiders, pluralistic separationists tend to view themselves as prophets who expose the clay feet of the political order rather than reform it from within.

The second position, *institutional separationism,* traces its origins to America's Puritan legacy. While this position maintains a clear separation of ecclesial and political institutions, it also believes that God has authority over the political realm as well as the church. Consequently, institutional separationists view political life as meaningful and within the proper vocation of the Christian. Like the Puritans, contemporary institutional separationists believe that religious bodies have a special obligation to participate in public life. Unlike the Puritans, however, this group claims no special legal status for any particular religious institution. Institutional separationists typically have affirmed the church's special obligation to maintain republican political structures as the best mechanism to maintain healthy public debate.

The conflict between pluralistic separationists and institutional separationists is a perennial feature of American public life. The substantive issues that first divided Roger Williams and John Cotton in colonial New England have never been resolved. Indeed, these issues may be unresolvable, since each of the two parties defends important truths that strike to the heart of the Christian faith. In contemporary American Christian ethics, this perennial argument has been reincarnated in the conflicts between those Christian intellectuals who ground Christian truth in a "narrative theology" and those who call on the church to vivify its "public theology." Metaphorically, the first of these models pictures the church as a resident alien within the political order, while the second pictures it as a responsible, yet critical, citizen. The remainder of this chapter will sketch out the parameters of these two positions and indicate their respective capacities to make sense of the place of the church in the American polity.

The Church as Resident Alien

Within recent years a movement has converged from diverse traditions within American Christian ethics that expresses profound unease about what it perceives as an unfortunate alliance between American Christianity and liberal democracy. This view is apparent in Pope John Paul II's indictments of Western culture, in philosopher Alasdair MacIntyre's work on virtue and character,[2] and in such perennial critics of secular culture as the American Mennonites and other peace churches.[3] Perhaps the most engaging of these critics is the United Methodist and Duke University seminary professor Stanley Hauerwas. Provocative, combative, and insightful, Hauerwas plays the role of gadfly in contemporary Protestant Christian ethics. His work will be the chief focus of this section.[4]

Hauerwas is convinced that the tensions between the Christian faith and democratic liberalism are so fundamental that the church can only be described as a resident alien living in the midst of the worldly kingdom. In the legal context, a resident alien is a person living and working within one state but whose citizenship remains in another. For Hauerwas, even as the church sojourns in this age, its true citizenship is in the Kingdom of Heaven. Like other pluralistic separationists, Hauerwas employs metaphors that connote tension and estrangement with the world to describe the identity of the church: the church is "a beachhead, an outpost, an island of one culture in the middle of another."[5] The church's most vital task, then, is not to save the world but to nurture its distinctive identity, pass this identity on to its young, and proclaim its witness in a voice that the world can only regard as strange and other. Hauerwas does affirm that the church can work for proximate justice in its alien home, so long as it preserves its independence and eschews the coercive tactics of the state.[6]

Hauerwas believes that the alien status of the church in the world is not accidental, for the moral imperatives that guide the church are utterly foreign to the political order. Following the lead of the historic peace churches, Hauerwas dates the "fall" of the church at 313, when Emperor Constantine's Edict of Milan wedded church to empire. From this point forward, the church had to relinquish the purity of the definitive Christian virtues: agapic love, hospitality, and especially nonviolence. Hauerwas rejects the mainstream American church as "accommodationist" or "Constantinian." This church measures its moral voice not by faithfulness to agapic love, "but rather on the basis of how much Christian ethics Caesar can be induced to swallow without choking."[7]

Hauerwas anchors this antagonistic stance toward the American culture in a theological movement called narrative theology. This now widely influential theological model emerged from a collection of scholars at Yale University in the mid-twentieth century, including such luminaries as Hans Frei, H. Richard Niebuhr (the early work but assuredly not his mature work), and especially the theologian Julian Hartt.[8] Central to this model is the conception that all communities, and not merely the church, form their identities and define their mission by the stories they tell about who they are. Narrative theologians believe that this model is especially appropriate for Christian communities. They point to the narrative genre that forms the bulk of the scriptural tradition. But even more, they believe that the Christian scriptures picture a God who leads the faithful through time. This history, like a good story, defines a beginning, develops the plot throughout the middle, and places its hopes in a consummation at the end of time. "We are 'storied people,'" Hauerwas writes, "because the God that sustains us is a 'storied God,' whom we come to know only by having our character formed appropriate to God's character."[9]

Many critics of narrative theology counter that the movement valorizes a tradition that is closed, patriarchal, and static. The more thoughtful of the narrative theologians respond that simply retelling the same old story is not enough, for traditions can grow moribund and die. Truly vital societies are best understood as an extended argument. The inherited tradition must be reexamined and reinterpreted continually so that its latent possibilities and limitations can be exposed. Hauerwas writes that the real depth of a tradition is measured by its ability to form people who are willing to put its inherited understandings of truth to the test.[10]

Narrative theology is closely tied with a moral theory that places a renewed emphasis on virtue and character. Narrative theologians believe that the stories a community tells form its self-identity and shape its character. So understood, the Christian virtues are profoundly social in nature. Character is formed slowly over time as one participates in a community that is committed to the common task of modeling its behavior after the stories it tells about the life of Jesus.[11]

This emphasis on character and virtue provides a basis for narrative ethicists to claim a common cause with historic Catholic moral theology. Both schools reject obligation-oriented ethical systems, which conceive moral reasoning as application of abstract principles like love, justice, or beneficence to concrete cases. This latter approach typically has dominated Protestant ethics since Kant. Despite superficial agreements in method, however, narrative and historical Catholic moral theologians build their ethical systems on entirely different foundations. Catholic moral theologians typically have grounded ethical theory in an Aristotelean conception of virtue: the virtues are those durable traits that enable a person to achieve happiness (*eudaimonia*), which is the proper end of human life. Aristotle was convinced that the true nature of happiness could be determined through reason. Ethics, a form of practical reason, is the reflective process of determining how to live out the virtues in concrete situations. Thomas Aquinas believed that the ultimate ground of human happiness is made known through revelation, but he never abandoned the conviction that the content of revelation is at least consistent with human reason. Catholic moral theology thus has consistently maintained that true human virtues reflect not simply the truth "for us," but the Truth, at least insofar as it can be known in a particular time and place. This conviction provides Catholic moral theologians a foundation for engagement with the public sphere. Non-Catholics, and even non-Christians, can be addressed from a shared foundation in common human reason.

Hauerwas utterly rejects the possibility that the virtues can be anchored in a single human end that is consistent in common human reason. "We must choose between ways of life that are inherently incompatible," he writes.[12] Character is shaped, rather, by living within a distinctive community whose first principles are not shared by outsiders. The Christian narrative *does* make universal claims, Hauerwas maintains, but these are appropriated by becoming part of a particular community living out its distinctive story.[13] He concedes to his critics that narrative theology renders impossible any truly moral discourse between persons from different customs and beliefs. He acknowledges that the Christian story simply cannot provide the foundations for a common morality that can support the diversity of communities that liberal society produces. However, Hauerwas argues that the church's task is not to provide social order but to be faithful to its own story in a divided world. The church must simply bear witness to its own story with the hopes that others will hear it and be converted.

At this point we are at last able to see the true source of Hauerwas's great distaste for liberal democracy. Liberal political theory alone, he argues, is founded on the myth that social life can be organized without reference to any common narrative. Liberalism is founded on the proposition that "the good society is that in which each person gets to be his or her own tyrant."[14] It promises to ground social cooperation not in a common story or common conception of justice but in a set of procedures that ensure fairness even as people disagree about who they are and where they are going. On its face, liberalism seems an ingenious device to coordinate political life in a world made up of strangers that share no common story. Paradoxically, however, liberal society is parasitic on coherent narrative communities. Hauerwas makes the now commonplace observation that the founders of the American republic themselves knew that liberal society is itself dependent on communities that can form character in the private sphere. The problem, however, is that the liberal vision has so thoroughly affected private life that Americans are increasingly strangers to one another within their own families and churches. Hauerwas concludes that contemporary American public life, deprived a common narrative, cannot be other than shallow, bureaucratic, and litigious.[15]

Hauerwas is quite willing to concede that liberal democracy, despite its inadequacies, is a real historical achievement and is far better than most political systems that preceded it. Moreover, he acknowledges that liberal democracy is so fully entrenched that there is no ready alternative to it in American political life. Still, Hauerwas believes that the deficiencies of liberal democracy are severe, are built into the founding assumptions of American democracy, and are reinforced by even its best political theory and practices.[16] "We are all liberals," Hauerwas concludes, but this statement must be read more as a lament than a positive affirmation.[17]

Hauerwas thus finds the quest to develop a public theology to be fundamentally misguided. He believes that public theology is grounded on false assumptions about the universality of reason and the universal accessibility of moral values. Hauerwas asks, if Christians are able to understand God's will for humanity apart from the unique revelation of Jesus Christ and through the life of the Christian community, then why be Christian at all?[18]

The Christian as Citizen

Stanley Hauerwas's appreciation for the narrative structure of human community, his emphasis on virtue and character, and his profound criticism of liberalism are widely shared within contemporary Christian ethics. More contentious is his claim that these theoretical commitments render impossible any substantive engagement in the public sphere between Christians and others. Opposing Hauerwas and other narrative ethicists is that movement in contemporary American Christian social ethics that is endeavoring to establish the basis for a public theology. The term *public theology* was first coined by Martin Marty to indicate those churches whose discourse is directed outward, engaging others in the public square in order to bring about a transformation of society. According to this model, the proper metaphor for the place of the Christian in liberal democratic society is not that of a resident alien, but that of a responsible, yet critical, citizen.

At the risk of glossing over important differences between individual theorists, this model tends to perceive a common set of features that characterizes public discourse. First, public discourse concerns common things. "Common" here does not mean that public participation requires homogenous sameness or even that all citizens affirm the same slate of fundamental values. Rather, it refers to those common commitments that arise when persons consent to live together in a body politic. John Dewey termed them the "consequences of our social interaction."[19] Hauerwas may or may not be correct in his assessment that liberal society produces relative strangers who share little in common in their private lives. Dewey was convinced, however, that even strangers create a common history when they consent to form a society. To the degree that Christians and others create and maintain a coherent society, they share a common good.

Public theologians thus share Hauerwas's assessment that American society is excessively subjective and privatistic. Unlike Hauerwas, however, these theorists believe that the church itself can help heal these great ills by appeals to common convictions upon which the society is founded. As public discourse goes about its work of expanding public space, concerns formerly deemed private will be exposed for public examination and debate. In recent years, for example, patriarchal gender roles, child abuse, and spousal sexual abuse have become topics of moral discourse in the American public square.

Second, public discourse concerns not simply common things, but a common *good*. Public discourse is thus inherently *moral* discourse. Public discourse is concerned what it means to live the good life, what priorities a society holds, what virtues it rewards, what moral obligations it must maintain. *Pacem* liberal social theories that reduce the common good to the aggregate sum of individual goods, public theorists believe that public discourse directs speakers to recall shared intersubjective norms that arise from normative traditions that they hold in common.[20] The prolific sociologist of religion Robert Wuthnow describes public discourse as "the process of arriving at collective values."[21]

Third, the mode of public discourse is reason and persuasion rather than coercion or manipulation. The German social philosopher Jürgen Habermas defines a "communication community" as a public forum in which those affected, as participants in a practical discourse, test the validity claims of norms and, to the extent they accept them with reasons, arrive at the conviction that in the given circumstances the proposed norms are "right."[22] In similar terms, Richard Bernstein describes "public" as a space in which individuals can debate one another and clarify and test values, and in which "judgment, deliberation, and *phronesis* can flourish."[23] In sum, public speech, even that which is guided by religious faith, must be accessible to common experience and reason.[24]

Like other institutional separatists, public theologians thus stake their agenda on the belief that Americans both inside and outside the church share a common life, affirm at least some common moral convictions, and should seek consensus through the medium of reason and persuasion. Public theologians believe that these beliefs are not simply accurate descriptions of contemporary American society but that they rest on deeper convictions about the nature of God and human community. Many contemporary Catholic public theologians, for example, reaffirm their tradition's emphasis on the efficacy of common human reason, affirmation of a common human nature, and belief in a strong doctrine of creation.

An emphasis on public theology is especially associated with those Protestant theorists who work within the perspective of covenantal ethics. These theologians argue that public theology can be particularly vibrant in democratic federal republics, which they believe embody especially well the covenantal foundations of human social life. These theorists see it as no accident that federal republican political structures emerged in the early modern period in those free cities along the Rhine River that embraced covenantal theology. Federalism and covenantalism share foundations that are both extensive and deep: the relational nature of human life, the centrality of promise-making and consent in moral anthropology, the need to measure the popular will against some transcendent standard, and a political model that stresses the need for a healthy pluralism of associations.[25] Unlike Hauerwas, many covenantal ethicists believe that the church *does* have a stake in democratic republicanism, for the church has played a vital role in the formation of republican political structures in Western history and shares many of its values concerning public life.

A belief that the church and American society share some common moral convictions does not mean that these convictions are easily determined. Indeed, when public theologians indicate historical examples that best illustrate responsible public leadership by the church, they typically point to periods of great conflict in which Americans have redefined their moral convictions only by struggling through intensive national conflict. One such example in this century is the civil rights movement. The movement truly was a watershed event in the national consciousness, for it required a fundamental transformation of beliefs, attitudes, and even patterns of social interaction. Church participation in the movement was key. Yet, this participation was not simply a matter of proclamation of God's justice to an unjust world. Churches aligned themselves on both sides of the issue. The national debate forced the church to come to terms with its own moral convictions in order for it to speak to the world. The civil rights movement thus appears to be a clear example of a mutually beneficial dialogue between the church and a society whose institutions and values themselves had been heavily shaped by Judeo-Christian conceptions of justice.

Of all figures in this epic struggle, Dr. Martin Luther King, Jr., emerges as one of the most towering personalities. King regularly is named as one of the finest public theologians that America has produced. Public theologians maintain that King called for systemic political change of grossly unjust racial structures by an appeal to the nation to own up to its most fundamental moral convictions. King believed that these convictions were rooted in the Judeo-Christian moral tradition and were reaffirmed in America's founding documents, most especially the

Declaration of Independence. Public theologians thus conclude that Americans shared a common set of values that were sufficiently coherent that they could support a deep public consensus for racial healing and sufficiently prophetic that they could prompt substantive political change. To the degree that this picture of King is an accurate one, it would seem to call into question Hauerwas's indictment of the moral bankruptcy of the liberal tradition.[26]

Hauerwas understands King and the civil rights movement differently. He believes that King's moral convictions arose from his particular "embeddedness" in the black church with its distinctive memories and stories. His vision of justice was thoroughly infused with the radicality of the eschatological kingdom far richer and deeper than liberalism's purely procedural justice. Hauerwas argues that King's commitment to liberal society was largely instrumental. In the end, Hauerwas believes that King was successful not because he addressed American society as a whole, but because he managed to put together a highly particular, and highly unstable, coalition.[27] In short, Hauerwas pictures King as a missionary for a particular narrative rather than a disinterested prophet for the common good. An adequate treatment of King is beyond the scope of this essay. The issue is instructive, however, in that it illustrates the very different interpretations given to recent American social history by these two ethical movements.

Reflections

We have seen that contemporary public and narrative theologians define the church's task in the world in sharply divergent terms. Public theologians believe that substantive moral discourse in the public square is made possible by the existence of at least some common core values shared between communities with different moral traditions, that this common ground concerns moral convictions and not merely incidental matters of taste, and that different groups share at least a minimal understanding of what constitutes valid moral reasoning. Narrative theology in general—and Stanley Hauerwas in particular—rejects all of these claims. Hauerwas responds that communities from different moral communities really hold very little that is meaningful in common, that this essential strangeness prevents any truly moral discourse between such groups, and that any political change that might emerge from an encounter between groups would be produced through conversion or naked exercise of social power and not a genuine consensus reached through rational discourse.

As the most vocal proponent of narrative theology, Hauerwas has done a great service to the church. He rightly diagnoses the danger that the mainline churches may lose sight of their distinctive self-understanding and mission as they make their home in a society that is at least superficially "Christianized." Narrative theology also promises to more firmly connect Christian ethics to the local congregation, where individual persons are shaped into a people of God by the stories they hear and retell. The contributions of narrative theology are recognized even by many Christian ethicists who do not consider themselves to be narrative theologians. For example, no contemporary American Christian ethicist is more committed to substantive dialogue between groups from differing moral traditions than is James Gustafson. Yet, Gustafson readily acknowledges that abstract moral reasoning has a limited function, for it cannot "stir the imagination" or "induce dreams" in the way that a community's moral narratives can. Gustafson calls narrative "first-order religious discourse," for it shapes a durable identity that can survive the tests of engagement and dialogue.[28]

Despite Hauerwas's great contributions to the ongoing debate concerning the American church's role in public life, several difficulties remain in his project. First, one regrets a certain disingenuousness in some of Hauerwas's rhetoric. Throughout *Resident Aliens*, for example, Hauerwas and William Willimon describe the true church as a "colony in an alien culture" and label all churches who seek some sort of active engagement with the culture as "Constantinian." Neither of these terms is terribly helpful in describing the complexity of the church's relationship to American public life. Must a faithful church view the American culture as utterly alien to its mission? Despite its great deficiencies, the American state is not simply "the beast out of the abyss" (Revelation 13:11) that has declared war on the church. Rather, the American state is relatively just and its Constitution grants unprecedented protection to religious conscience. As Augustine so clearly understood, a church oriented toward the peace of the City of God can nevertheless make its home in and make use of the provisional peace found in the earthly city. The church is never purely "at home" in the world nor purely estranged from it. Describing the culture as simply "alien" obscures the delicate task assigned Christian ethics to map out what it means to engage a culture to which the church can give more or less provisional—but nevertheless very real—loyalty.

The second term is the charge of "Constantinianism." It is difficult to discern what this term might mean in the American context. On the one side, the "church" in America is not early Catholicism's monolithic body ruled by a single hierarchy, but rather an uncountable multitude of separate and competing institutions. On the other side, the American polity is not an imperial state led by an emperor who can meddle at will in matters of church doctrine and order, but a democratically elected authority that is constitutionally prohibited from establishing religion and interfering in matters of conscience without compelling state interest.

The terms "colony" and "Constantinianism" are thus so inaccurate in their description of the American context that they simply cannot be taken at face value. One can only assume that they are rhetorical terms intended to produce an effect. The reader is left wondering, however, what the effect is intended to be. Hauerwas may employ these terms to indicate simply that the church "depends on more profound moral convictions than our secular polity can politically acknowledge" and that Christians must "challenge the moral presuppositions of our polity and society."[29] These convictions are by no means special insights of narrative theology, however, but are enduring themes in the history of Christian ethics. The public theologians comprehend more clearly than Hauerwas that "challenging the moral presuppositions" of society is complementary to, and not an alternative to, substantive engagement of the church in public life.

A second area of difficulty concerns the role of narrative in Christian ethics. Even if one recognizes the formative role of narrative in establishing Christian identity, Hauerwas has not sufficiently shown that the stories the church tells about its life in Christ are fundamentally at odds with the stories in the wider American public that establish a national identity. One only need recall here the great impact of Martin Luther King's ringing address at the march on Washington. King's theme for the speech was "I have a dream that is deeply rooted in the American dream." This classic in American rhetoric is a skillful interweaving of sacred and secular themes: prophetic calls for justice from Isaiah, lines from African American spirituals, and phrases lifted from the Declaration of Independence and the U.S. Constitution. Certainly the most natural reading of King's mission—Hauerwas's protestations aside—is that he sought to transform the whole nation from the perspective of faith and not simply to advance the interests of one segment within it.

A third and related concern is that Hauerwas has not sufficiently demonstrated that a people whose identities are shaped by the "first-order" discourse of narrative cannot, without denying that identity, also choose to engage in public dialogue through the "second-order" moral discourse of rational argumentation. To be sure, the church always risks a watering down of its message as it translates it into publicly accessible terms. Nevertheless, the enterprise can be rejected out of hand only if one sees no common ground between reason and revelation, justice and love, Christian perfection and the general conditions for human flourishing. Some minority voices in the Christian tradition have denied these linkages in order to preserve the purity of the gospel, and indeed these claims ring true in those instances that the church must struggle to survive in a hostile environment. It is doubtful, however, that such conditions prevail in contemporary America. Hauerwas himself recognizes that the greatest challenge facing the American church is not outright opposition but a subtle pressure from a quasi-Christian culture to set aside the more radical obligations of the Christian gospel.

Stanley Hauerwas sees rightly the danger that the church will become too comfortable with its place in the world. Nevertheless, given the particularly rich historical interactions between religious faith and the formation of American democratic political institutions, the church cannot understand itself as simply a "resident alien" in a hostile land. As the church rediscovers its true identity, it no doubt must affirm many moral commitments that truly are untranslatable to the wider public. But it will also find rumblings of faith that have resounded deeply throughout the American polity. Indeed, a full telling of the church's "storied past" should include not only memories of martyrdom, but also legitimate engagement with the public sphere as a responsible, yet critical citizen.

Notes

1. The terms *pluralistic separationism* and *institutional separationism* were coined by the legal historian Carl H. Esbeck. Actually, Esbeck perceives five categories in his typology of church-state relations in America, but the two discussed here dominate in the contemporary American church's self-understanding. In addition, what he terms *strict separationism* received much judicial support during the decades of the 1960s and 1970s. *Nonpreferentialism* and *restorationism* are manifested by some quarters of the Religious Right but have never garnered widespread popular support. Carl H. Esbeck, "Five Views of Church-State Relations in Contemporary American Thought," *Brigham Young University Law Review* (1986): 371-404.

2. See especially MacIntyre's *After Virtue,* 2d ed. (Notre Dame, Ind.: University of Notre Dame Press, 1984). See also Alasdair MacIntyre, *Whose Justice? Which Rationality?* (Notre Dame, Ind.: University of Notre Dame Press, 1988).

3. The work of John Howard Yoder is perhaps the best representative of the Mennonite tradition. See especially his recently published work coauthored with Glen H. Stassen and D. M. Yeager, *Authentic Transformation: A New Vision of Christ and Culture* (Nashville, Tenn.: Abingdon Press, 1996).

4. Hauerwas's work is especially frustrating because he is not above painting a caricature of the work of his interlocutors—or even his own work—in order to provoke an argument. He sets forth his position most carefully and constructively in *A Community of Character: Toward a Constructive Christian Social Ethic* (Notre Dame, Ind.: University of Notre Dame Press, 1981). This chapter will draw most heavily from this work, supplementing the analysis from Hauerwas's other writings as necessary to flesh out his argument.

5. Stanley Hauerwas and William Willimon, *Resident Aliens: Life in the Christian Colony* (Nashville, Tenn., Abingdon Press, 1989), 12.

6. Hauerwas, *Community of Character,* 110.

7. Hauerwas, *Resident Aliens,* 18-19.

8. Jonathan R. Wilson traces out these connections in "From Theology of Culture to Theological Ethics: The Hartt-Hauerwas Connection," *Journal of Religious Ethics* 23 (Spring 1995): 149-63.

9. Hauerwas, *Community of Character,* 91.

10. The conception of tradition as extended argument is most closely identified with Alasdair MacIntyre, whose works are cited above. Hauerwas develops this concept in *Community of Character,* 14.

11. Hauerwas, *Community of Character,* 91-105.

12. Hauerwas, *Community of Character,* 143. See the extended discussion in the whole of chapter 7.

13. Hauerwas, *Community of Character,* 12.

14. Hauerwas, *Resident Aliens,* 33.

15. Hauerwas, *Community of Character,* 81.

16. Hauerwas, *Community of Character,* 77.

17. Gustafson, *Theology and Ethics* (Oxford: Basil Blackwell, 1981), 321-22.

18. Hauerwas, *Community of Character,* 39.

19. See John Dewey, *The Public and Its Problems* (New York: Henry Holt & Co., 1927).

20. See José Casanova, *Public Religions in the Modern World* (Chicago: University of Chicago Press, 1994), 229.

21. Robert Wuthnow, ed., *Between States and Markets: The Voluntary Sector in Comparative Perspective* (Princeton, N.J.: Princeton University Press, 1991), 22.

22. Jürgen Habermas, *Legitimation Crisis*, trans. Thomas McCarthy (Boston: Beacon Press, 1973), 103-105.

23. Richard Bernstein, "The Meaning of Public Life," in *Religion and American Public Life: Interpretations and Explorations*, ed. Robin W. Lovin (New York: Paulist Press, 1986), 46.

24. See, for example, Franklin I. Gamwell, "Religion and Reason in American Politics," in *Religion and American Public Life*, 105.

25. For an excellent study of public theology made possible by the deep connections between covenantal theology and federalism, see William Johnson Everett, *God's Federal Republic: Reconstructing Our Governing Symbol* (New York: Paulist Press, 1988). See also Daniel J. Elazar's majestic four-volume series, *The Covenant Tradition in Politics* (New Brunswick, N.J.: Transaction, 1995-1998).

26. See Christopher Beem, "American Liberalism and the Christian Church: Stanley Hauerwas versus Martin Luther King, Jr.," *Journal of Religious Ethics* 23 (Spring 1995): 119-33.

27. Stanley Hauerwas, "Remembering Martin Luther King, Jr., Remembering," *Journal of Religious Ethics* 23 (Spring 1995): 135-48.

28. James F. Gustafson, *Intersections: Science, Technology and Ethics*(Cleveland, Ohio: Pilgrim Press, 1996), 49-52.

29. Hauerwas, *Community of Character*, 73-74.

Chapter 11

Inverted Morality

Brad Lowell Stone

My concerns in this brief chapter are both practical and theoretical. I employ classical liberal moral theory to criticize the moral practices of the American middle class, as described by Alan Wolfe in *One Nation, After All,*[1] and I defend classical liberalism against certain theoretical arguments advanced by theologian Stanley Hauerwas. I discuss Hauerwas for two reasons. First, he is representative of a group of antiliberal theorists whose criticisms of liberalism result from what I believe is selective misrepresentation and, second, he is unique among antiliberal theorists in that his own thoroughly Christian moral theory is largely compatible with classical liberalism properly understood. I commence with the discussion of middle-class morality, after which I turn to Hauerwas.

If we trust John Stuart Mill, H. L. Mencken, and Professor Wolfe, the historic transformation of middle-class morality has been nothing short of a complete inversion. According to Mill and Mencken, the salient features of the old middle-class morality were its parochialism, exclusivity, uniformity, and intolerance.[2] Today, according to Wolfe, middle class morality is cosmopolitan, inclusive, pluralistic, and nonjudgmental. No longer the sworn enemy of Mill's "one very simple principle," the middle class now embodies that principle. The middle class believes that no one has the right or obligation to impede the choices of another and that any and all self-regarding actions must be tolerated. "Judge not, lest ye be judged." Indeed, as Wolfe says, this morality is "tolerant to a fault." Although generally friendly to the middle class and its morality, he observes that the middle class would be "better off with a little more Kantian backbone in their moral assembly kit."[3]

Wolfe calls this morality "a morality writ small" because its *content* is modest and wishy-washy and because it is limited to a *sphere* "below politics," the local sphere of close personal relations. It is a private, not a public, morality, a fact that Wolfe laments because it inhibits civic actions and fosters a sense of powerlessness. Still, for the most part, Wolfe finds middle-class morality more admirable than blamable. He is impressed by the absence of rancor among the middle class, and he is convinced that the "culture war" is being waged by the clerisy far from comfortable, suburban middle-class homes. He is also impressed by the "maturity and moderation" of this morality and by its pragmatic, commonsensical, *bricolage* nature.[4]

Wolfe's account of middle-class morality is very convincing, but in the spirit of the middle class itself, Wolfe is, I believe, tolerant to a fault. There is precious little that is admirable in this morality. I would like to maintain, in fact, that the *content* of this morality is wholly inappropriate to its *sphere* and that this confused morality is at the source of most social ills about which middle-class Americans claim concern. It is antimorality parading as morality.

I say these things not because I am impressed with rigorous moral systems such as those of Rousseau, Kant, or Durkheim, each of which requires the submission of individual inclinations to the great demands of duty. I say these things based upon my admiration for the naturalistic ethics of Locke, Hume, and Adam Smith, a humble and rather amiable moral theory important to the American founding and to much of the American experience.[5] It was, in fact, these classical liberals who first firmly distinguished between the private and public spheres and who cast their moral theory in terms of the very different virtues appropriate to each sphere.

The classical liberals sought to promote a cosmopolitan, inclusive, pluralistic, and tolerant *public* morality, one appropriate to relations among nonintimates. At the center of this morality was universalistic justice, a negative virtue that could be expressed by doing nothing, but which more commonly would regulate the mercenary exchanges of rational and self-interested strangers. The cosmopolitan and tolerant public morality espoused by the classical liberals was deemed a much-needed alternative to the harsh virtues of archaic morality because such virtues fostered hatred, constrained one's sense of humanity, and impelled adherents toward war. The commercial republic envisioned by the classical liberals would soften rigorous morals, pacify the citizenry, and promote universal opulence.

It is possible that the classical liberals were too successful in their efforts to promote this public morality if indeed middle-class private morality is cosmopolitan, inclusive, and nonjudgmental. For the classical liberals most emphatically did not believe that the moral relations of intimates could possess these qualities. Private morality, they believed, should be guided by natural obligation and benevolence to one's kin and friends, a morality that is particularistic, exclusive, finely discriminating, and dependent upon the praise and harsh censure of one's significant fellows. Unlike justice, the breach of which requires sanctions codified in law, the maintenance of benevolence, the classical liberals believed, requires regular monitoring by our intimates and the willingness of the same to show their disapprobation when we fall short of our duties. Indeed, for the classical liberals, a willingness to judge and censure the acts of others was seen as a necessary check upon temptations to evil, one that in the liberal scheme made the Hobbesian check unnecessary.

For the classical liberals, we are not naturally political beings, but we are naturally sociable. Although we are naturally sociable or communal, however, the extent of our sociability is limited. By nature, we are partial to our fellow parishioners, neighbors, friends, and especially our kin. Universal benevolence is impossible. Our good will knows no limits, but our good offices are inherently limited. Benevolence looks its object in the face, and particular people are recommended by nature to our care. Accordingly, and most important in this view, parents have a natural and unilateral obligation to raise their children to maturity.

Although quite modest in its moral demands, liberal moral theory sets standards well beyond the reach of many middle-class Americans. Wolfe found few middle-class Americans willing to say that any family type is as good as any other, but few seemed willing or capable of describing the rearing of children as the natural and transcendent purpose of marriage. According to Wolfe, the notion that emerged most consistently among his middle-class interviewees is "that people ought to decide for themselves what kind of family form is appropriate for them."[6] There are no natural obligations, no transcendent ends, when the choosing-self is sanctified.

On one point the classical liberal view—at least that of Adam Smith—was probably wrong. Smith argued that the natural moral sentiments could be "somewhat warpt" but not "entirely perverted" by custom or culture.[7] He shuddered with horror at the thought of what else a people might be capable of if custom enabled them to kill children because supporting those children would be "inconvenient."[8] Nonetheless, Smith knew well that assaults on nature and natural moral sentiments would always have dramatic and demonstrable effects. Indeed, I believe a dispassionate survey of American life suggests that our chief problems do not lie with the public institutions of commerce and government or with our public morality, as pallid as it may be. Our problems instead lie with our private morality and with our familiar institutions. In any event, contemporary empirical evidence on family form and its consequences sustains what nature recommends, and, although I cannot do justice to this evidence, I can mention some of it as an indictment of the moral lassitude of middle-class Americans.

A good place to begin this brief bill of particulars is with poverty, because critics of the American public order regularly see poverty as an unfortunate consequence of capitalism, a consequence that belies the classical liberal hope that capitalism would provide universal opulence. At the risk of sounding indifferent to the real plight of the poor, I am compelled to mention that among the poor in America 40 percent own their own homes, 97 percent have televisions, two-thirds have air-conditioning, and a fourth have two cars.[9] By any reasonable historic or contemporary world standard, Americans have indeed achieved the classical liberal dream of universal opulence. More directly to my point, indifference to family composition on the part of middle-class Americans is hardly laudable because American poverty is a function of household composition. Single-parent households are five times more likely to be in poverty than intact households, and intact households—white, black, other—are now virtually immune to long-term poverty.[10] Similarly, children from intact households are twice as likely as single-parent children to be educational high achievers and half as likely to drop out of school.[11] Single women are four times more likely than married women to be victims of violent crime.[12] Regarding domestic violence specifically, never-married women are four times as likely as married women to suffer domestic abuse, and divorced and separated women are ten times more likely to suffer abuse.[13] Almost nine of ten American children who are victims of neglect are from single-parent households, and children with a stepparent are forty times more likely to be victims of abuse than children living with both biological parents.[14] Moreover, children from intact households are half as likely as single-parent children to abuse drugs; they are less than a third as likely to be institutionalized for emotional and psychological problems, and they are less than half as likely to be arrested for a crime.[15] Seventy percent of all juveniles in state reform institutions, 70 percent of long-term prison inmates, 60 percent of rapists, and 72 percent of adolescent murderers are from fatherless homes.[16]

These associations or correlations are easily shown to be causal relationships, and a case can be made in most instances that family form is the chief cause of these different social problems.[17] Nonetheless, it is certainly not true that family composition is the only cause of these or other social maladies. Moreover, the family does not stand alone among the institutions within the private sphere because religious institutions are essential to the maintenance of private morality within liberal nations. In this regard, the writings of Hauerwas are especially intriguing because he insists upon the role of Christian communities in the formation of moral character, while indicting liberalism for the disruption of these communities.

Hauerwas has blistered many Christians for their bland ecumenicalism and universalism; his writings are especially noteworthy for their insistence upon the singularity of the Christian life. More forcefully and eloquently than any other contemporary theologian, he has demonstrated the peculiarity of the Christian virtues of hope, peaceableness, patience, obedience, forgiveness, and, above all, *caritas*. The Christian virtues, for Hauerwas, are simply not compatible with pagan or civic virtues, and they are formed in but one context—a community of Christians. There is no salvation outside disciplined Christian communities that make the Christian life meaningful and *demanding*. Indeed, though a pacifist, he regularly asserts the need for Christians to prepare themselves to die for their faith—not as holy warriors but as martyrs.[18] Such views have led Hauerwas to be accused of fideism and sectarianism, but his views are both refreshing and illuminating in this regard.

Unfortunately, Hauerwas attributes the cosmopolitan and universalizing tendencies of contemporary Christianity to the pernicious influence of liberalism. He states that liberalism has turned "Christianity into a set of beliefs to legitimate the false universalism of liberalism" itself by promoting justice as the highest good and by transforming Christian charity into an indolent expression of universal compassion or benevolence. This, though, is just one of the many liberal sins enumerated by Hauerwas in characteristically virile tones. Indeed, though it may seem odd that in a century that has seen states butcher untold millions of their own citizens in the name of civil religions such as Marxism and which provides numerous examples demonstrating the intrinsic link between industrial socialism and strident secularism, Hauerwas's political animus is almost always directed against liberalism and liberal societies. In Hauerwas's view, liberalism's many sins include making "rationality qua rationality" the basis of morality. It has promoted "individualistic fictions" and a blind commitment to individual rights; it has promulgated an unfortunate distinction between the public realm and a private realm of individuals; and it has "forced Christians to divorce their convictions from their practices." Liberalism, he says, made the family into a "voluntary institution," and it has led to a view of morality "strong on choice and independence of mind" but ignorant of obligation. Additionally, according to Hauerwas, liberalism advances political doctrines "based upon a denial of death and sacrifice," but those very doctrines aspire to nothing higher than the preservation of life. It has led to political institutions designed "to create people incapable of killing other people in the name of God" but which "form those that would make war in the name of universal ideals."[19]

Such statements are admirable and memorable for their vigor. With the exception of the assertion that liberalism sought to "create people incapable of killing others in the name of God," however, none of these assertions is true of the variety of theoretical liberalism that most influenced the American founders and has most influenced the American experience—the classical liberalism of Locke, Hume, and Smith. Indeed, Hauerwas avoids treating real existing liberalism as it has influenced American life through two means typical among contemporary antiliberals such as Jürgen Habermas, Robert Bellah, Michael Sandel, and Alasdair MacIntyre.[20] Both means involve bait and switch. What he calls "liberalism" is in fact either an implausible form of Hobbesianism or a variety of liberalism—typically Millian or Kantian—completely irrelevant to the American founding and largely irrelevant to contemporary Americans outside philosophy and political studies departments. By whichever means, however, liberalism is portrayed as having an asocial, unencumbered, ahistorical, and hedonistic view of human nature, a view which in fact the classical liberal tradition, so influential in America, eschewed and hoped to refute at least as vigorously as Hauerwas himself. For we are by nature sociable or communal, according to the classical liberals, and in the classical liberal view the private/public distinction was not between a private realm of isolated individuals and a sociable public realm. It was rather between a communal private realm in which people seek common goods, in which certain obligations are natural and unilateral, in which virtues are formed, and wherein individuals regulate one another through approbation and disapprobation, and a public realm in which indifferent and self-interested strangers meet and peaceably coordinate their activities because laws of justice provide that tranquil feeling of security Montesquieu called "liberty."

Properly conceived, this distinction is congenial to the Augustinian distinction between the City of God and the City of Man. Each of the classical liberals favored the disestablishment of religion, freedom of religious conscience, and religious pluralism. For example, Hume, who feared enthusiastic religion perhaps more than any other eighteenth-century thinker, believed that sectarian religion was more friendly to civil liberty and public order than priestly religion.[21] And for his part, Smith wrote eloquently and at great length about sectarian religion providing a disciplined community capable of inculcating an orderly and austere system of morals.[22] Indeed, Smith anticipated Hauerwas's own concerns over universal benevolence. Smith spoke of "universal benevolence," a vague sense supportive of justice; yet, he says, "It is the source of no solid happiness," and adds "The administration of the great system of the universe . . . the core of the happiness of all rational and sensible beings is the business of God and not of man."[23] Our duties lie close to home. Genuine benevolence recommends those to our care who are closest to us, according to Smith. He says, "The most sublime speculation of the contemplative philosopher can scarce compensate the neglect of the smallest active duty."[24] For Smith, genuine benevolence or love is particularistic and only expressed within a community of intimates. Such a view may not perfectly express the Christian idea of charity, but it certainly accommodates it.

In short, the liberalism that most informed the American Founding and has most influenced the American experience is not the liberalism criticized by Hauerwas and most other contemporary antiliberals. It is a variety of liberalism whose truths are in fact often the very truths asserted by Hauerwas.

In conclusion, then, I would like to suggest that there are two contemporary problems of religion and the American experience. The first is a problem of religious and especially civic education: too often we fail to understand our own religious and political traditions, which makes us susceptible to curious and false accusations against both. The second is that although liberalism properly conceived cannot be said to have corrupted Christianity, Christianity has largely failed itself and in so doing has failed liberalism and the liberal public order because it has lost its character-forming role. This is a problem of the self-willed collapse of Christianity, a crisis of faith especially among its elites, where this problem has emerged, ironically, within the context of the only type of modern public order well suited to religious flourishing. To indict liberalism and the liberal public order for the problems of Christianity, I believe, is to misidentify the source of these problems and wholly misdirect efforts at addressing them.

Notes

1. Alan Wolfe, *One Nation, After All* (New York: Viking Press, 1998).

2. John Stuart Mill, *On Liberty* (New York: Norton, 1975), and H. L. Mencken, *A Carnival of Buncombe* (Chicago: University of Chicago Press, 1984). Mill describes the middle class in Victorian England, while Mencken writes about the American middle class of the 1920s and 1930s. Mencken characterized the middle class as the "booboisie" and as "homo boobiens" and was especially disdainful toward Protestant evangelicals.

3. Wolfe, *One Nation*, 318.

4. Wolfe, *One Nation*, 310.

5. My characterization of classical liberal moral theory relies chiefly upon John Locke, *Second Treatise of Government* (Indianapolis, Ind.: Hackett, 1980); David Hume, *An Inquiry concerning the Principles of Morals* (Indianapolis, Ind.: Bobbs-Merrill, 1957); Adam Smith, *The Theory of Moral Sentiments* (Indianapolis, Ind.: Liberty Press, 1982); and Adam Smith, *An Inquiry into the Nature and Causes of the Wealth of Nations*, 2 vols. (Indianapolis, Ind.: Liberty Press, 1981). For a more elaborate survey of classical liberalism, see Brad Lowell Stone, "Classical Liberalism and Sociology," *Sociological Forum* 12 (September 1997): 497-512.

6. Wolfe, *One Nation*, 108.

7. Smith, *Moral Sentiments*, 200.

8. Smith, *Moral Sentiments*, 210.

9. For a discussion of the poor, see Thomas Sowell, *The Quest for Cosmic Justice* (New York: Free Press, 1999), 53-55.

10. Sara McLanahan and Gary Sandefur, *Growing Up with a Single Parent* (Cambridge, Mass.: Harvard University Press), 82. In 1995, married-couple families had a median income of $47,062, while female-headed families earned $19,691. U.S. Census Bureau, "Families by Median and Mean Income, Race and Hispanic Origin of Householder, 1947 to 1995," table F-7, <http://www.census.gov/hhes/income/histinc/f07.html> (accessed September 25, 1999).

11. See McLanahan and Sandefur, *Growing Up with a Single Parent*, 41, 67. Also see Daniel Patrick Moynihan, *Family and Nation* (San Diego: Harcourt Brace Javanovich, 1986), 92-93.

12. David Blankenhorn, *Fatherless America* (New York: Basic Books, 1995), 55-56.

13. Bureau of Justice Statistics, "Violence between Intimates," <http://ojp.usdoj.gov/bjs/-pub/ascii/vbi.txt> (accessed September 25, 1999), 2.

14. On neglect, see National Clearinghouse on Child Abuse and Neglect Information, "Answers to Frequently Asked Questions on Child Abuse and Neglect," <http://www.calib.com/nccanch/pubs/factsheet/infact.htm> (accessed September 25, 1999), 3. On abuse, see Lee Dugatkin, *Cheating Monkeys and Citizen Bees* (New York: Free Press, 1999), 65. Dugatkin summarizes data provided in Martin Daly and Margo Wilson, *Homicide* (New York: Aldine deGruyter, 1988).

15. See Sylvia Ann Hewlett, *When the Bough Breaks* (New York: Basic Books, 1991).

16. David Popenoe, *Life without Father* (New York: Free Press, 1996), 63.

17. Perhaps the strongest case for a causal relationship between single-parent households and various social pathologies is made by McLanahan and Sandefur in *Growing Up with a Single Parent.*

18. Stanley Hauerwas, *After Christendom?* (Nashville, Tenn.: Abingdon Press, 1991), and Stanley Hauerwas and Charles Pinches, *Christians among the Virtues* (South Bend, Ind.: University of Notre Dame Press, 1997).

19. Hauerwas, *After Christendom?* and Hauerwas and Pinches, *Christians among the Virtues.*

20. See Jürgen Habermas, *Between Facts and Norms*, trans. William Rehg (Cambridge, Mass.: MIT Press, 1996); Michael Sandel, *Democracy's Discontent* (Cambridge, Mass.: Belknap, 1996); Robert Bellah, Richard Madsen, William Sullivan, Ann Sidler, and Steven Tipton, *Habits of the Heart*, updated ed. (Berkeley: University of California Press, 1996); and Alasdair MacIntyre, *After Virtue* (South Bend, Ind.: University of Notre Dame Press, 1981).

21. David Hume, *Essays: Moral, Political, Literary* (Indianapolis, Ind.: Liberty Press, 1985), 73-79.

22. Smith, *The Wealth of Nations*, 788-814.

23. Smith, *Moral Sentiments*, 235-237.

24. Smith, *Moral Sentiments*, 237.

Chapter 12

From Virtues to Values:
Some Opening Thoughts

Alan Woolfolk

> Morality is character, character is that which is engraved; but the sand
> and the sea have no character and neither has abstract intelligence, for
> character is really inwardness. Immorality, as energy, is also character;
> but to be neither moral nor immoral is merely ambiguous, and
> ambiguity enters into life when the qualitative distinctions are weakened
> by a gnawing reflection. The revolt of the passions is elemental, the
> dissolution brought about by ambiguity is a silent sorites that goes on
> night and day. The distinction between good and evil is enervated by a
> superficial, superior and theoretical knowledge of evil, and by a
> supercilious cleverness which is aware that goodness is neither
> appreciated nor worth while in this world, that it is tantamount to
> stupidity.
>
> –Soren Kierkegaard

The conception of *morality as character*,[1] which one finds advanced in the work
of more than a few formidable theorists (while given scant consideration by social
scientists),[2] assumes that all genuine ethical and spiritual life is grounded in
personality dispositions formed through disciplines of self-denial. This assumption
is widely doubted today, as is the very idea of morality as character. It is one of the
hallmarks of the therapeutic metanarrative of our time that we have increasingly
ceased to comprehend morality in terms of some ongoing inner struggle of the self
with its own corrupt tendencies. We have advanced beyond the inhibitions of ethics
of conscience and responsibility toward de-inhibited ethics of engagement and
disengagement that have evolved beyond their early modern capitalist and Marxist
forms. Under the cultural revolution that has been ongoing for some time,
therapeutic criteria of health and sickness, psychologically functional and
dysfunctional, have gradually effaced our inherited criteria of good and evil, right

and wrong, dramatically transforming the priorities of our lives in ways that we have only begun to understand.

Today, we are all more or less members of highly particular cultures of "critical discourse" that, as Alvin Gouldner understood, have "the profound consequence of making all *authority-referring* claims potentially problematic"[3]—especially those claims which invoke the moral authorities of the past or demand unconditional commitment on the part of the individual. For these emergent and by now dominant cultures in all their varieties, morality has become less a question of conflict between higher and lower motives of the self and more a matter of opening the self to the possibilities of life in all of its sinuous diversity. Where once character was clearly understood as a restrictive shaping of the individual personality which defined a stable and limited self, in contemporary culture it has acquired pejorative connotations of neurotic rigidity and inward impoverishment. And even though morality as character may retain some residual aura of integrity, that aura has faded before implications of ignorance and narrow-mindedness, which have resulted in charges of prejudice and intolerance being added to the diagnosis of psychological disease. Indeed, much of contemporary morality consists of overcoming within oneself and others the lingering prejudices of older moralities against what were once considered to be the "worldly" aspects of human nature. Those prejudices are now looked upon with disdain and disgust by all but the least enlightened. At the beginning of the twenty-first century, morality, much more often than not, begins with values rather than virtues, world affirmation rather than world rejection, therapy rather than asceticism, even when employing a language of world rejection and self-denial. Nietzsche's charge of the late nineteenth century that "the whole morality of self-denial must be questioned mercilessly and taken to court" has succeeded in ways that he never intended.[4]

Nonetheless, even moralities of self-affirmation frequently preserve something of what Bernard Williams has described as a "special notion of obligation."[5] Insofar as they are continuations of what he calls, in a Nietzschean vein, "the peculiar institution," moralities of self-affirmation can be just as categorical and non-negotiable as older moralities of self-denial. Both modes of morality appear to reduce ethical and spiritual life to a matter of commanding "thou shalts." But where the older "thou shalts" brought into play complex orders of "shalt nots," the newer "thou shalts" generally oppose interdictory forms of moral commitment, thereby pitting morality against character. The new moralities, while no less militant at times than older moralities, are more expressive than repressive, more impulsive than inhibitive. Dostoyevsky's underground man long ago broke to the surface of modernity: his contention that "an intelligent man in the nineteenth century must and *morally ought* to be pre-eminently a characterless creature" is no longer a hidden minority opinion. Likewise, his scornful assertion that "a man of character, an active man, is pre-eminently a *limited creature*" expresses sentiments that are widely, if ambivalently, shared today.[6]

In our ambivalence, we desire, on the one hand, to deny the very notion of moral obligation. Commanding "thou shalts" are to go the way of commanding "shalt nots," as the assumption that ethical and spiritual life depend upon mandatory commitments is viewed askance. On the other hand, the conception of morality as character resists easy dismissal from our individual and collective lives, for every culture is what Lionel Trilling once described as a dialectic of Yes and No, the interaction of whose expressions defines a particular culture.[7] In these dialectical expressions, it may well be the No's in the form of what Philip Rieff has called *interdicts*, rather than the Yeses, that ensure the members of a culture their collective identity, just as it is internalized, variant readings of interdicts deeply instilled as inhibitions that anchor individual character. Our ambivalence about moralities of self-denial and even moral obligations per se betrays our suspicion that all personal and cultural development may ultimately require mandatory, interdictory forms. Indeed, even Nietzsche, who generally opposed all mandatory moralities of self-denial, on occasion revealed his own ambivalence and acknowledged the necessity of just such moral systems.[8]

Negative Dispositions

Every culture, as a condition of its very existence, must limit the breadth and depth of experiences available to its members. Each necessarily defines a "common symbolic" that is, first of all, "a pattern of moral demands, a range of standard self-expectations about what we may and may not do, in the face of infinite possibilities"; for although "everything is possible to human beings; we are members of a culture in the sense that everything is not permitted to us, nor even conceivable by us."[9] According to Philip Rieff's theory of culture, all social order and cultural development depend upon the circumscription of sheer possibility, just as personal development begins with a similar narrowing of options within the individual. Moreover, in order to establish a stable self-identity and to limit the human penchant for destructiveness, human beings need cultural forms thrust deeply enough into the self that they are beyond conscious choice and the ability to change voluntarily. Definition and depth of self depend upon acquiring the capacity to reject the assaults of experience without asking why. The achievement of a certain freedom from the treacherous involvements of life is a positive cultural achievement.[10]

Clifford Geertz's conception of culture as a "set of control mechanisms" for the "governing of behavior" complements Rieff's theory in certain important respects. According to Geertz, symbolic controls perform the primary function of narrowing the extreme generality, diffuseness, and variability of innate human capacities.[11] Without "cultural patterns," we would become, in Geertz's language, "functionally incomplete . . . a kind of formless monster with neither sense of direction nor power of self-control, a chaos of spasmodic impulses and vague emotions."[12] Although clearly far more than laws and external authorities, such controls are not adequately described under the standard social scientific, namely functionalist, rubric of "values" and "norms," any more than morality can be stipulated as either the simple or reflective application of rules and precepts. Such understandings of controls focus too exclusively on the conscious and cognitive dimensions of culture and encourage the notion that socialization into a particular culture is primarily a matter of internalizing certain core values and learning and applying various normative conventions. Likewise, the analyses of symbolic codes by semiotic and Durkheimian theorists also tend to exhibit a cognitive bias, as does Weberian theory insofar as it has been influenced by Weber's typology of action. Generally, cognitive approaches to the study of culture miss the extent to which membership in a culture is unconscious and dispositional; they elide the affective and the habitual, eliminating the significance of what Paul Connerton calls "social habit-memory" and that dimension of culture which is "a habit of affectation and conduct."[13] More to the point of this chapter, the focus on the cognitive side of culture is itself a manifestation of what Weber called the intellectualization and rationalization of the modern world that has devalued the significance of negative dispositions for the personality, even as habits of self-denial and world rejection have declined in Western culture(s).

Emotivist Sociology

Recent studies of American society, such as Alan Wolfe's *One Nation, After All*, have inadvertently helped to document the continuing influence both within sociology and in the larger culture of what Alasdair MacIntyre has described as the doctrine of emotivism—the doctrine that moral judgments are nothing but expressions of personal preference.[14] Under this reigning therapeutic doctrine, the very conception of morality was transformed in the twentieth century from that of *morality as character* to *morality as values*. Within sociology, the emotivist language of values can be traced back to the work of Weber, who inherited the term from both Nietzsche and the Marburg School and, within the United States in particular, to the work of W. I. Thomas and Florian Znaniecki in their seminal study *The Polish Peasant in Europe and America*.[15] In both instances, the use of the term *values* was linked with a theoretical shift away from habits and dispositions toward the study of attitudes and conscious intentions.

Take, for example, Weber's preference for *zweckrational* and *wertrational* action over traditional and emotion-based action in his typology of action: the larger vision behind much of Weber's scholarly work may be understood as an effort to clarify for the modern world the ideal of a rational, ethical personality type that rises above the merely habitual, in spite of his consistent reliance upon concepts such as disposition and *habitus* in his studies of religion and traditional cultures. In addition, Weber played a decisive role in making the cognitive term *value* central to the vocabularies of modern social science and Western culture(s). Those two vocabularies have become increasingly one since Weber's day and have never been completely separate, not simply because sociology has influenced its host cultures but also due to the impact of host cultures upon sociology. The rising moral capital in the twentieth century of the notion of values over older concepts such as virtue and character can be directly traced to the failure of those character traits that once defined a range of virtues and the ascent of a moral individualism that emphasizes the achievement of self-awareness and a "rational" freedom from the older cultural controls. The virtuous dispositions of the Victorian age, the German ideal of personal cultivation (*Bildung*), the nineteenth-century American model of "the balanced character,"[16] and the Kantian ethical personality are examples of exacting character ideals that were discredited in the late nineteenth and early twentieth centuries, if not earlier, by the idealization of an intellectual-aesthetic approach to life among the culturally sophisticated and the widespread public acceptance of a variety of habits formerly considered unacceptable among the general populace of the United States and Europe.[17] With respect to the former, Weber's use of the term "value" (*Wert*) was not simply inherited from both Nietzsche and the Marburg School but was also indicative of the advance of an "intellectualist civilization" which he otherwise diagnosed and opposed. In criticism of this civilization, Weber wrote that "the rejection of responsibility for ethical judgment and the fear of appearing bound by tradition, which come to the fore in intellectualist periods, shift judgments whose intention was originally ethical into an aesthetic key. Typical is the shift from the judgment 'reprehensible' to the judgment 'in poor taste.'"[18] Nonetheless, by employing the concept of value to describe the various priorities of highly differentiated spheres of life in an increasingly fragmented culture, Weber helped to ratify the recession of morality as character that stands at the center of the intellectualization and disenchantment of the modern world. That intellectualization has paradoxically overseen the *emotivist* reduction of moral judgments to mere personal preferences and ushered in the therapeutic commandment: Thou shalt not judge.[19]

The rise of the notion of values within sociology was also undoubtedly associated, especially in the United States, with the efforts of the social sciences to distinguish themselves from the behaviorism of academic psychology. As Charles Camic has cogently argued, American sociologists, for all intents and purposes, purged the concept of habit from their vocabulary early in the twentieth century in an effort to secure the integrity of the field and to distance it from Watsonian behaviorism, which was seen as an extension of the biological sciences.[20] Thomas and Znaniecki were leaders in this effort. In *The Polish Peasant*, they wrote that "the indistinct use of the term 'habit' to indicate any uniformities of behavior . . . should be restricted to the biological field. . . . The uniformity of behavior [that society] tends to impose upon the individual is not a uniformity of organic habits but of consciously followed *rules*."[21] More specifically, Thomas and Znaniecki identified attitudes, as opposed to habits, as the proper data for sociologists to study. The concept of attitude, as Camic has pointed out, helped to redefine sociology by shifting the theoretical focus to conscious, purposeful aspects of the personality that were concerned with more reflective types of real or possible action.

Thomas and Znaniecki, however, went farther than has been generally recognized. First, they did *not* identify all attitudes with reflective types of action. *Temperamental attitudes* referred to attitudes that tend to be habitual and "essentially instinctive," which exist independently of social influences with no conscious connection to one another. *Character* referred to attitudes determined by conscious reflection that shape and organize the personality; it was "the set of organized and fixed groups of attitudes developed by social influences operating upon the temperamental basis."[22] Second, Thomas and Znaniecki identified the social complement of an attitude associated with character as a "social value"—for values were defined as determining the meaningful objects of action within a particular social group. In practice, reflective attitudes and actions presuppose the existence of values. "The attitude is thus the individual counterpart of the social value; activity, in whatever form, is the bond between them."[23] By focusing on attitudes and values, Thomas and Znaniecki were decisive influences in moving sociology toward the still-prevailing cognitive approach to the study of culture. They did not reject the concept of morality as character per se but rather eliminated one of its most important theoretical supports—the concept of habit—and emphasized the role of values in shaping human conduct. In the case of attitudes, the negative or inhibitory dispositions associated with militant character ideals were denied significance; in the case of values, the rationalization of a broad range of human action was highlighted. As a consequence, the focus on attitudes and values effectively undermined the concept of morality as character within sociology and prepared for the rise of morality as values.

Thou Shalt Not Judge

Wolfe's discovery of an antipolitical "morality writ small" among contemporary Americans that has as its primary commandment "Thou shalt not judge" not only confirms the dominance of an emotivistic morality of values within American culture but also illustrates the influence of therapeutic emotivism within current sociology. To be more precise: interpretations of empirical findings depend upon the theory that the theorist brings to bear upon the facts because data do not stand by or speak for themselves. In Wolfe's case, which is representative of many lesser examples, the author misses the decline of militant character ideals that defines what is perhaps most significant about American culture at the turn of the century. What is *not* illuminated in Wolfe's analysis may be what is most telling.

Wolfe finds little evidence for the existence of the much-publicized *Kulturkampf* between what James Davison Hunter has called "the orthodox" and "the progressivists" in recent American history.[24] "I have found little support," Wolfe concludes, "for the notion that middle-class Americans are engaged in bitter cultural conflict with each other over the proper way to live." In Wolfe's reading, Americans are united precisely because they are "accommodating, pluralistic, tolerant, and expansive." Americans are "reluctant to pass judgment, they are tolerant to a fault. . . . Above all moderate in their outlook on the world, they believe in the importance of leading a virtuous life but are reluctant to impose values they understand as virtuous for themselves on others; strong believers in morality, they do not want to be considered moralists."[25] However, Gertrude Himmelfarb contends that Wolfe obscures the reality of polarization in American culture, that in fact a vital "dissident culture" continues to oppose the dominant progressivists with what Adam Smith called a "strict or austere" system of morality. Indeed, Himmelfarb suggests that Wolfe's intolerance toward the absolutist judgments of such strict systems is itself symptomatic of his adherence to the more "liberal" or "loose system" of morality that characterizes Hunter's progressivists.[26]

Nonetheless, Himmelfarb fails to consider adequately the possibility that the "dissident culture" of strict morality may suffer from a discrepancy between belief and action, values and conduct, that plagues therapeutic cultures generally. To the extent that therapeutic culture has triumphed in American society (and Wolfe and Himmelfarb, in addition to many others, implicitly confirm that it has), it is doubtful that a "strict or austere" system of morality has remained intact and vital. In his recent study, James Nolin argues that the therapeutic has triumphed by penetrating the institutions of the state and, beyond that, even the hearts and minds of the very individuals whom one might expect to be most opposed to any such victory.[27] With respect to the state, Nolin presents compelling evidence that the therapeutic ethos has made dramatic gains in civil law, criminal justice, public education, welfare policy, and political rhetoric in recent decades. In public education, for instance, Nolin contends that therapeutic assumptions became more pronounced and unchallenged with the rise of the self-esteem movement that followed upon the heels of the values-clarification movement of the 1960s, 1970s, and early 1980s. Implicit in his analysis is an important, underemphasized point: the self-esteem movement triumphed where the values-clarification did not—namely, with many of Hunter's defenders of so-called cultural orthodoxy. Democrats and Republicans, liberals and conservatives, defenders of public schools and champions of private Christian education and "school choice," despite their many and real differences, all appear to accept the centrality of self-esteem to education, even though American students regularly score at or near the bottom on standardized, international tests and at the top on measures of self-esteem among advanced industrial and postindustrial societies. According to Nolin, discontent with American education does not translate into a critique of therapeutic assumptions but rather a narrow focus on the problem of declining academic abilities. Another example: with the election of the 104th Congress and efforts to "end welfare as we know it" during the 1990s, one might assume that many of the therapeutic assumptions underlying the welfare state would have been challenged. But Nolin argues that the therapeutic state cannot be equated with the welfare state;

for while Republicans attempted to reign in the welfare state, they continued to employ the same therapeutic-emotivist code of moral understanding as their opponents. Democrats and Republicans alike appealed to the "value" of self-esteem as they defended and attacked various welfare programs, with Republicans simply arguing that programs in question robbed individuals of self-respect and that reform bills encouraging work increased self-esteem.

Wolfe's finding that Americans "prefer to sit in the seat of nonjudgment"[28] points toward the failure of all public moralities, both liberal and strict, and beyond that to the failure of our "morality writ small" to instill militant character ideals that might result in a genuine ethic of self-denial. As Nolin remarks, "Where once the self was to be surrendered, denied, sacrificed, and died to, now the self is to be esteemed, actualized, affirmed, and unfettered."[29] Americans have learned, as Wolfe argues, that "rules are not made to be broken . . . but they are made to be bent." But Wolfe's tolerance of American tolerance and his own acceptance of *morality as values* obscures what has been lost with the decline of militant character ideals—the possibility of cultivating spiritual heights and depths that would put the present "moral mediocrity"[30] into an appropriate and sharply critical perspective.

Notes

1. Soren Kierkegaard, *The Present Age*, trans. Alexander Dru (New York: Harper & Row), 43.

2. Indeed, the concept of character itself has scarcely received consideration by social scientists. One exception is the work of Colin Campbell, whose analysis, important as it is, suffers from being too strongly influenced by what he calls "the nineteenth-century cult of character" and Weber's typology of social action. "Character," Campbell observes, "is not a term one normally finds in the conceptual tool kit of the average sociologist. Indeed the term is notable in sociological discourse only by its absence. Thus it is not listed as a heading in *Sociological Abstracts*, nor included in the majority of sociology dictionaries or encyclopedias. . . . On those odd occasions when it is encountered, it is usually accompanied by the view that it is better dealt with under some other heading. Thus the entry for 'Character' in *The International Encyclopedia of the Social Sciences* (1968) reads 'See "Character Disorders"; "Ethics"; "Moral Development"; "National Character"; "Personality"; "Psychopathic Personality"; "Traits."' The clear message here would appear to be that either the concept is so marginal to the concerns of sociologists that there is really no need to discuss it, or there is no particular need for the term, as there are others (the notable candidate being 'personality') which are considered better adapted to serve the same purpose." Colin Campbell, "Detraditionalization, Character, and the Limits of Agency," in *Detraditionalization: Critical Reflections on Authority and Identity*, ed. Paul Heelas, Scott Lash, and Paul Morris (Cambridge: Blackwell, 1996), 151-52.

3. Alvin Gouldner, *The Future of Intellectuals and the Rise of the New Class* (New York: Continuum, 1979), 3, 28-42.

4. Friedrich Nietzsche, *Beyond Good and Evil: Prelude to a Philosophy of the Future*, trans. Walter Kaufmann (New York: Vintage Books, 1966), 45.

5. Bernard Williams, *Ethics and the Limits of Philosophy* (Cambridge, Mass.: Harvard University Press, 1985), 174.

6. Fyodor Dostoyevsky, *Notes from Underground and The Grand Inquisitor*, trans. Ralph Matlaw (New York: Dutton, 1960), 5.

7. Lionel Trilling, *The Liberal Imagination* (New York: Anchor Books, 1953), 7.

8. "Every morality is, as opposed to *laisser aller*, a bit of tyranny against 'nature'; also against 'reason'; but this in itself is no objection, as long as we do not have some other morality which permits us to decree that every kind of tyranny and unreason is impermissible. What is essential and inestimable in every morality is that it constitutes a long compulsion: to understand Stoicism or Port Royal or Puritanism, one should recall the compulsion under which every language so far has achieved strength and freedom—the metrical compulsion of rhyme and rhythm. . . . What is essential 'in heaven and on earth' seems to be, to say it once more, that there should be *obedience* over a long period of time and in a *single* direction: given that, something always develops, and has developed, for whose sake it is worth while to live on earth; for example, virtue, art, music, dance, reason, spirituality—something transfiguring, subtle, mad, and divine. . . . Consider any morality with this in mind: what there is in it of 'nature' teaches hatred of the *laisser aller*, of any all-too-great freedom, and implants the need for limited horizons and the nearest tasks—teaching the *narrowing of our perspective*, and thus in a certain sense stupidity, as a condition of life and growth." Nietzsche, *Beyond Good and Evil*, 100-102. See Philip Rieff's comments about this passage in his *Triumph of the Therapeutic* (New York: Harper & Row, 1966), 14.

9. Philip Rieff, "Toward a Theory of Culture," in *The Feeling Intellect: Selected Writings*, ed. Jonathan Imber (Chicago: University of Chicago Press, 1990), 323.

10. Chamfort makes the link between character, inward freedom, and the ability to reject experience in the following maxim: "Almost all men are slaves, for the reason that the Spartans gave for the servitude of the Persians: the inability to pronounce the syllable 'no.' The ability to pronounce this word, and the ability to live to oneself, are the only two ways of preserving one's liberty and one's character." Sebastien Chamfort, *Products of the Perfected Civilization, Selected Writings of Chamfort*, trans. W. S. Merwin (San Francisco: North Point Press, 1984), 159.

11. Clifford Geertz, *The Interpretation of Cultures* (New York: Basic Books, 1973), 44.

12. Geertz, *The Interpretation of Cultures*, 99.

13. Paul Connerton, *How Societies Remember* (Cambridge: Cambridge University Press, 1989). See especially pages 28-36 for a discussion of conventionalism and the importance of Michel Oakeshott's distinction between cognitive and noncognitive types of morality. See further pages 93-95 for a defense of the theoretical superiority of the concept of habit over disposition.

14. Alan Wolfe, *One Nation, After All* (New York: Penguin Books, 1998); and Alasdair MacIntyre, *After Virtue: A Study in Moral Theory*, 2d ed. (Notre Dame, Ind.: University of Notre Dame Press, 1984), 11-12.

15. William Thomas and Florian Znaniecki, *The Polish Peasant in Europe and America*, vol. 2 (New York: Dover Publications, 1958).

16. See Daniel Walker Howe, *Making the American Self: Jonathan Edwards to Abraham Lincoln* (Cambridge, Mass.: Harvard University Press, 1997).

17. On the widespread acceptance of what were formerly considered "bad habits" by Americans in the twentieth century, see John C. Burnham, *Bad Habits: Drinking, Smoking, Taking Drugs, Gambling, Sexual Misbehavior, and Swearing in American History* (New York: New York University Press, 1993).

18. Max Weber, *Economy and Society*, vol. 1, ed. G. Roth and C. Wittich (Berkeley: University of California, 1978), 608.

19. Wolfe, *One Nation, After All*, 54.

20. Charles Camic, "The Matter of Habit," *American Journal of Sociology* 91, no. 5 (March 1986): 1039-87.

21. Thomas and Znaniecki, *The Polish Peasant*, 2:1851-52.

22. Thomas and Znaniecki, *The Polish Peasant*, 2:1844.

23. Thomas and Znaniecki, *The Polish Peasant*, 2:22.

24. James Davison Hunter, *Culture Wars: The Struggle to Define America* (New York: Basic Books, 1991), 107-32.

25. Wolfe, *One Nation, After All*, 278, 315.

26. Gertrude Himmelfarb, *One Nation, Two Cultures* (New York: Alfred A. Knopf, 1999), 3, 124, 135-37. On Adam Smith's two systems of morality, see also *The Essential Adam Smith*, ed. Robert Heilbroner (New York: W. W. Norton, 1986), 308-10.

27. James Nolin, *The Therapeutic State: Justifying Government at Century's End* (New York: New York University Press, 1998).

28. Wolfe, *One Nation, After All*, 298.

29. Nolin, *The Therapeutic State*, 3.

30. Wolfe, *One Nation, After All*, 300, 308.

Index

About the Contributors

David Oki Ahearn is Chair of the Humanities Division at LaGrange College in Georgia. He teaches and writes in the area of Christian social ethics, most particularly about the intersection of religion and public life.

Michael Bailey is Assistant Professor of Government at Berry College where he teaches American politics. His research examines the importance of political tensions in the American Constitution.

John P. Bartkowski is Associate Professor of Sociology at Mississippi State University. Much of his work examines the intersection of religion, social inequality, and identity. His most recent books include *Charitable Choices: Religion, Race, and Poverty in the Post-Welfare Era* (NYU Press, 2003) (co-authored with Helen A. Regis) and *The Promise Keepers: Servants, Soldiers, and Godly Men* (Rutgers University Press, 2003).

Steven P. Brown is Assistant Professor of Political Science at Auburn University where he teaches constitutional law. He is the author of *Trumping Religion: The New Christian Right, the Free Speech Clause, and the Courts* (2002). His current research focuses on the local implementation of federal guidelines for religious expression in public schools.

Beverly Gaddy is Assistant Professor of Political Science at Georgia Southwestern State University. She writes and teaches in the field of American politics, with an emphasis on religion and politics. Her publications have dealt with religion and political behavior in the United States and abroad. Her current research and forthcoming publications are on the politics of Presbyterian clergy and theories of church and state.

Joshua P. Hochschild is Assistant Professor of Philosophy at Wheaton College. His primary research interest is medieval philosophy.

Peter Augustine Lawler is Dana Professor of Government at Berry College. He is author or editor of nine books, including *Aliens in America: The Strange Truth about Our Souls* (ISI Books, 2002), and executive editor of the quarterly journal *Perspectives on Political Science.*

Dale McConkey is Associate Professor of Sociology at Berry College. His research examines the role of traditional religion in contemporary society. He has co-edited several books with Peter Augustine Lawler, including *Faith, Reason, and Political Life Today* (Lexington Books, 2001).

Kevin Pybas is Visiting Assistant Professor of Political Science at Miami University. His current research focuses on the political and social thought that underlies competing interpretations of the Establishment Clause, and he is working on a book on liberalism and civic education.

Helen A. Regis is Assistant Professor of Anthropology at Louisiana State University. Research interests include racial subjects, performance, neoliberalism, and state-community relations in postcolonial contexts. Her work has appeared in *American Ethnologist* and *Cultural Anthropology,* and she recently published *Fulbe Voices: Marriage, Islam and Medicine in Northern Cameroon* (Westview Press, 2003). She also recently co-authored *Charitable Choices: Religion, Race, and Poverty in the Post-Welfare Era* (NYU Press, 2003) with John P. Bartkowski.

Brad Lowell Stone is Professor of Sociology and Director of American Studies at Oglethorpe University in Atlanta. He is the author of *Robert Nisbet: Communitarian Traditionalist* and has written the introduction for the recently republished edition of Robert Nisbet's *Conservatism: Dream and Reality.*

Alan Wolfe is Professor of Political Science and Director of the Boisi Center for Religion and American Public Life at Boston College. He is the author or editor of more than ten books including *Marginalized in the Middle* (1997) and *One Nation, After All* (1998). His most recent books are *Moral Freedom: The Search for Virtue in a World of Choice* (2001) and *School Choice: The Moral Debate* (editor, 2002). Wolfe is currently writing a book on the ways in which Americans actually practice their religious faith.

Alan Woolfolk is Professor of Sociology, Director of the Core Curriculum, and Manning M. Pattillo Professor of Liberal Arts at Oglethorpe University in Atlanta. He has published many articles on the sociology of culture and intellectuals, is a member of the editorial board of *Society,* and co-editor of *Constructive Sociological Theory: Thomas G. Masaryk* (Transaction Publishers, 1994). He is currently completing a book on the relation of character to therapeutic culture.